KU-530-243

Information Security
FUNDAMENTALS

Thomas R. Peltier
Justin Peltier
John Blackley

AUERBACH PUBLICATIONS

A CRC Press Company
Boca Raton   London   New York   Washington, D.C.

Library of Congress Cataloging-in-Publication Data

Peltier, Thomas R.
   Information security fundamentals / Thomas R. Peltier, Justin Peltier, John Blackley.
      p.   cm.
   Includes bibliographical references and index.
   ISBN 0-8493-1957-9 (alk. paper)
   1. Computer security. 2. Data protection. I. Peltier, Justin. II. Blackley, John A. III.
Title.

QA76.9.A25P427 2004
005.8—dc22   2004051024

This book contains information obtained from authentic and highly regarded sources. Reprinted material is quoted with permission, and sources are indicated. A wide variety of references are listed. Reasonable efforts have been made to publish reliable data and information, but the author and the publisher cannot assume responsibility for the validity of all materials or for the consequences of their use.

Neither this book nor any part may be reproduced or transmitted in any form or by any means, electronic or mechanical, including photocopying, microfilming, and recording, or by any information storage or retrieval system, without prior permission in writing from the publisher.

The consent of CRC Press does not extend to copying for general distribution, for promotion, for creating new works, or for resale. Specific permission must be obtained in writing from CRC Press LLC for such copying.

Direct all inquiries to CRC Press, 2000 N.W. Corporate Blvd., Boca Raton, Florida 33431.

Trademark Notice: Product or corporate names may be trademarks or registered trademarks, and are used only for identification and explanation, without intent to infringe.

Visit the CRC Press Web site at www.crcpress.com

© 2005 by CRC Press LLC
Auerbach is an imprint of CRC Press LLC

No claim to original U.S. Government works
International Standard Book Number 0-8493-1957-9
Library of Congress Card Number 2004051024
Printed in the United States of America 1 2 3 4 5 6 7 8 9 0
Printed on acid-free paper

Information Security
FUNDAMENTALS

OTHER INFORMATION SECURITY BOOKS FROM AUERBACH

Asset Protection and Security Management Handbook
POA Publishing
ISBN: 0-8493-1603-0

Building a Global Information Assurance Program
Raymond J. Curts and Douglas E. Campbell
ISBN: 0-8493-1368-6

Building an Information Security Awareness Program
Mark B. Desman
ISBN: 0-8493-0116-5

Critical Incident Management
Alan B. Sterneckert
ISBN: 0-8493-0010-X

Cyber Crime Investigator's Field Guide
Bruce Middleton
ISBN: 0-8493-1192-6

Cyber Forensics: A Field Manual for Collecting, Examining, and Preserving Evidence of Computer Crimes
Albert J. Marcella, Jr. and Robert S. Greenfield
ISBN: 0-8493-0955-7

The Ethical Hack: A Framework for Business Value Penetration Testing
James S. Tiller
ISBN: 0-8493-1609-X

The Hacker's Handbook: The Strategy Behind Breaking into and Defending Networks
Susan Young and Dave Aitel
ISBN: 0-8493-0888-7

Information Security Architecture: An Integrated Approach to Security in the Organization
Jan Killmeyer Tudor
ISBN: 0-8493-9988-2

Information Security Fundamentals
Thomas R. Peltier
ISBN: 0-8493-1957-9

Information Security Management Handbook, 5th Edition
Harold F. Tipton and Micki Krause
ISBN: 0-8493-1997-8

Information Security Policies, Procedures, and Standards: Guidelines for Effective Information Security Management
Thomas R. Peltier
ISBN: 0-8493-1137-3

Information Security Risk Analysis
Thomas R. Peltier
ISBN: 0-8493-0880-1

Information Technology Control and Audi
Fredrick Gallegos, Daniel Manson, and Sandra Allen-Senft
ISBN: 0-8493-9994-7

Investigator's Guide to Steganography
Gregory Kipper
0-8493-2433-5

Managing a Network Vulnerability Assessn
Thomas Peltier, Justin Peltier, and John A. Black
ISBN: 0-8493-1270-1

Network Perimeter Security: Building Defe In-Depth
Cliff Riggs
ISBN: 0-8493-1628-6

The Practical Guide to HIPAA Privacy and Security Compliance
Kevin Beaver and Rebecca Herold
ISBN: 0-8493-1953-6

A Practical Guide to Security Engineering Information Assurance
Debra S. Herrmann
ISBN: 0-8493-1163-2

The Privacy Papers: Managing Technology Consumer, Employee and Legislative Actie
Rebecca Herold
ISBN: 0-8493-1248-5

Public Key Infrastructure: Building Truste Applications and Web Services
John R. Vacca
ISBN: 0-8493-0822-4

Securing and Controlling Cisco Routers
Peter T. Davis
ISBN: 0-8493-1290-6

Strategic Information Security
John Wylder
ISBN: 0-8493-2041-0

Surviving Security: How to Integrate Peop Process, and Technology, Second Edition
Amanda Andress
ISBN: 0-8493-2042-9

A Technical Guide to IPSec Virtual Private Networks
James S. Tiller
ISBN: 0-8493-0876-3

Using the Common Criteria for IT Security Evaluation
Debra S. Herrmann
ISBN: 0-8493-1404-6

AUERBACH PUBLICATIONS
www.auerbach-publications.com
To Order Call: 1-800-272-7737 • Fax: 1-800-374-3401
E-mail: orders@crcpress.com

Dedication

To our spouses, friends, children, and colleagues; without them we would be without direction, support, and joy.

Contents

Chapter 8   Risk Analysis and Risk Management 181

Acknowledgments

An organization that has moved to the forefront of creating usable information for the information security professional is the National Institute of Standards and Technology (NIST). The NIST 800 Series of Special Publications is a great source of information that many security professionals have provided over the years. Joan Hash and the other dedicated people who work at NIST have added greatly to the profession.

The Computer Security Institute (CSI) has been the leader in the information security industry since 1974 and continues to provide leadership and direction for its members and the industry as a whole. John O'Leary has been the constant in all the changes seen in this industry. The new CSI management team of Julie Hogan, Chris Keating, and Jennifer Stevens continues to provide the tools and classes that the security professional needs to be successful. The new team has blended well with the CSI seasoned veterans of Pam Salaway, Kimber Heald, Frederic Martin, Nancy Baer, and Joanna Kaufman.

No one has all of the answers to any question, so the really "smart" person cultivates good friends. Having been in the information security business for nearly 30 years, I have had the great good fortune of having a number of such friends and fellow professionals. This group of long-time sources of great information include Mike Corby, Terri Curran, Peter Stephenson, Merrill Lynch, Bob Cartwright, Pat Howard, Cheryl and Carl Jackson, Becky Herold, Ray Kaplan, Genny Burns, Anne Terwilliger, Patrice Rapalus, David Lynas, John Sherwood, Herve Schmidt, Antonio and Pietro Ruvolo, Wayne Sumida, Caroline Hamilton, Dan Erwin, Lisa Bryson, and William H. Murray.

My working buddies must also be acknowledged. My son Justin is the greatest asset any father — and more importantly, any information security team — could ever hope for. Over the past two years, we have logged nearly 150,000 air miles together, and each day we learn something new from each other.

The other working buddy is John Blackley, a strange Scotsman who makes our life more fun and interesting. I have worked with John since 1985 and have marveled at how well he takes obtuse concepts and condenses them so that even management types understand.

Who can leave out their publisher? Certainly not me; Rich O'Hanley has taken the time to discuss security issues with numerous organizations to understand what their needs are and then presented these findings to us. A great deal of our work here is a direct result of what Rich discovered the industry wanted. Rich O'Hanley, not only the world's best editor and task master, but a good friend and source of knowledge. Thanks Rich!

And finally I extend a thank-you to my editor Andrea Demby. She takes the time to take the raw manuscript and put it into a logically flowing work. She sometimes has to ask me the same question more than once, but finally I get what needs to be done.

Introduction

The purpose of information security is to protect an organization's valuable resources, such as information, computer hardware, and software. Through the selection and application of appropriate safeguards, security helps the organization's mission by protecting its physical and financial resources, reputation, legal position, employees, and other tangible and intangible assets. To many, security is sometimes viewed as thwarting the business objectives of the organization by imposing poorly selected, bothersome rules and procedures on users, managers, and systems. Well-chosen security rules and procedures do not exist for their own sake — they are put in place to protect important assets and thereby support the overall business objectives.

Developing an information security program that adheres to the principle of security as a business enabler is the first step in an enterprise's effort to build an effective security program. Organizations must continually (1) explore and assess information security risks to business operations; (2) determine what policies, standards, and controls are worth implementing to reduce these risks; (3) promote awareness and understanding among the staff; and (4) assess compliance and control effectiveness. As with other types of internal controls, this is a cycle of activity, not an exercise with a defined beginning and end.

This book was designed to give the information security professional a solid understanding of the fundamentals of security and the entire range of issues the practitioner must address. We hope you will be able to take the key elements that comprise a successful information security program and implement the concepts into your own successful program.

Chapter 1

Overview

The purpose of information protection is to protect an organization's valuable resources, such as information, hardware, and software. Through the selection and application of appropriate safeguards, security helps the organization meet its business objectives or mission by protecting its physical and financial resources, reputation, legal position, employees, and other tangible and intangible assets. We will examine the elements of computer security, employee roles and responsibilities, and common threats. We will also examine the need for management controls, policies and procedures, and risk analysis. Finally, we will present a comprehensive list of tasks, responsibilities, and objectives that make up a typical information protection program.

1.1 Elements of Information Protection

Information protection should be based on eight major elements:

1. Information protection should support the business objectives or mission of the enterprise. This idea cannot be stressed enough. All too often, information security personnel lose track of their goals and responsibilities. The position of ISSO (Information Systems Security Officer) has been created to support the enterprise, not the other way around.
2. Information protection is an integral element of due care. Senior management is charged with two basic responsibilities: a *duty of*

1

loyalty — this means that whatever decisions they make must be made in the best interest of the enterprise. They are also charged with a *duty of care* — this means that senior management is required to protect the assets of the enterprise and make informed business decisions. An effective information protection program will assist senior management in meeting these duties.

3. Information protection must be cost effective. Implementing controls based on edicts is counter to the business climate. Before any control can be proposed, it will be necessary to confirm that a significant risk exists. Implementing a timely risk analysis process can complete this. By identifying risks and then proposing appropriate controls, the mission and business objectives of the enterprise will be better met.

4. Information protection responsibilities and accountabilities should be made explicit. For any program to be effective, it will be necessary to publish an information protection policy statement and a group mission statement. The policy should identify the roles and responsibilities of all employees. To be completely effective, the language of the policy must be incorporated into the purchase agreements for all contract personnel and consultants.

5. System owners have information protection responsibilities outside their own organization. Access to information will often extend beyond the business unit or even the enterprise. It is the responsibility of the information owner (normally the senior level manager in the business that created the information or is the primary user of the information). One of the main responsibilities is to monitor usage to ensure that it complies with the level of authorization granted to the user.

6. Information protection requires a comprehensive and integrated approach. To be as effective as possible, it will be necessary for information protection issues to be part of the system development life cycle. During the initial or analysis phase, information protection should receive as its deliverables a risk analysis, a business impact analysis, and an information classification document. Additionally, because information is resident in all departments throughout the enterprise, each business unit should establish an individual responsible for implementing an information protection program to meet the specific business needs of the department.

7. Information protection should be periodically reassessed. As with anything, time changes the needs and objectives. A good information protection program will examine itself on a regular basis and make changes wherever and whenever necessary. This is a dynamic

and changing process and therefore must be reassessed at least every 18 months.

8. Information protection is constrained by the culture of the organization. The ISSO must understand that the basic information protection program will be implemented throughout the enterprise. However, each business unit must be given the latitude to make modifications to meet its specific needs. If your organization is multinational, it will be necessary to make adjustments for each of the various countries. These adjustments will have to be examined throughout the United States. What might work in Des Moines, Iowa, may not fly in Berkeley, California. Provide for the ability to find and implement alternatives.

Information protection is a means to an end and not the end in itself. In business, having an effective information protection program is usually secondary to the need to make a profit. In the public sector, information protection is secondary to the agency's services provided to its constancy. We, as security professionals, must not lose sight of these goals and objectives.

Computer systems and the information processed on them are often considered critical assets that support the mission of an organization. Protecting them can be as important as protecting other organizational resources such as financial resources, physical assets, and employees. The cost and benefits of information protection should be carefully examined in both monetary and nonmonetary terms to ensure that the cost of controls does not exceed the expected benefits. Information protection controls should be appropriate and proportionate.

The responsibilities and accountabilities of the information owners, providers, and users of computer services and other parties concerned with the protection of information and computer assets should be explicit. If a system has external users, its owners have a responsibility to share appropriate knowledge about the existence and general extent of control measures so that other users can be confident that the system is adequately secure. As we expand the user base to include suppliers, vendors, clients, customers, shareholders, and the like, it is incumbent upon the enterprise to have clear and identifiable controls. For many organizations, the initial sign-on screen is the first indication that there are controls in place. The message screen should include three basic elements:

1. The system is for authorized users only
2. That activities are monitored
3. That by completing the sign-on process, the user agrees to the monitoring

1.2 More Than Just Computer Security

Providing effective information protection requires a comprehensive approach that considers a variety of areas both within and outside the information technology area. An information protection program is more than establishing controls for the computer-held data. In 1965 the idea of the "paperless office" was first introduced. The advent of third-generation computers brought about this concept. However, today the bulk of all of the information available to employees and others is still found in printed form. To be an effective program, information protection must move beyond the narrow scope of IT and address the issues of enterprisewide information protection. A comprehensive program must touch every stage of the information asset life cycle from creation to eventual destruction.

1.2.1 Employee Mind-Set toward Controls

Access to information and the environments that process them are dynamic. Technology and users, data and information in the systems, risks associated with the system, and security requirements are ever changing. The ability of information protection to support business objectives or the mission of the enterprise may be limited by various factors, such as the current mind-set toward controls.

A highly effective method of measuring the current attitude toward information protection is to conduct a "walk-about." After hours or on a weekend, conduct a review of the workstations throughout a specific area (usually a department or a floor) and look for just five basic control activities:

1. Offices secured
2. Desk and cabinets secured
3. Workstations secured
4. Information secured
5. Diskettes secured

When conducting an initial "walk-about," the typical office environment will have a 90 to 95 percent noncompliance rate with at least one of these basic control mechanisms. The result of this review should be used to form the basis for an initial risk analysis to determine the security requirements for the workstation. When conducting such a review, employee privacy issues must be remembered.

1.3 Roles and Responsibilities

As discussed, senior management has the ultimate responsibility for protecting the organization's information assets. One of these responsibilities is the establishment of the function of Corporate Information Officer (CIO). The CIO directs the organization's day-to-day management of information assets. The ISSO and Security Administrator should report directly to the CIO and are responsible for the day-to-day administration of the information protection program.

Supporting roles are performed by the service providers and include Systems Operations, whose personnel design and operate the computer systems. They are responsible for implementing technical security on the systems. Telecommunications is responsible for providing communication services, including voice, data, video, and fax.

The information protection professional must also establish strong working relationships with the audit staff. If the only time you see the audit staff is when they are in for a formal audit, then you probably do not have a good working relationship. It is vitally important that this liaison be established and that you meet to discuss common problems at least each quarter.

Other groups include the physical security staff and the contingency planning group. These groups are responsible for establishing and implementing controls and can form a peer group to review and discuss controls. The group responsible for application development methodology will assist in the implementation of information protection requirements in the application system development life cycle. Quality Assurance can assist in ensuring that information protection requirements are included in all development projects prior to movement to production.

The Procurement group can work to get the language of the information protection policies included in the purchase agreements for contract personnel. Education and Training can assist in developing and conducting information protection awareness programs and in training supervisors in the responsibility to monitor employee activities. Human Resources will be the organization responsible for taking appropriate action for any violations of the organization's information protection policy.

An example of a typical job description for an information security professional is as follows:

1.3.1 Director, Design and Strategy

Location: Anywhere, World

Practice Area: Corporate Global Security Practice

Grade:

Purpose: To create an information security design and strategy practice that defines the technology structure needed to address the security needs of its clients. The information security design and strategy will complement security and network services developed by the other Global Practice areas. The design and strategy practice will support the clients' information technology and architecture and integrate with each enterprise's business architecture. This security framework will provide for the secure operation of computing platforms, operating systems, and networks, both voice and data, to ensure the integrity of the clients' information assets. To work on corporate initiatives to develop and implement the highest quality security services and ensure that industry best practices are followed in their implementation.

Working Relationships: This position reports in the Global Security Practice to the Vice President, Global Security. Internal contacts are primarily Executive Management, Practice Directors, Regional Management, as well as mentoring and collaborating with consultants. This position will directly manage two professional positions: Manager, Service Provider Security Integration; and Service Provider Security Specialist. Frequent external contacts include building relationships with clients, professional information security organizations, other information security consultants; vendors of hardware, software, and security services; and various regulatory and legal authorities.

Principle Duties and Responsibilities: The responsibilities of the Director, Design and Strategy include, but are not limited to, the following:

■ Develop global information security services that will provide the security functionality required to protect clients' information assets against unauthorized disclosure, modification, and destruction. Particular focus areas include:
■ Virtual private networks
  – Data privacy
  – Virus prevention
  – Secure application architecture
  – Service provider security solutions

- Develop information security strategy services that can adapt to clients' diverse and changing technological needs.
- Work with Network and Security practice leaders and consultants; create sample architectures that communicate the security requirements that will meet the needs of all client network implementations.
- Work with practice teams to aid them from the conception phase to the deployment of the project solution. This includes a quality assurance review to ensure that the details of the project are correctly implemented according to the service delivery methodology.
- Work with the clients to collect their business requirements for electronic commerce, while educating them on the threats, vulnerabilities, and available risk mitigation strategies.
- Determine where and how you should use cryptography to provide public key infrastructure and secure messaging services for clients.
- Participate in security industry standards bodies to ensure that strategic information security needs will be addressed.
- Conduct security focus groups with the clients to cultivate an effective exchange of business plans, product development, and marketing direction to aid in creating new and innovative service offerings to meet client needs.
- Continually evaluate vendors' product strategies and future product statements, and advise which will be most appropriate to pursue for alliances, especially in the areas of:
  - Virtual private networks
  - Data privacy
  - Virus prevention
  - Secure application architecture
  - Service provider security solutions
- Provide direction and oversight of hardware- and software-based cryptography service development efforts.

Accountability: Maintain the quality and integrity of the services offered by the Global Security Practice. Review and report impartially on the potential viability and profitability of new security services. Assess the operational efficiency, compliance with industry standards, and effectiveness of the client network designs and strategies that are implemented through the company's professional service offerings. Exercise professional judgment in making recommendations that may impact business operations.

Knowledge and Skills:

■ 10 Percent Managerial and Practice Management:
  - Ability to supervise a multidisciplinary team and a small staff; must handle multiple tasks simultaneously; ability to team with other Practice Directors and Managers to develop strategic service offerings
  - Willingness to manage or to personally execute necessary tasks, as resources are required
  - Excellent oral, written, and presentation skills
■ 40 Percent Technical:
  - In-depth technical knowledge of information processing platforms, operating systems, and networks in a global distributed environment
  - Ability to identify and apply security techniques to develop services to reduce clients' risk in such an environment
  - Technical experience in industrial security, computer systems architecture, design, and development, physical and data security, telecommunications networks, auditing techniques, and risk analysis principles
  - Excellent visionary skills that focus on scalability, cost effectiveness, and implementation ease
■ 20 Percent Business:
  - Knowledge of business information flow in a multinational, multiplatform networked environment
  - Solid understanding of corporate dynamics and general business processes; understanding of multiple industries
  - Good planning and goal-setting skills
■ 20 Percent Interpersonal:
  - Must possess strong consulting and communication skills
  - Must have the ability to work with all levels of management to resolve issues
  - Must understand and differentiate between tactical and strategic concepts
  - Must be able to weigh business needs with security requirements
  - Must be self-motivating

Attributes: Must be mature, self-confident, and performance oriented. Will clearly demonstrate an ability to lead technological decisions. Will establish credibility with personal dedication, attention to detail, and a hands-on approach. Will have a sense of urgency in establishing security designs and strategies to address new technologies to be deployed addressing clients' business needs. Will also be capable of developing strong relationships with all levels of management. Other important characteristics include the ability to function independently, holding to the highest levels of personal and professional integrity. Will be an excellent communicator and team player.

Specific requirements include:

- Bachelor's degree (Master's degree desirable)
- Advanced degree preferred
- Fifteen or more years of information technology consulting or managerial experience, eight of those years spent in information security positions
- CISM or CISSP certification preferred (other appropriate industry or technology certifications desirable)

Potential Career Path Opportunities: Opportunities for progression to a VP position within the company.

1.4 Common Threats

Information processing systems are vulnerable to many threats that can inflict various types of damage that can result in significant losses. This damage can range from errors harming database integrity to fires destroying entire complexes. Losses can stem from the actions of supposedly trusted employees defrauding a system, from outside hackers, or from careless data entry. Precision in estimating information protection-related losses is not possible because many losses are never discovered, and others are hidden to avoid unfavorable publicity.

The typical computer criminal is an authorized, nontechnical user of the system who has been around long enough to determine what actions would cause a "red flag" or an audit. The typical computer criminal is an employee. According to a recent survey in "Current and Future Danger: A CSI Primer on Computer Crime & Information Warfare," more than

80 percent of the respondents identified employees as a threat or potential threat to information security. Also included in this survey were the competition, contract personnel, public interest groups, suppliers, and foreign governments.

The chief threat to information protection is still errors and omissions. This concern continues to make up 65 percent of all information protection problems. Users, data entry personnel, system operators, programmers, and the like frequently make errors that contribute directly or indirectly to this problem.

Dishonest employees make up another 13 percent of information protection problems. Fraud and theft can be committed by insiders and outsiders, but it more likely to be done by a company's own employees. In a related area, disgruntled employees make up another 10 percent of the problem. Employees are most familiar with the organization's information assets and processing systems, including knowing what actions might cause the most damage, mischief, or sabotage.

Common examples of information protection-related employee sabotage include destroying hardware or facilities, planting malicious code (viruses, worms, Trojan horses, etc.) to destroy data or programs, entering data incorrectly, deleting data, altering data, and holding data "hostage."

The loss of the physical facility or the supporting infrastructure (power failures, telecommunications disruptions, water outage and leaks, sewer problems, lack of transportation, fire, flood, civil unrest, strikes, etc.) can lead to serious problems and make up 8 percent of information protection-related problems.

The final area comprises malicious hackers or *crackers*. These terms refer to those who break into computers without authorization or exceed the level of authorization granted to them. While these problems get the largest amount of press coverage and movies, they only account for five to eight percent of the total picture. They are real and they can cause a great deal of damage. But when attempting to allocate limited information protection resources, it may be better to concentrate efforts in other areas. To be certain, conduct a risk analysis to see what the exposure might be.

1.5 Policies and Procedures

An information protection policy is the documentation of enterprisewide decisions on handling and protecting information. In making these decisions, managers face difficult choices involving resource allocation, competing objectives, and organization strategy related to protecting both technical and information resources as well as guiding employee behavior.

When creating an information protection policy, it is best to understand that information is an asset of the enterprise and is the property of the organization. As such, information reaches beyond the boundaries of IT and is present in all areas of the enterprise. To be effective, an information protection policy must be part of the organization's asset management program and be enterprisewide.

There are as many forms, styles, and kinds of policy as there are organizations, businesses, agencies, and universities. In addition to the various forms, each organization has a specific culture or mental model on what and how a policy is to look and who should approve the document. The key point here is that every organization needs an information protection policy. According to the 2000 CSI report on Computer Crime, 65 percent of respondents to its survey admitted that they do not have a written policy. The beginning of an information protection program is the implementation of a policy. The program policy creates the organization's attitude toward information and announces internally and externally that information is an asset and the property of the organization and is to be protected from unauthorized access, modification disclosure, and destruction.

This book leads the policy writer through the key structure elements and then reviews some typical policy contents. Because policies are not enough, this book teaches the reader how to develop standards, procedures, and guidelines. Each section provides advice on the structural mechanics of the various documents, as well as actual examples.

1.6 Risk Management

Risk is the possibility of something adverse happening. The process of risk management is to identify those risks, assess the likelihood of their occurrence, and then taking steps to reduce the risk to an acceptable level. All risk analysis processes use the same methodology. Determine the asset to be reviewed. Identify the risk, issues, threats, or vulnerabilities. Assess the probability of the risk occurring and the impact to the asset or the organization should the risk be realized. Then identify controls that would bring the impact to an acceptable level.

The book entitled *Information Security Risk Analysis* (CRC Press, 2001) discusses effective risk analysis methodologies. It takes the reader through the theory of risk analysis:

1. Identify the asset.
2. Identify the risks.

3. Prioritize the risks.
4. Identify controls and safeguards.

The book will help the reader understand qualitative risk analysis; it then gives examples of this process. To make certain that the reader gets a well-rounded exposure to risk analysis, the book presents eight different methods, concluding with the Facilitated Risk Analysis Process (FRAP).

The primary function of information protection risk management is the identification of appropriate controls. In every assessment of risk, there will be many areas for which it will not be obvious what kinds of controls are appropriate. The goal of controls is not to have 100 percent security; total security would mean zero productivity. Controls must never lose sight of the business objectives or mission of the enterprise. Whenever there is a contest for supremacy, controls lose and productivity wins. This is not a contest, however. The goal of information protection is to provide a safe and secure environment for management to meet its duty of care.

When selecting controls, one must consider many factors, including the organization's information protection policy. These include the legislation and regulations that govern your enterprise along with safety, reliability, and quality requirements. Remember that every control will require some performance requirements. These performance requirements may be a reduction in user response time; additional requirements before applications are moved into production or additional costs.

When considering controls, the initial implementation cost is only the tip of the "cost iceberg." The long-term cost for maintenance and monitoring must be identified. Be sure to examine any and all technical requirements and cultural constraints. If your organization is multinational, control measures that work and are accepted in your home country might not be accepted in other countries.

Accept residual risk; at some point, management will need to decide if the operation of a specific process or system is acceptable, given the risk. There can be any number of reasons that a risk must be accepted; these include but are not limited to the following:

■ The type of risk may be different from previous risks.
■ The risk may be technical and difficult for a layperson to grasp.
■ The current environment may make it difficult to identify the risk.

Information protection professionals sometimes forget that the managers hired by our organizations have the responsibility to make decisions. The job of the ISSO is to help information asset owners identify risks to the assets. Assist them in identifying possible controls and then allow them to determine their action plan. Sometimes they will choose to accept the risk, and this is perfectly permissible.

1.7 Typical Information Protection Program

Over the years, the computer security group responsible for access control and disaster recovery planning has evolved into the enterprisewide information protection group. This group's ever-expanding roles and responsibilities include:

- Firewall control
- Risk analysis
- Business Impact Analysis (BIA)
- Virus control and virus response team
- Computer Emergency Response Team (CERT)
- Computer crime investigation
- Records management
- Encryption
- E-mail, voice-mail, Internet, video-mail policy
- Enterprisewide information protection program
- Industrial espionage controls
- Contract personnel nondisclosure agreements
- Legal issues
- Internet monitoring
- Disaster planning
- Business continuity planning
- Digital signature
- Secure single sign-on
- Information classification
- Local area networks
- Modem control
- Remote access
- Security awareness programs

In addition to these elements, the security professional now has to ensure that standards, both in the United States and worldwide, are examined and acted upon where appropriate. This book discusses these new standards in detail.

1.8 Summary

The role of the information protection professional has changed over the past 25 years and will change again and again. Implementing controls to be in compliance with audit requirements is not the way in which a program such as this can be run. There are limited resources available for controls. To be effective, the information owners and users must accept the controls. To meet this end, it will be necessary for the information protection professionals to establish partnerships with their constituencies. Work with your owners and users to find the appropriate level of controls. Understand the needs of the business or the mission of your organization. And make certain that information protection supports those goals and objectives.

Chapter 2

Threats to Information Security

2.1 What Is Information Security?

Information security is such a wide-ranging topic that it can be rather difficult to define precisely what it is. So when it came time for me to try to define it for the introduction of this chapter, I was stuck for a long period of time. Following the recommendation of my wife, I went to the best place to find definitions for anything — the dictionary. I pulled up the Merriam-Webster dictionary online and came up with these entries:

Main Entry: in·for·ma·tion

Pronunciation: "in′fər mā ′shən

Function: noun

1: the communication or reception of knowledge or intelligence

2 a (1): knowledge obtained from investigation, study, or instruction

   (2): INTELLIGENCE, NEWS

   (3): FACTS, DATA b : the attribute inherent in and communicated by one of two or more alternative sequences or arrangements of something (as nucleotides in DNA or binary digits in a computer

program) that produce specific effects c (1) : a
signal or character (as in a communication system
or computer) representing data (2) : something
(as a message, experimental data, or a picture)
which justifies change in a construct (as a plan
or theory) that represents physical or mental
experience or another construct d : a quantitative
measure of the content of information; specifically : a numerical quantity that measures the
uncertainty in the outcome of an experiment to
be performed

3: the act of informing against a person

4: a formal accusation of a crime made by a prosecuting
officer as distinguished from an indictment presented
by a grand jury
—in'for·ma'tion·al, adjective
—in'for·ma'tion·al·ly, adverb

And for security, my result was this:

Main Entry: se·cu·ri·ty

Pronunciation: sikyur'i t ē

Function: noun

Inflected Form(s): *plural* **-ties**

1: the quality or state of being secure: as a : freedom
from danger : SAFETY b: freedom from fear or anxiety
c: freedom from the prospect of being laid off <job
security>

2a: something given, deposited, or pledged to make
certain the fulfillment of an obligation b: SURETY

3: an evidence of debt or of ownership (as a stock
certificate or bond)

4a: something that secures: PROTECTION b (1): measures taken to guard against espionage or sabotage,
crime, attack, or escape (2): an organization or department whose task is security

So even after looking up information security in this dictionary, I still did not have a good way to describe and explain what information security was. Considering that I have worked in information security for almost nine years now, it was a little unsettling to not be able to define, at the most basic level, what I really did. The greatest difficulty in defining information security is, to me, because it is a little bit like trying to define infinity. It just seems far too vast for me to easily comprehend. Currently, information security can cover everything from developing the written policies that an organization will follow to secure its information, to the implementation of a user's access to a new file on the organization's server. With such a wide range of potential elements, it often leaves those in information security feeling as if they are a bit of the "Jack of all trades — and master of none." To give you a better feeling of the true breadth of information security, we will cover some of the more common aspects of information security in brief. All of the facets that we cover in the next few paragraphs are discussed in more detail throughout the remainder of the book.

The first and probably most important aspect of information security is the security policy (see Figure 2.1). If information security were a person, the security policy would be the central nervous system. Policies become the core of information security that provides a structure and purpose for all other aspects of information security. To those of you who may be a bit more technical, this may come as a surprise. In the documentation for

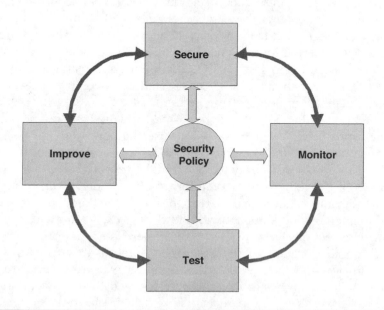

FIGURE 2.1 Security Wheel

their Cisco PIX® product, the folks at Cisco® even refer to the security policy as the center of security. RFC 2196 "Site Security Handbook" defines a security policy as "a formal statement of the rules by which people who are given access to an organization's technology and information assets must abide." Because of the central nature of security policies, you cannot discuss information security without mentioning security policies.

Another aspect of information security is organizational security. Organizational security takes the written security policy and develops the framework for implementing the policy throughout the organization. This would include tasks such as getting support from senior management, creating an information security awareness program, reporting to an information steering committee, and advising the business units of their role in the overall security process. The role of information security is still so large that there are many other aspects beyond just the organizational security and security policy.

Yet another aspect of information security is asset classification. Asset classification takes all the resources of an organization and breaks them into groups. This allows for an organization to apply differing levels of security to each of the groups, as opposed to security settings for each individual resource. This process can make security administration easier after it has been implemented, but the implementation can be rather difficult. However, there is still more to information security.

Another phase of information security is personnel security. This can be both fun and taxing at the same time. Personnel security, like physical security, can often be a responsibility of another person and not the sole responsibility of the information security manager. In small organizations, if the word "security" is in your job description, you may be responsible for everything. Personnel security deals with the people who will work in your organization. Some of the tasks that are necessary for personnel security are creating job descriptions, performing background checks, helping in the recruitment process, and user training.

As mentioned in the previous paragraph, physical security is a component of information security that is often the responsibility of a separate person from the other facets of information security. Even if physical security is some other person's responsibility, the information security professional must be familiar with how physical security can impact information security as a whole. Many times when an organization is thinking of stopping a break-in, the initial thought is to stop people from coming in over the Internet — when in fact it would be easier to walk into the building and plug into the network jack in the reception area. For years I have heard one particular story, which I have never been able to verify, that illustrates this example very well.

Supposedly, the CEO of a large company stands up in the general session of a hacker conference and announces, "This is a waste of time. My organization is so secure that if anyone here can break into our computers, I'll eat my hat."

Someone in the audience decides that the CEO needs to learn a lesson. The attacker decides to break into the organization, not by using the Internet or their telecommunication connection, but instead decides to take a physical approach to the attack. The attacker walks in the front door of the organization, walks to the second floor server room and proceeds to enter. Supposedly, the server room was having HVAC problems, so the door had to be propped open to allow the excess heat out. The attacker walks through the rows of devices in the server room and walks up to each of the cabinets and reads the electronically generated label on each device. When he finds the rack with the device marked "Firewall," he realizes he has found what he was seeking. The attacker then proceeded to turn off the firewall, disconnect the cables, and remove the firewall from the rack. The attacker followed this by hoisting the firewall up onto his shoulder and walking into the CEO's office.

When the attacker entered the CEO's office, he had only one thing to say. He asked, "What kind of sauce would you like with your hat?"

Physical security is much like information security in that it can be immense in its own right. Physical security can encompass everything from closed-circuit television to security lighting and fencing, to badge access and heating, ventilation, and air conditioning (HVAC). One area of physical security that is often the responsibility of the information security manager is backup power. The use of uninterruptible power supplies (UPS) are usually recommended even if your organization has other power backup facilities such as a diesel generator.

However, there is still more to information security. Another area of information security is communication and operations management. This area can often be overlooked in smaller organizations because it is often mistakenly considered "overhead." Communication and operations management encompass such tasks as ensuring that no one person in an organization has the ability to commit and cover up a crime, making sure that development systems are kept separate from production systems, and making sure that systems that are being disposed of are being disposed in a secure manner. While it is easy to overlook some of these tasks, doing so can create large security holes in an organization.

Access control is another core component of information security. Following the analogy used previously, if information security is the central nervous system of information security, access control would be the skin. Access control is responsible for allowing only authorized users to have access to your organization's systems and also for limiting what access an authorized user does have. Access control can be implemented in many different parts of information systems. Some common places for access control include:

- Routers
- Firewalls
- Desktop operating system
- File server
- Applications

Some organizations create something often referred to as a "candyland." A "candyland" is where the organization has moved the access to just one or two key points, usually on the perimeter. This is called a "candyland" because the organization has a tough crunchy exterior, followed by a soft gooey center. In any organization, you want access control to be in as many locations as your organization's support staff can adequately manage.

In addition to the previously mentioned components of information security, system development and maintenance is another component that must be considered. In many of the organizations that I have worked for, we never followed either of these principles. One area of system development and maintenance has been getting a lot of attention lately. Patch management would be a task from the maintenance part of system development and maintenance. This is a task that has many information security professionals referring to themselves as "patch managers." With such a large number of software updates coming out so frequently for every device on the network, it can be difficult — if not impossible — for support staff to keep everything up-to-date. And all it takes is one missed patch on any Internet-facing system to provide attackers a potential entry point into your organization. In addition to keeping systems up-to-date with patches, system development is another area that should be security-minded. When a custom application is written for your organization, each component or module of the application must be checked for security holes and proper coding practices. This is often done quickly or not at all, and can often lead to large exposure points for the attacker.

In addition to keeping our systems secure from attackers, we also need to keep our systems running in the event of a disaster — natural or otherwise. This becomes another facet of information security, and is often called business continuity planning. Every information security professional should have some idea of business continuity planning. Consider what you would do if the hard drive in your primary computer died. Do you have a plan for restoring all your critical files?

If you are like me, you probably never plan for a hard drive failure until after the first one happens. For me, it actually took many failed hard drives before I became more diligent in performing home backups of my critical files. In a large organization, just having an idea what you would do in the event of a disaster is not enough. A formal plan must be written, tested, and revised regularly. This will ensure that when something much worse than a hard drive dying happens to your organization, everyone will know exactly what to do.

The last aspect of information security discussed here is compliance. Now you may be thinking that compliance is someone else's job. And you might be telling the truth; but if we go back to our analogy that if information security were a person with security policy being the backbone and access control being the skin, then compliance would be the immune system. I know that might be a rather odd comparison, but compliance is a component of information security and I like to think of the compliance folks like a partner to the security folks. Many information security professionals spend some time reviewing and testing an information system for completeness and adequacy, and that is compliance.

So maybe now you see why information security is so difficult to define — it is just huge! With all the phases from policy to telecommunications, there is a lot to it. All the phases are equally important, because when it comes to threats to an organization, a breakdown in any of the phases of information security can present a gaping hole to the attacker. This is why the information security professional must have an understanding of all the aspects of information security.

2.2 Common Threats

From the hacker sitting up until all hours of the night finding ways to steal the company's secrets, to the dedicated employee who accidentally hits the delete key, there are many foes to information security. Due to the many different types of threats, it is a very difficult to try to establish and maintain information security. Our attacks come from many different sources, so it is much like trying to fight a war on multiple fronts. Our good policies can help fight the internal threats and our firewall and intrusion detection system can help fight the external threats. However, a failure of one component can lead to an overall failure to keep our information secure. This means that even if we have well secured our information from external threats, our end users can still create information security breaches. Recent statistics show that the majority of successful compromises are still coming from insiders. In fact, the Computer Security

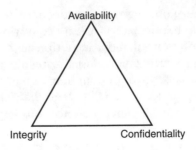

FIGURE 2.2   CIA Triad

Institute (CSI) in San Francisco estimates that between 60 and 80 percent of network misuse comes from inside the enterprise.

In addition to the multiple sources of information security attacks, there are also many types of information security attacks. In Figure 2.2, a well-known model helps illustrate this point. The information security triad shows the three primary goals of information security: integrity, confidentiality, and availability. When these three tenets are put together, our information will be well protected.

The first tenet of the information security triad is integrity. Integrity is defined by ISO-17799 as "the action of safeguarding the accuracy and completeness of information and processing methods." This can be interpreted to mean that when a user requests any type of information from the system, the information will be correct. A great example of a lack of information integrity is commonly seen in large home improvement warehouses. One day, I ventured to the local home improvement mega-mart looking for a hose to fix my sprinkler system. I spent quite some time looking for the hose before I happened upon a salesperson. Once I had the salesperson's attention, I asked about the location and availability of the hoses for which I was looking. The salesperson went to his trusty computer terminal and pulled up information about the hose I needed. The salesperson then let me know that I was in luck and they had 87 of the particular type of hose I needed in stock. So I inquired as to where these hoses could be found in the store and was told that just because the computer listed 87 in the store, this did not mean that there really were any of the hoses. While this example really just ruined my Sunday, the integrity of information can have much more serious implications. Take your credit rating; it is just information that is stored by the credit reporting agencies. If this information is inaccurate, or does not have integrity, it can stop you from getting a new home, a car, or a job. The integrity of this type of information is incredibly important, but is just as susceptible to integrity errors as any other type of electronic information.

The second tenet of the information security triad is confidentiality. Confidentiality is defined by ISO-17799 as "ensuring that information is accessible only to those authorized to have access to it." This can be one of the most difficult tasks to ever undertake. To attain confidentiality, you have to keep secret information secret. It seems easy enough, but remember the discussion on threat sources above. People from both inside and outside your organization will be threatening to reveal your secret information.

The last tenet of the information security triad is availability. Once again, ISO-17799 defines availability as ensuring that authorized users have access to information and associated assets when required. This means that when a user needs a file or system, the file or system is there to be accessed. This seems simple enough, but there are so many factors working against your system availability. You have hardware failures, natural disasters, malicious users, and outside attackers all fighting to remove the availability from your systems. Some common mechanisms to fight against this downtime include fault-tolerant systems, load balancing, and system failover.

Fault-tolerant systems incorporate technology that allows the system to stay available even when a hardware fault has occurred. One of the most common examples of this is RAID. According to the folks over at linux.org, the acronym RAID means redundant array of inexpensive disks. I have heard much debate as to what those letters actually stand for, but for our purposes, let us just use that definition. RAID allows the system to maintain the data on the system even in the event of a hard drive crash. Some of the simplest mechanisms to accomplish this include disk mirroring and disk duplexing. With disk mirroring, the system would have two hard drives attached to the same interface or controller. All data would be written to both drives simultaneously. With disk duplexing, the two hard drives are attached to two different controllers. Duplexing allows for one of the controllers to fail without the system losing any availability of the data. However, the RAID configuration can get significantly more complex than disk mirroring or disk duplexing. One of the more common advanced RAID solutions is RAID level 5. With level 5, RAID data is striped across a series of disks, usually three or more, so that when any one drive is lost, no information is destroyed. The disadvantage with using any of the systems mentioned above is that you lose some of the storage space from the devices. For example, a RAID 5 system with five 80-gigabyte hard drives would only have 320 gigabytes of actual storage. For more information on RAID, see Table 2.1.

The technologies just mentioned provide system tolerance but do not provide improved performance under heavy utilization conditions. To improve system performance with heavy utilization, we need load balancing. Load balancing allows the information requests to be spread across

TABLE 2.1   RAID Chart

RAID Level	Activity	Name
0	Data striped over several drives. No redundancy or parity is involved. If one volume fails, the entire volume is unusable. It is used for performance only.	Striping
1	Mirroring of drives. Data is written to two drives at once. If one drive fails, the other drive has the exact same data available.	Mirroring
2	Data striping over all drives at the bit level. Parity data is created with a hamming code, which identifies any errors. This level specifies the use of up to 39 disks: 32 for storage and 7 for error recovery data. This is not used in production today.	Hamming code parity
3	Data striping over all drives and parity data held on one drive. If a drive fails, it can be reconstructed from parity drive.	Byte-level parity
4	Same as level 3, except data is striped at the block level instead of the byte level.	Block-level parity
5	Data is written in disk sector units to all drives. Parity is written to all drives also, which ensures that there is not a single point of failure.	Interleave parity
6	Similar to level 5 but with added fault tolerance, which is a second set of parity data written to all drives.	Second parity data (or double parity)
10	Data is simultaneously mirrored and striped across several drives and can support multiple drive failures.	Striping and mirroring

a large number of servers or other devices. Usually a front-end component is necessary to direct requests to all of the back-end servers. This also provides tolerance, due to the fact that the front-end processor can just redirect the requests to the remaining servers or devices.

A technology that would lie between load balancing and RAID in terms of most availability would be system failover. With a failover environment, when the primary processing device has a hardware failure, a secondary device begins processing. This is a common technology to use with firewalls. In most organizations, to avoid having the firewall be a single point of failure on the network, the organization implements two firewalls that communicate with each other. In the event that the primary firewall cannot communicate with the secondary firewall, the secondary firewall takes over and begins processing the data.

As discussed, the job of the information security manager is difficult. There are many tasks that must be done to adequately protect the resources of an organization, and one slip along any of them can lead to a system breach. This is why the task of defending information systems is rather difficult. In the next section we look at other ways that your systems can be attacked.

2.2.1   Errors and Omissions

While error and omissions do not get the headlines of international hackers and the latest work propagating through the e-mail system, it is still the number-one threat to our systems. Because we cannot deny access to all of the user community, it becomes difficult to protect our systems from the people who need to use it day in and day out. Errors and omissions attack the integrity component of the CIA triad. To help fight these mistakes, we can use some of the following security concepts.

The first security concept that will help fight error and omissions is "least privilege." If we give our users only the most minimal set of permissions they need to perform their job functions, then we reduce the amount of information that can be accidentally contaminated. Using least privilege can create additional overhead on the support staff members who are tasked with applying the access controls to the user community. However, it will be worth the additional changes to keep the integrity of our information systems.

Another principle that can help is performing adequate and frequent backups of the information on the systems. When the user causes loss of the integrity of the information resident on the system, it may be easiest to restore the information from a tape backup made the night before. Tape backups are one of the essential tools of the information security manager and can often be the only recourse against a successful attack.

2.2.2   Fraud and Theft

If your end users are not accidentally destroying data but are maliciously destroying the information, then you may have a completely different type of attack. For most employees it is difficult to imagine a fellow employee coming into work every day under a ruse, but it does happen. As previously stated, employees are responsible for more successful intrusions than outsiders. It becomes very difficult to find the source of internal attacks without alerting the attacker that you suspect him of wrong-doing. The best line of defense against fraud and theft by your internal employees is to have well-defined policies. Policies can make it easier for the information security manager to collect data on the suspected wrong-doer to prove what bad acts the employee has performed.

If you have well-defined policies in your organization, the information security manager can use forensic techniques to gather evidence that will help provide proof of who performed the attack. While the entire breadth of forensics is beyond the scope of this book, we do spend a little time here discussing forensics from a high level.

Computer forensics allows a trained person to recover evidence from computer systems. The first rule of computer forensics is: "do no harm." This means that if you are not sure what to do, do not do anything to the system. The first goal of computer forensics is to leave the system in as pristine condition as possible. This may run counter-intuitive to the technology professional whose instincts want to look at the system to determine exactly what is going on and how it happened. Every time the technical professional moves the mouse or touches the keyboard to enter a command, the system is changing. This makes the evidence gathered from the system more suspect. After all, how would one determine what was done by the suspected employee and what was done by the professional investigating the activity?

There are many places that evidence of the activity may be left. Firewalls, server logs, and the client workstation are all places that should be investigated to determine if any evidence remains. When it comes to the client workstation, the first step in computer forensics is very non-technical. In this first step the security or support staff should be contacted to see what details they know about the system. One of the biggest potential problems would be if the client is using a hard drive encryption utility. The reason for this is that the second step is to "pull the plug." If you pull the plug on a system that has an encrypted hard drive, you may never be able to determine what information is on that system. We talk more about encryption in a later chapter of this book.

Assuming that you are able to confirm that there is no hard drive encryption on the suspect system, the next step is as mentioned above — pull the plug. Now, if the system is a laptop, pulling the plug will not shut down the system; it will just run off of a battery. In the case of the laptop, you need to pull the plug and remove the battery as well. In any case, once the system is powered off, the hard drive in the system should be turned over to a qualified professional. Please note that there are actually many more steps in the forensic process that are just beyond on the scope of this book.

Once the qualified professional has the suspect system, or at least the hard drive, he or she will then make a bit-stream backup of the hard drive. A bit-stream backup is different from a regular tape backup in that it makes an exact copy of the hard drive. A bit-stream backup does not just copy the files and the file system; it copies everything. The blank space, the slack space, file fragments, and everything else get copied to a second hard drive. The reason for this is that all the data recovery processes will be done on the second hard drive, leaving the original hard drive in its pristine state and it will not be modified. All data recovery processes performed on the system will also be performed on the backup copy of the hard drive.

Once the copy is made, a comparison of the hard drives will be done using an integrity technology called an MD5 hash (see Figure 2.3). The definition of an MD5 hash, as taken from the MD5 Web page, is as follows:

> [The MD5 algorithm] takes as input a message of arbitrary length and produces as output a 128-bit "fingerprint" or "message digest" of the input. It is conjectured that it is computationally infeasible to produce two messages having the same message digest, or to produce any message having a given prespecified target message digest.
>
> In essence, MD5 is a way to verify data integrity, and is much more reliable than checksum and many other commonly used methods.

Once the MD5 hashes are made from each hard drive, the corresponding values can then be compared. If these values are the same, then the two drives are identical; if the MD5 values are different, then the bit-stream backup failed and the drives are different. MD5 hashes are quite commonly used to verify the integrity of a file. The values can be used to ensure that a file was not modified during download and can also be used as a component of a digital signature.

After the hard drives have been compared and found to be identical, the forensic professional would then begin looking at the hard drive for evidence that the attack was launched from that machine. The forensics professional will try to recover deleted files, will look for file fragments in slack space, and will also look through the data files on the suspect system to see if any evidence is present. If any evidence is found on the system, the forensic professional will document the evidence and turn it into a final written report.

Because we have been looking at the damage that internal employees can carry out against our information systems, let us look at the other community that can also cause destruction to our data — the outsiders.

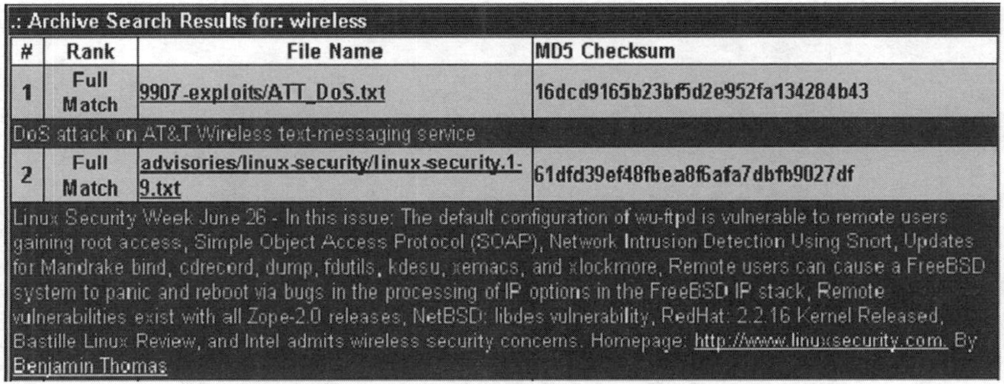

.: Archive Search Results for: wireless

#	Rank	File Name	MD5 Checksum
1	Full Match	9907_exploits/ATT_DoS.txt	16dcd9165b23bf5d2e952fa134284b43
		DoS attack on AT&T wireless text-messaging service	
2	Full Match	advisories/linux-security/linux-security-1-9.txt	61dfd39ef48f6ea8f6afa7dbfb9027df

Linux Security Week June 26 - In this issue: The default configuration of wu-ftpd is vulnerable to remote users gaining root access, Simple Object Access Protocol (SOAP), Network Intrusion Detection Using Snort, Updates for Mandrake bind, cdrecord, dump, fdutils, kdesu, xemacs, and xlockmore, Remote users can cause a FreeBSD system to panic and reboot via bugs in the processing of IP options in the FreeBSD IP stack, Remote vulnerabilities exist with all Zope-2.0 releases, NetBSD: libdes vulnerability, RedHat: 2.2.16 Kernel Released, Bastille Linux Review, and Intel admits wireless security concerns. Homepage: http://www.linuxsecurity.com. By Benjamin Thomas

FIGURE 2.3 Web Site with MD5 Values

2.2.3   Malicious Hackers

There are several groups of Internet users out there that will attack information systems. The three primary groups are hackers, crackers, and phreaks. While common nomenclature is to call all three of the groups "hackers," there are some differences between the groups. A hacker is a user who penetrates a system just to look around and see what is possible. The etiquette of hackers is that after they have penetrated the system, they will notify the system administrator to let the administrator know that the system has a vulnerability. It is often said that a hacker just wants security to be improved on all Internet systems. The next group, the crackers, are the group to really fear. A cracker has no etiquette on breaking into a system. Crackers will damage or destroy data if they are able to penetrate a system. The goal of crackers is to cause as much damage as possible to all systems on the Internet. The last group, phreaks, tries to break into an organization's phone system. The phreaks can then use the free phone access to disguise the phone number from which they are calling, and also stick your organization with the bill for long-distance phone charges.

The ways a hacker will attack a system can vary tremendously. Each attacker has his own bag of tricks that can be used to break into a system. There are several books on just the subject of hacking currently available, but we will cover the basic hacker methodology briefly here.

The basic hacker methodology has five main components: reconnaissance, scanning, gaining access, maintaining access, and covering tracks. It might seem odd to think of a methodology for hackers; but as with anything else, time matters. So to maximize time, most hackers follow a similar methodology.

The first phase in the methodology is the reconnaissance phase. In this phase, the attacker tries to gain as much information as possible about the target network. There are two primary ways an attacker can do this: active and passive. Most attackers would generally begin with passive attacks. These passive attacks can often generate a lot of good information about the network or organization the hacker wants to attack. The hacker would often begin by reading through the target organization's Web site to see if any information can be gained. The attacker would look for contact information for key employees (this can be used for social engineering), information on the types of technology used at the organization, and any other nugget of information that could be used in an attack. After the attacker has gone through the Web site, he would probably move to Internet search engines to find more information about the network he wishes to attack. He would be looking for bad newsgroup postings, posts at sites for people who are upset with the company, and any other details that could help in the attack. The attacker would then look for information in the DNS servers for the attack organization. This would provide a list of server and corresponding IP addresses. Once this is done, the hacker would move to active attacking.

To perform an active reconnaissance attack, a hacker would perform ping sweeps, SNMP network scans, banner grabbing, and other similar attacks. The attacks would help the attacker weed out the number of dead IP addresses and find the live hosts to move on to the next phase — scanning.

An attacker would begin scanning, looking for holes to compromise to gain access to the network. The attacker would scan all servers that are available on the Internet, looking for known vulnerabilities. These vulnerabilities could be in a poorly written Web-enabled application or from applications that have known security vulnerabilities in them. The attacker would also look at the organization's firewall and routers to see if vulnerabilities exist there as well. Once an attacker has compiled a list of vulnerabilities, he would then move on to the next stage — gaining access.

There are many ways for an attacker to gain access to the target network. Some of the more common entry points into the network are through the target server's OS (operating system), through an application that was developed in-house, as well as through an application with known vulnerabilities, through the network devices that can be seen from the Internet, and if all else fails the attacker will perform a denial-of-service attack. Once the attacker has access, all he wants to do is make sure that he can keep it.

To maintain access, an attacker would commonly upload a custom application onto the compromised server. This application would then be a back door into the target organization, and would allow the attacker to come and go at will. In addition to uploading new programs, an attacker can alter existing programs on the system. The advantage of doing this is that a well-informed administrator may know the files on his system and he might recognize that new files have been installed on his servers. By modifying already-existing files, the system would appear to be unmodified at first glance. A common way of doing this is with a group of files called a rootkit. A rootkit allows an attacker to replace normal system files with files of the same name that also have Trojan horse functionality. The new system files would allow the attacker in just as if he added additional files to the target server. An attacker may not need long access to the system and he might just wish to download the existing programs or data off the target server. Once an attacker has determined his mechanism for getting back into the server, the last step in the hacker methodology is to cover his tracks.

To cover his tracks, an attacker would go through the system audit log files and remove any trace of the attacker on the system. This would hide his access from the system administrator and would also leave less evidence behind in case the system administrator wishes to have a forensics examination performed on the compromised host. The level of skill of an attacker is often apparent in this phase. A crude attacker might delete an entire log file, thus making it easy for the system administrator to determine that someone has been in the system; but a more skillful attacker might just modify his log entries to show that the traffic was originating from a different IP address.

2.2.4 Malicious Code

While malicious users can attack your system, programs released by the same group of people will often be more successful in reaching the protected parts of your organization. Malicious code is defined as any code that is designed to make a system perform any operation with the knowledge of the system owner. One of the fastest ways to introduce malicious code into a target organization's protected network is by sending the malicious code via e-mail.

There are many different types of malicious code. This chapter discusses a few of the more common ones, including virus, worm, Trojan horse, and logic bomb. The most commonly thought of type of malicious code is the virus. A virus is a code fragment, or a piece of code, that can be injected into target files. A virus then waits, usually until the file is opened or accessed, to spread to another file where the malicious code is then injected into that file. With a virus-infected system, one can often find in excess of 30,000 infected files. There are many different types of viruses; there are viruses that attack the boot sector of the hard drive, there are file system infectors, there are macro viruses that use the Office scripting functionality, and there are viruses for all major operating systems.

Another type of malicious code is the worm. A worm is typically a complete file that infects in one place on a given system and then tries to replicate to other vulnerable systems on the network or Internet. A number of the highly publicized attacks have been worms. Nimda is one example of a recent, highly publicized attack that was a worm.

Trojan horses are a different type of malicious code and can be quite deceiving to the end user. A Trojan horse appears to have a legitimate function on the surface, but also has malicious code underneath. There are a number of freeware programs on the Internet that allow an attacker to insert malicious code into most of the common executables. The only way to help stop the Trojan horses is to educate the end user to not open file attachments unless they know exactly what the attachment will do.

The final type of malicious code discussed here is the logic bomb. "Logic bomb" is a generic term for any type of malicious code that is waiting for a trigger event to release the payload. This means that the code could be waiting for a period of time (e.g., one month) before it executes. A well-known example of a logic bomb was the Michelangelo attack. This logic bomb was waiting for Michelangelo's birthday before it would trigger the malicious code.

2.2.5   Denial-of-Service Attacks

As an attacker if you cannot get access to the target network, often the best thing that you can do is make sure that no one gets access to the network. Enter the denial-of-service attack. The denial-of-service or DoS attack is designed to either overwhelm the target server's hardware resources or overwhelm the target network's telecommunication lines. For years there were a number of common "one-to-one" DoS attacks. In these attacks, the hacker would launch an attack from his system against the target server or network. Syn floods, Fin floods, Smurfs, and Fraggles are all examples of these "one-to-one" attacks. While all these attacks remain successful on some target networks today, most organizations have implemented technology to stop these attacks from causing a service disruption in their organizations.

In February 2000, DoS attacks hit the next level. In this month, a number of high-profile targets were taken offline by the next generation of DoS attacks — the distributed denial of service (DDoS) attack. These DDoS attacks were no longer the familiar "one-to-one" attacks of the past. These attacks used zombie hosts to create a "many-to-one" attack. These zombie hosts were devices that were compromised and had code uploaded onto them that would allow for a master machine to contact them, and have them all release the DoS attack at the same time. There were tens of thousands of zombie hosts available and the attacker could use a number of common tools from which to launch the attack. Some of the common tools were Trinoo, TFN2K, and stacheldraht. These tools were pretty straightforward to use and allowed an attacker to release a devastating attack against the target.

The new DDoS attacks are very difficult to defend against. Most of the tools denied service not by overwhelming the processing server, but by flooding the telecommunications lines from the Internet service provider (ISP). Most organizations are still vulnerable to this type of attack. The mechanism that has curtailed most DDoS attacks is by trying to minimize the number of zombie-infected hosts available. As soon as a new and better infection mechanism surfaces, another round of DDoS attacks is sure to spring up.

2.2.6 Social Engineering

Social engineering is the name given to a category of security attacks in which someone manipulates others into revealing information that can be used to steal data, access to systems, access to cellular phones, money, or even your own identity. Such attacks can be very simple or very complex. Gaining access to information over the phone or through Web sites that you visit has added a new dimension to the role of the social engineer.

This section examines ways in which people, government agencies, military organizations, and companies have been duped into giving information that has opened them up to attack. Low-tech as well as the newer forms of electronic theft are discussed.

Social engineering is the acquisition of sensitive information or inappropriate access privileges by an outsider, based upon the building of an inappropriate trust relationship with insiders. Note that the term "outsider" does not refer only to nonemployees; an outsider can be an employee who is attempting to circumvent established policies and standards.

The goal of social engineering is to trick someone into providing valuable information or access to that information or resource. The social engineering exploiter preys on qualities of human nature, such as:

■ *The desire to be helpful.* We have trained our employees well. Make sure the customer is satisfied. The best way to a good appraisal is to have good responses from those needing assistance. Most of our employees want to be helpful and this can lead to giving away too much information.

■ *A tendency to trust people.* Human nature is to actually trust others until they prove that they are not trustworthy. If someone tells us that he is a certain person, we usually accept that statement. We must train our employees to seek independent proof.

■ *The fear of getting into trouble.* Too many of us have seen negative reaction by superiors because verification of identity took too long or because some official was offended. Management must support all employees who are doing their assignment and protecting the information resources of the enterprise.

■ *The willingness to cut corners.* Sometimes we get lazy. We post passwords on the screen or leave important material lying out for anyone to see.

What scares most companies about social engineers is that the sign of truly successful social engineers is that they receive what they are looking for without raising any suspicion. It is the bad social engineers we know about, not the good ones.

According to the *Jargon Dictionary,* "wetware" is the human being attached to a computer system. People are usually the weakest link in the security chain. In the 1970s, we were told that if we installed access control packages, we would have security. In the 1980s, we were encouraged to install effective antivirus software to ensure that our systems and networks were secure. In the 1990s, we were told that firewalls would lead us to security. Now in the 21st century, it is intrusion detection systems or public key infrastructure that will lead us to information security. In each and every iteration, security has eluded us because the silicon-based products must interface with carbon-based units. It is the human factor that will continue to appear in our discussion on social engineering.

A skilled social engineer will often try to exploit this weakness before spending time and effort on other methods to crack passwords or gain access to systems. Why go to all the trouble of installing a sniffer on a network when a simple phone call to an employee will gain the needed user id and password. Social engineering is the most difficult form of attack to defend against because it cannot be defended with hardware or software alone. A successful defense will require an effective information security architecture, starting with policies and standards and following through with a vulnerability assessment process.

2.2.7 Common Types of Social Engineering

While the greatest area for success is human-based interaction by the social engineer, there are also some computer-based methods that attempt to retrieve the desired information using software programs to either gather information or deny service to a system. One of the most ingenious methods was first introduced into the Internet in February 1993. The user attempting to log on to the system was met with the normal prompt, and, after entering the correct user id and password, had the system begin the prompt all over again. What happened was that a social engineer managed to get a program installed in front of the normal sign-on routine, gathered the information, and then passed the prompt to the real sign-on process. According to published articles at the time, more than 95 percent of regular users had their access codes compromised.

Today we see the use of Web sites as a common ploy to offer something free or a chance to win something on the Web site or to gain important information. At a Michigan firm in 1998, the network administrator installed a 401(k) information Web site that required employees to register with the site to obtain information on their 401(k) program. After giving such information as account id, password, social security number, and home address, the Web site returned a message that indicated it was still under construction. Within a week, nearly every employee with a 401(k) plan, including senior management, had attempted to register on the Web site.

Other forms of social engineering have been classified into various groups. The first two are *Impersonation* and *Important User.* These are often used in combination with one another. The 1991 book *Cyberpunk* by Katie Hafner and John Markoff describes the actions of one Susan Hadley (aka Susan Thunder). Using an easily accessible military computer directory, she was able to obtain the name of the individual in charge. She used her basic knowledge of military systems and terminology as she called a military base to find out the commanding officer of the secret compartmentalized information facility. She sweet-talked her way into obtaining the name of the major's secretary and then hung up.

Using this information, she changed tactics. She switched from being nonchalant to authoritative. Her boss, the major, was having problems accessing the system and she wanted to know why. Using threats, she got the access and, according to her, was in the system within 20 minutes.

Pretending to be someone you are not, or schmoozing your way to the information you need; these are typical examples of how social engineers work to obtain the information they need. They will often contact the help desk and drop names of other employees. Once they have what they need to gain further access, they will attack a more vulnerable person — one who has information but not necessarily the clout to challenge anyone of "authority."

Perhaps two of the oldest forms of social engineering are *dumpster diving* and *shoulder surfing.* The dumpster diver is willing to get dirty to get the information he needs. Too often companies throw out important information. Sensitive information, manuals, and phone directories should be shredded before disposing.

The shoulder surfer will look over someone's shoulder to gain passwords or PIN numbers. A few years ago, one of the news magazine shows did a session on phone card fraud. During one sequence, the reporter was given a new phone calling card and told to use it at Grand Central Station in New York City. While she made the call, the undercover police counted at least five people surfing her PIN number. One even turned to the cameraman to make sure he got the number too.

The final two types of human-based social engineering are *third-party authorization* and *tech support.* The typical third-party authorization occurs when the social engineer drops the name of a higher-up who has the authority to grant access. It is usually something like "Ms. Shooter says its OK" or "Before she went on vacation, Ms. Shooter said I should call you to get this information." The social engineer may well have called the authority's' office to find out if she was out. Remember that most social engineers are internal.

The tech support method is where the social engineer pretends to be someone from an infrastructure group and wants a user to access the system while the social engineer scopes out the connection. They will normally ask for the user's account id and password so that they can see it cross the network. In a recent vulnerability assessment of a large Texas-based insurance provider, 12 employees were called by "network administration," which was actually the security staff posing as network administration. The employees were told that the network was experiencing connection problems, that they had installed a scope on the fiber connections, and then asked the employees to log on to the system. They requested the account id and password to use as a verification that the data was being properly sent. Three employees did not answer the phone call. Eight out of the other nine gave the information requested. One employee was not able to give out his password because he could not find the Post-It note on which he had it written.

Some potential security breaches are so mundane that they hardly seem to be a concern. With all the fires that we have to fight each day and the deadlines we have to meet, sometimes the most obvious are often overlooked:

- *Passwords.* The number-one access point for social engineers is the good old-fashioned password. After all of the awareness programs and reminder cards, we still find that employee-generated passwords are too short or too easy to guess. System-generated passwords are too long and employees have to write them down to remember them. Even today, some systems do not require that passwords be changed. We find this most often in e-mail systems and Internet accounts. We recommend an assessment of the password length and interval for change standards; determine if they still meet the current needs of the user community.
- *Modems.* Every company has more modems than they know about. Employees and contractors will add a modem to a system and then install products such as *pcAnywhere* or *Carbon Copy* to improve their remote access time. We recommend that war dialers be used at least twice a year to check on modems.
- *Help desk.* Put in place processes that can assist the help-desk employee in verifying who is on the other end of the phone call.
- *Web sites.* There are two problems here: the dummy site that gathers information and the legal site that gives away too much information. Many hackers use the information they gather from the enterprise Web site to launch attacks on the network. Make certain that the information available will not compromise the information resources of the enterprise.

A social engineer can simply walk in and behave like an employee. Our employees have not been trained to challenge strangers. Or if they have been trained, there has not been enough reinforcement of the challenge process. Require that all personnel on site wear appropriate identification. Some organizations require only visitors to wear badges. Therefore, to become an employee, a visitor must simply remove the badge. Sell the principle that employee identification is not just a security measure, but rather a process to protect the employees in the workplace. By ensuring that only authorized personnel are permitted access, the employees will have a safe work environment.

Because there is neither hardware nor software available to protect an enterprise against social engineering, it is essential that good practices be implemented. Some of those practices might include:

- Require anyone there to perform service to show proper identification.
- Establish a standard that passwords are never to be spoken over the phone.
- Implement a standard that forbids passwords from being left lying about.
- Implement caller ID technology for the help desk and other support functions.
- Invest in shredders and have one on every floor.

Policies, procedures, and standards are an important part of an overall antisocial engineering campaign. To be effective, a policy should:

- Not contain standards or directives that may not be attainable
- Stress what can be done and stay away from what is not allowed as much as possible
- Be brief and concise
- Be reviewed on a regular basis and kept current
- Be easily attainable by the employees and available via the company intranet

To be effective, policies, procedures, and standards must be taught and reinforced to the employees. This process must be ongoing and must not exceed six months between reinforcement times. It is not enough to just publish policies and expect employees to read, understand, and implement what is required. They need to be taught to emphasize what is important and how it will help them do their jobs. This training should begin at new employee orientation and continue throughout employment. When a person becomes an ex-employee, a final time of reinforcement should be done during the exit interview process.

Another method to keep employees informed and educated is to have a Web page dedicated to security. It should be updated regularly and should contain new social engineering ploys. It could contain a "security tip of the day" and remind employees to look for typical social engineering signs. These signs might include behaviors such as:

■ Refusal to give contact information
■ Rushing the process
■ Name-dropping
■ Intimidation
■ Small mistakes
■ Requesting forbidden information or access

As part of this training or education process, reinforce a good catch. When employees do the right thing, make sure they receive proper recognition. Train the employees on who to call if they suspect they are being social engineered.

Apply technology where you can. Consider implementing trace calls if possible, or at least caller ID where available. Control overseas long-distance services to most phones. Ensure that physical security for the building.

A social engineer with enough time, patience, and resolve will eventually exploit some weakness in the control environment of an enterprise. Employee awareness and acceptance of safeguard measures will become our first line of defense in this battle against the attackers. The best defense against social engineering requires that employees be tested and that the bar of acceptance be raised regularly.

2.3 Summary

Security professionals can begin this process by making available a broad range of supporting documentation available to all personnel. Many employees respond positively to anecdotes relating to social engineering attacks and hoaxes. Keep the message fresh and accurate.

Include details about the consequences of successful attacks. Do not discuss these attacks in terms of how security was circumvented, but rather their impact on the business or mission of the enterprise. These attacks can lead to a loss of customer confidence, market share, and jobs.

Employees at all levels of the enterprise need to understand and believe that they are important to the overall protection strategy. Without all employees being part of the team, the enterprise, its assets, and its employees will be open to attack from both external and internal social engineers. With training and support, one can lessen the impact of these kinds of attacks.

Chapter 3

The Structure of an Information Security Program

3.1 Overview

The structure of an information security program is its performance at every level of the organization. The reach of the program, how each business unit supports the program, and how every individual carries out his or her duties as specified in the program all determine how effective the program will be.

Uniform participation in the program is necessary if its results are to justify an organization's investment. From senior management, through business unit management, to every individual member of an organization, all must be seen — for varying reasons — to give the same level of support to the information security program's aims and objectives. If there are levels or areas in an organization where support is seen as weak, this will cause gaps in the effectiveness of the program and weaken the entire information security structure. Like an unpopular law (the 55 mph speed limit comes to mind), when a requirement to follow good business practices is ignored by some — and effective information security is good business practice, more will come to think they need not comply either.

LIVERPOOL
JOHN MOORES UNIVERSITY
AVRIL ROBARTS LRC
TEL. 0151 231 4022

3.1.1 Enterprisewide Security Program

The aim of the information security practitioner should be to have a uniform information security program that spans the whole enterprise. Many organizations have strong and weak areas; a good example might be a financial services organization in which everyone but the stock traders abides by strong information security standards. The stock traders, however, feel that they work under so much pressure that learning and complying with information security standards would be too much of an impediment to their work. In an organization such as this, the management of the stock traders might have enough influence to hold off efforts to enforce compliance.

If we use a castle as an analogy for a strong information security program, then having all but one department in compliance with standards is equivalent to leaving open a gate in the castle walls. Having said that, information security practitioners cannot — by themselves — ensure that the information security program is applied in a uniform way across the entire organization. Only the organization's management can do this job. Of course, it is the job of the information security practitioner to provide the organization's management with the tools necessary to do that job.

A measured security strategy based on the organization's business objectives and attitude toward risk is the foundation for a uniform program. Building information security policies and standards on that strategy is the next step, and helping the organization achieve compliance with those policies and standards follows. The information security practitioner can help the organization achieve a uniform, enterprisewide security program by leading efforts to create and implement policies and standards, by educating all levels of employees within the organization on acceptable security-related practices, and by acting as a consultant to help business units address specific problems in a way that is consistent with practice in other parts of the organization.

An enterprisewide security program then is necessary to make sure that everyone knows the rules and abides by them and, by doing so, makes sure that the enterprise information is given the protection desired by the enterprise's senior management. An organization structure must be set up to ensure effective communication — both of policy and standards to the entire organization and of issues from the entire organization to the decision makers. The organization structure should involve:

- Information Security Management who provide direction for the program, advice to the entire organization, and a focal point for resolving security issues
- Internal Audit who report on information security practices to the Audit Committee and, through the Audit Committee, to the organization's directors and other senior management

- A Steering Committee composed of the heads of all business units who — among their other duties — take direction from the organization's senior management and make sure it is translated into working practices
- Security Coordinators in each business unit who, with the support and cooperation of Information Security Management, implement the instructions of the steering committee
- Security Administrators in each business unit who maintain the access controls and other tools used as controls to protect information
- A Security Working Team that gets its support and direction from Information Security Management and the Steering Committee and that focuses on plans to implement new and amended information security processes and tools so that the implementation has the lowest possible impact on the organization

Of course, no information security practitioner should attempt to impose this structure on an organization where it clearly does not fit, but the broad responsibilities outlined above must be carried out if the information security program is to have robust support in the organization. An illustration of the organization structure — and suggested lines of report — is shown in Figure 3.1.

3.2 Business Unit Responsibilities

When discussing business unit responsibilities, it makes sense to separate them into two areas: the creation and implementation of policies and standards and compliance with those policies and standards.

3.2.1 Creation and Implementation of Policies and Standards

The development of policies and standards requires the involvement of every business unit. Each business unit — at some point in its chain of authority to senior management — must be represented in the process to review and approve policies.

For the policies to be as robust as possible and to represent the needs of the entire enterprise, each business unit must be represented in two ways: (1) some member of the chain of authority for each business unit must have the opportunity to approve policies (or withhold approval); and (2) a number of members of the chain of authority must be given the opportunity to review and comment on the policies. See Table 3.1

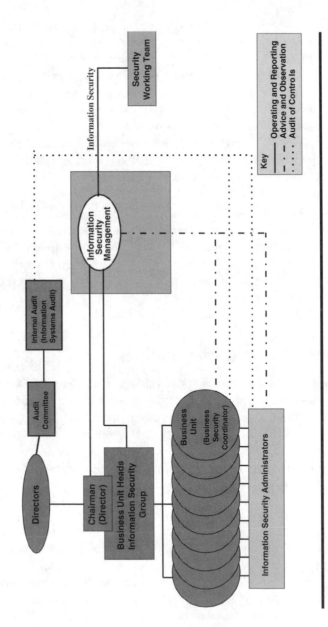

FIGURE 3.1 Organization Structure

TABLE 3.1   Sample Responsibilities

Policy Reviewer	Info. Sec.	Sec. Organization	Asset Classification	Personnel	Physical	Network Management	System Access	Systems Devel.	BCP	Compliance
CEO										
SVP, Refining										
SVP, Marketing										
SVP, Dev. & Tech.										
President, Asphalt Ref.										
VP, Finance										
General Auditor										
General Counsel										
VP, Corp. Planning										
GM, HR										
GM, Risk Mgmt.										
Senior Consultant										
CISO										

for a sample table in which the responsibilities in the policy development process can be laid out. A simple table, we lay out the officers and managers involved in the process on one axis and the policies we intend to review or develop on the other. At each intersection, we place an R — indicating the responsibility to review indicated policy. Some organizations use a table like this but make a difference between those responsible for only review — where their comments may or may not be included in revisions, at the discretion of the Information Security Manager. Other may be denoted with a C, which indicates that they have the right to comment on policy and, of course, their comments must be incorporated in revised drafts.

Generally, in large organizations, this means that management at the Director or Vice President level approves policy after management and staff at lower levels have reviewed it and provided their comments. The approval at the higher level usually involves a Steering Committee approach (discussed later).

In the process for drafting and implementing standards, the responsibilities change slightly. In this case, business units have the responsibility for writing information security standards for their area of responsibility. For example, standards for Personnel security could best be written by Human Resources (with input from Information Security, of course). Once again, however, each business unit must provide someone who can review information security standards for their impact on their business unit. That person will then advise their representative on the group that approves standards for the enterprise.

When policies and standards have been approved, it is the responsibility of each business unit to assist in their implementation.

3.2.2 Compliance with Policies and Standards

Moving beyond the drafting and implementation of policies and standards, each business unit — through its management — has the responsibility to ensure constant compliance with those policies and standards. It is of little use to ignore information security policies and standards until an audit is performed and then have to devote a significant effort to remedial or "catch-up" work. This culture will tend to repeat itself (rather than viewing compliance as a normal business practice) and thus will continually create gaps in protection and exposure to risk for the company's information. A better practice is for business unit management to learn what is necessary for compliance with information security policies and standards and then use that knowledge to improve the business practices within the unit.

Another responsibility within business units is, of course, the enforcement of compliance. If there is confusion about the difference between compliance itself and the enforcement of compliance, perhaps one can view compliance as a normal practice and enforcement as the action to be taken when one finds noncompliance. For example, the management of a business unit might consider making compliance with information security policies and standards a performance issue — at least in the exception. While it might — for many reasons — be difficult to have information security made part of the performance improvement and measurement process across an entire organization, it is less difficult to persuade business unit managers that it can be made so in cases where failure to comply has been found.

Consider, for example, a policy statement that says all means of access — IDs, passwords, tokens, etc. — are confidential to the individual to whom they are issued. If an individual is known to habitually share his ID or password (or seek to share others'), then that individual's performance review or performance plan could include a requirement to change that behavior in a fixed time — "John Doe will ensure that, over the course of the next 12 months, he will not be found sharing his or others' means of access. Otherwise, further disciplinary action (and it can be specified here) will ensue. It is expected that, even after this 12-month period expires, John Doe will continue to comply with company policies."

3.3 Information Security Awareness Program

The purpose of a security awareness program is in clearly demonstrating the "who, what, and why" of the policies and standards. Reading alone is not the most effective method of absorbing information and, once read, the message of the policies and standards are easily forgotten in the stress of the working day. If an organization wishes its policies and standards to have perpetual effect, it should commit to a perpetual program of reinforcement and information — a security awareness program.

Problems with budget may stop your employee information security awareness program before it gets properly started. Those who control budgets need to show due diligence by demonstrating the effect or the potential return on investment for every dollar spent and information security awareness programs are notoriously difficult to quantify in this way. What is the return on investment? Increased employee awareness? And how does that contribute to the profitability of the enterprise? These are difficult numbers to demonstrate.

However, if we look at things that an organization would like to avoid, justifying the cost of an employee information security awareness program can get easier. Most information security programs struggle with things such as access control (password management, sharing computer sessions, etc.), e-mail practices, and virus management; so, if your Information Security staff can find a way to address these issues as benefits of the information security awareness program, then you have a way to justify expense for that program.

The way to address these issues is through measurement. Information Security staff must understand what it is that they are trying to improve (and "security awareness" is too fuzzy a subject to talk about improving). If your organization is trying to improve users' access control habits, then Information Security start must start by finding ways to measure them. These can include password cracking software such as lophtcrack or sampling walk-throughs where a given number of workstations are observed and a record made of how many are left unattended and logged on.

Similarly, if your organization wants to improve e-mail habits, observation of e-mail traffic before any security awareness activity will be necessary. Some organizations have made use of "honeypot" e-mails — in other words, e-mails that coax users into behavior that we will later teach them to avoid practicing — to measure the effect of their information security awareness program on e-mail habits.

Audit findings and workpapers will also provide valuable measurements at no cost to the Information Security department.

As for the content and mechanics of the awareness program, the following general advice should prove useful.

3.3.1 Frequency

One of the main factors in the success of the employee information security awareness program will be the frequency with which the message is delivered to staff. If the message is delivered too often, it will become background noise — easily ignored. On the other hand, we want the message to be in employees' minds as much as possible, so delivering the message too infrequently can be as damaging as delivering it too often.

Information security awareness programs are basically advertising — with an educational message. The messages might begin with a PowerPoint presentation, which focuses heavily on:

- Information security policies
- Information ownership
- Information classification
- Good information security practices

Because employee information security awareness is an ongoing process, the messages will vary over the first year according to how much information security program activity has already taken place and how well the implementation of other information security program components has gone.

In the first year, you should aim to deliver the messages outlined above, plus messages on:

- Information security standards
- Information security monitoring
- Information security performance measurement
- More information security good practices

Of course, while delivering these messages, the employee information security awareness should also reinforce the original messages.

3.3.2 Media

One of the main factors in the success of the employee information security awareness program will be the composition of the media used. Each media element has its strengths and weaknesses and so media for delivery must be carefully selected to ensure that the message of the program is communicated as effectively as possible. To rely on one medium — that is, video, posters, PowerPoint presentations, etc. — would deaden the message. Staff would become used to seeing whatever medium or media were chosen and would begin to ignore it. The key is to use a mix of media and a frequency of message delivery that achieves the level of consciousness of security issues that the organization has chosen.

We live in a video generation. News, entertainment, streaming video on the Internet, advertising, and education all come at us in video format. It makes sense then to consider custom video as a medium for delivering the employee information security awareness message — at least in part. The main "plus" of custom video, of course, is the sense of immediacy. The "minus" — equally obvious — is cost. However, there are a number of organizations that offer already-made information security awareness videos.

However, most organizations still rely on presentation software such as PowerPoint. It is familiar and, if done right, can still add some "zip" to the message — the biggest "plus" of using it. Other plusses are that presentation software is easy to use and easy to modify. You should consider using PowerPoint for your initial employee information security awareness offering and should not plan to use any more PowerPoint presentations during the first year. (We have all been subjected to "death by PowerPoint," the feeling that comes when presentations lack presence, go on too long, *or are too frequent*. Too many PowerPoint presentations will quickly kill audience interest in the program.)

Whether using video or presentation software, you must consider putting the definitive version of the presentation on the organization's Web server. Note that this has the potential to create bandwidth problems and should be discussed with IT before any plans are made. However, having the definitive version of any presentation on the company's Web server does allow universal access and provides savings from lower travel and "training the trainer" costs. Some companies — rich in bandwidth — stream the presentation to all company sites; but for those who do not have this bandwidth (or do not want to use it for this purpose), putting the definitive version on the company's Web server is still a good idea, because it allows people to access the definitive version of the presentation at a time convenient to them.

In addition to the media outlined above, one must consider the use of booklets, brochures, newsletters, and "giveaway" items to supplement the core media of the program. Most people react well to something they can hold in their hand; and while the readership rate of booklets, etc., may be low, any number of employees who read this material enhances the effectiveness of the media already discussed.

3.4 Information Security Program Infrastructure

The "infrastructure" discussed here is the mechanism within the organization that supports good information security practices. From the senior management who sit on the Information Security Steering Committee, to the responsibilities of every employee to practice good information security habits, the infrastructure must be robust and educated in order for the information security program to bring full benefit to the organization.

3.4.1 Information Security Steering Committee

As previously stated, the Information Security Steering Committee should ideally be comprised of senior managers (director or VP level) representing every major business element of the organization. To round out the committee — to provide the best possible contribution at that level to the information security program — Internal Audit, Legal, Human Resources, and, where appropriate, organized labor should also sit on the committee.

The Information Security Steering Committee generally meets no more than monthly and, in some organizations, as infrequently as quarterly. The purpose of the committee is to provide a forum where major issues can be presented (along with proposed resolutions) and where the organization's wishes and needs for the information security program can be set out. When major changes in business processes, new business processes, and major new technologies are introduced, it is at the Information Security Steering Committee level that direction for the information security program — with respect to these changes — will be found. Generally, when such a situation is proposed, the management of the Information Security group will propose to the committee their views on what controls should look like in the changed environment and the Information Security Steering Committee will accept or amend those views.

For example, in the case of a merger or acquisition, the information security group will study the proposed action and decide on a strategy to bring the merged or acquired company to the same level of control as the parent organization. The information security group will then present the proposed action to the Information Security Steering Committee, which will approve the strategy or direct that changes be made. As the merger or acquisition proceeds, the Information Security group will report progress and details to the committee on a predefined frequency.

3.4.2 Assignment of Information Security Responsibilities

Even in the early stages of the 21st century, there are still organizations that look to the management of the Information Security unit to take complete responsibility for all information security activities in the organization. And almost every organization with that outlook has an information security program that is failing.

Information security is an organizationwide responsibility that touches every person. While the Information Security unit must act as a source of guidance and advice, the program can only succeed when all parties in the organization recognize their responsibility to protect information and exercise that responsibility. The protection of information is no more than a part of doing business — as much a part as making sure that more tangible assets as, say, money in a bank or products made by a manufacturing company are physically protected.

3.4.2.1   Senior Management

The simplest way to state senior management's responsibility for information security comes from Franklin Roosevelt's maxim — "The Buck Stops Here." Senior management personnel of any organization are the ultimate decision makers and, as such, have the ultimate responsibility for deciding how the organization will handle risk.

It is widely accepted that senior management, under the Foreign Corrupt Practices Act, has a responsibility to make sure that information security (as an element of risk) is adequately addressed in the organization. In some industries — government, financial services, and healthcare spring most quickly to mind — senior management has clearly defined, regulated responsibilities to ensure that information is protected to a level equal to its perceived value to the organization.

Outside the legal requirements, senior management is responsible for:

- Making sure that audit recommendations pertaining to the protection of information are addressed in a timely and adequate manner
- Participating in the activities of the Information Security Steering Committee (where such a body exists) to guide the activities of the information security effort
- Overseeing the formation, management, and performance of the information security unit; this includes providing adequate resources (budget, manpower, etc.) to make sure that senior management requirements for information security can be carried out
- Participating in the effort to educate the organization's staff about their responsibilities for protecting information
- Reviewing and approving information security policies and strategies for the organization
- Providing resolution for information security issues that are of such magnitude or urgency that they must be addressed on an organizationwide basis

3.4.2.2 Information Security Management

The function of Information Security Management has been likened, variously, to "corporate policeman" and "referee." In a well-ordered information security program, Information Security Management will avoid being seen as the corporate policeman but might end up doing a great deal of work as a referee. As this section makes clear, Information Security Management is responsible for the information security practices of the information security unit — and nowhere else. For other units, Information Security provides services and advice, but the responsibility for protection of information within those units lies squarely on the management and staff of those units. In cases where conflicts arise because of differing opinions on how to implement information security measures, Information Security Management can be seen as an arbiter — or referee — of what is acceptable (acting, of course, under the direction of the organization's senior management).

The Information Security Management of an organization must be able to:

- *Drive the effort to create, publish, and implement information security policies and standards.* While the responsibility for the creation of policies and standards does not belong to Information Security Management, they should be best equipped to act as an agent to make sure these things are created and to project-manage the effort to implement.
- *Coordinate the creation and testing of business continuity plans.* There is still some argument over whether or not business continuity planning ought to be a function of information security, and I recognize that there may be some environments where it is not desirable that information security and business continuity planning not be managed by the same organization. However, given the closeness of the objectives of information security and continuity planning, I wholeheartedly endorse the idea that business continuity planning is a function that should fall under the control of Information Security Management.
- *Manage the information security effort within the information security unit.* Just as all business unit managers have the responsibility of making sure that information stored and processed by their unit is protected to a level equal to its value, so Information Security Management must take care of security databases and paper files, and protect them from threats.
- *Administer information security software tools on behalf of the organization.* "On behalf of the organization" is a very powerful phrase here because no information security unit should make

decisions about access to information. The information is owned by other pieces of the organization and so the responsibility for deciding access rules lies with other parts of the organization (guided by policies and standards). Information Security Management is only responsible for making sure that those access rules are implemented.

■ *Provide enough education and awareness programs to the organization.* This begs the question, "What is enough?," and the glib answer is, "Whatever senior management decides is enough." A more useful answer, however, is that enough education and awareness is the amount that provides the information necessary for everyone in the organization to know what his or her information security responsibilities are.

In all the above responsibilities, the most important — from my point of view — is the responsibility to acquire and communicate knowledge within the organization. This should be a major part of an Information Security manager's job description and is the activity that will contribute most to an organization's successful effort to protect its information.

3.4.2.3   Business Unit Managers

As already discussed, the information security program can only work if it is supported throughout the organization, and business unit managers may be the most important group of people when it comes to making that happen. If business unit managers do not buy into the idea that information security is important, then no amount of effort on the part of the Information Security manager will make it work in that unit. Once one unit fails to support the concepts of good information security, a domino effect can happen with employees in other units taking an attitude of, "Well, if they don't bother, why should I?"

Business unit managers deserve special attention from Information Security Management for this reason. Efforts to persuade business unit managers to support the program will help make sure that the program is applied evenly across the organization and will reduce the number of weak spots in the organization's defense.

Business unit managers support the information security program by:

■ *Participating in the process of reviewing policies.* Business unit managers must feed comments to senior management on every information security policy proposed for the organization, because it is the business unit manager who will enforce the policy within the unit.

■ *Creating input for information security standards.* Standards are more business-unit specific than policies (network support writes network security standards, Human Resources writes personnel security standards, etc.) and, with help from Information Security, business unit managers must write standards that their unit can live with and that adequately protect the information used by the unit.

■ *Measuring information security within the unit.* While Information Security will provide the metrics and the mechanisms for measuring the effect of the information security program, the business unit managers themselves benefit from taking responsibility for the measurement. Less negative audit comments and fewer disruptive events are two clear benefits from this kind of proactive stance.

■ *Enforcing compliance with policies and standards.* Information Security can report violations of policy and standards, but only business unit managers can initiate remedial and disciplinary action in response. Without such remedial and disciplinary action, policies and standards are soon seen as "toothless" and are ignored very quickly afterward.

■ *Supporting information security education and awareness.* The information security education and awareness program can only succeed with the clear cooperation of business unit managers. From basic cooperation in providing resources and scheduling events to a directive to adopt the messages delivered by the program, business unit managers' support is crucial.

■ Making sure resources are available to draft, test, and maintain business continuity plans under the coordination of the Information Security manager or the IS manager's designee.

3.4.2.4   First Line Supervisors

Often seen as "the front line" in information security, first line supervisors are on the one hand seen to be examples to judge the level of support for information security and, on the other hand, enforcers of policies and standards. First line supervisors often carry out duties delegated by business unit managers and are a key piece of the communication chain that allows an organization to monitor its information security program.

First line supervisors:

■ Monitor their employees' activities in light of organization information security policies and standards — directing better compliance where appropriate and reporting incidents of noncompliance to business unit managers.

- Communicate security issues to Information Security, senior management (through business unit managers), and through them to the Information Security Steering Committee.
- In organizations where information security is included as a performance measurement, comment on individual employees' performance with respect to information security at performance appraisal time.
- Support the information security policy by reinforcing the messages contained in the education and awareness elements of the program.

3.4.2.5   Employees

When asked to describe the information security responsibilities of employees, it would be easy (but not helpful) to say, "Everything else" and in a sense it would be true. Generally, employees are asked to comply with information security policies and standards and little else.

However, information security programs only work well when all employees participate, and employees participate most willingly when they feel they have a real role to play. Simply complying with policies and standards seems passive and might be done by all employees given enough support from business unit managers and first line supervisors. More active participation from employees can be encouraged in areas such as reporting security concerns — and it should be stated like this. Most organizations talk of employees "reporting security breaches" to their supervisors but get very little cooperation as a result because very few employees feel comfortable telling tales about their co-workers.

From general security issues (perhaps seen in the press) to topics of concern that are specific to the organization, employees should be encouraged to see the process as simply passing on information or asking for clarification. This line of communication helps make sure that the scarce resources of the Information Security unit are party to as much information as possible about the state of the organization's program and about outside security news.

3.4.2.6   Third Parties

Third parties (contractors, vendors, etc.) are responsible for complying with the information security policies and standards of the organization with which they are contracted or to which they provide goods or services. This must be clearly stated in any contract that binds two organizations. Where any waiver to this rule is allowed, it must only be to state that the contractor or vendor must provide protection for the purchasing organization's information to an equal or greater degree than the purchasing organization itself. Such contractual terms should be the subject of any service level agreement (SLA) between the purchasing organization and any contractor or vendor.

Where contractors or vendors operate in a site operated by the purchasing organization, they are subject to the same rules and methods of enforcement as full-time employees of the organization. Where the contractors or vendors operate on their own or others' premises, the contract should state that the purchasing organization has the right to audit the contractors' or vendors' information security programs at the times of the purchasing organization's choosing.

3.5 Summary

The structure of an information security program is its performance in every level of the organization. The reach of the program, how each business unit supports the program, and how every individual carries out his or her duties as specified in the program all determine how effective the program is going to be. Uniform participation in the program is necessary if its results are to justify an organization's investment. From senior management, through business unit management, to every individual member of an organization, all must be seen — for varying reasons — to give the same level of support to the information security program's aims and objectives. If there are levels or areas in an organization where support is seen to be weak, this will cause gaps in the effectiveness of the program and will weaken the whole information security structure. Like an unpopular law (the 55 mph speed limit comes to mind), when a requirement to follow good business practices is ignored by some — and effective information security is good business practice — more will come to think that they need not comply either.

Chapter 4

Information Security Policies

4.1 Policy Is the Cornerstone

The cornerstone of effective information security architecture is a well-written policy statement. This is the wellspring of all other directives, standards, procedures, guidelines, and other supporting documents. As with any foundation, it is important to establish a strong footing. As will be discussed, a policy performs two roles: one internal and one external.

The internal portion tells employees what is expected of them and how their actions will be judged. The external portion tells the world how the enterprise is run, that there are policies that support sound business practices, and that the organization understands that protection of assets is vital to the successful execution of its mission.

In any discussion regarding written requirements, the term "policy" has more than one meaning. To some, a policy is the directive of senior management on how a certain program is run, what its goals and objectives are, and to whom responsibilities are assigned. The term "policy" may refer to the specific security rules for a particular system, such as ACF2 rule sets, RACF permits, or intrusion detection system policies. Additionally, policy may refer to entirely different matters, such as specific management decisions that set an organization's e-mail privacy policy or Internet usage policy.

This chapter examines three different forms of policy statements: the general program policy (Tier 1), the topic-specific policy (Tier 2), and the system- or application-specific policy (Tier 3).

4.2 Why Implement an Information Security Policy

Security professionals often view the overall objective of an information security program as being to protect the integrity, confidentiality, and availability. While this is true from a security perspective, it is not the organization objective. Information is an asset and is the property of the organization. As an asset, management is expected to ensure that an appropriate level of controls are in place to protect this resource.

An information protection program should be part of any organization's overall asset protection program. This program is not established to meet security needs or audit requirements; it is a business process that provides management with the processes needed to perform the fiduciary responsibility. Management is charged with a trust to ensure that adequate controls are in place to protect the assets of the enterprise. An information security program that includes policies, standards, and procedures will allow management to demonstrate a standard of care.

As information security professionals, it is our responsibility to implement policies that reflect the business and mission needs of the enterprise. This chapter examines the reasons why information security policies are needed and how they fit into all elements of the organization. The development of information security policies is not an information technology or audit responsibility, nor do they remain solely in these areas. The concept of information security must permeate through all of the organization's policies.

This chapter discusses eleven organizationwide policies and, at a minimum, what each should have with reference to information security. The policies initially discussed are high-level (Tier 1) organizationwide policies and include the following:

- Employment practices
- Employee Standards of Conduct
- Conflict of Interest
- Performance Management
- Employee Discipline
- Information Security
- Corporate Communications
- Procurement and Contracts
- Records Management
- Asset Classification
- Workplace Security
- Business Continuity Planning

We discuss the different levels of Tier 2 policies (topic specific) and Tier 3 policies (application specific) throughout the remainder of the book.

4.3 Corporate Policies

Most organizations have a standard set of policies that govern the way they perform their business (see Figure 4.1). There are at least eleven Tier 1 policies; this means that a policy is implemented to support the entire business or mission of the enterprise. There are also Tier 2 policies; these are topic-specific policies and address issues related to specific subject matter. The Tier 3 policies address the requirements for using and supporting specific applications. Later in the book we present examples of a number of each of these policies; for now we present the Tier 1 policy title and a brief description of what the policy encompasses.

4.4 Organizationwide (Tier 1) Policies

4.4.1 Employment

This is the policy that describes the processes required to ensure that all candidates get an equal opportunity when seeking a position with the organization. This policy discusses the organization's hiring practices and new employee orientation. It is during the orientation phase that new employees should receive their first introduction to the information security requirements. Included in this process is a Nondisclosure Agreement or Confidentiality Agreement. These agreements require the signatory to keep confidential information secret and generally remain in effect even after the employee leaves the organization.

The employment policies should also include condition-of-employment requirements such as background checks for key management levels or certain jobs. A side part to the Employment policy and the Performance policy is the publication of job descriptions for every job level. These descriptions should include what is expected of employees regarding information security requirements.

4.4.2 Standards of Conduct

This policy addresses what is expected of employees and how they are to conduct themselves when on company property or when representing the organization. This policy normally discusses examples of unacceptable

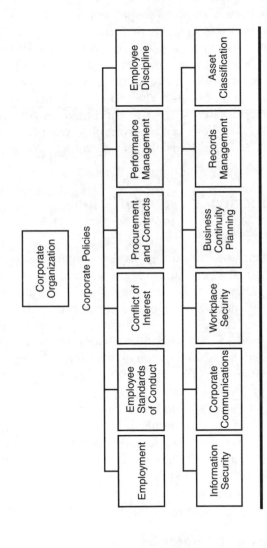

FIGURE 4.1 Corporate Policies

behavior (dishonesty, sleeping on the job, substance abuse, introduction of unauthorized software into company systems) and the penalties for infractions. Also included in this policy is a statement that "Company management has the responsibility to manage enterprise information, personnel, and physical properties relevant to their business operations, as well as the right to monitor the actual utilization of these enterprise assets."

Information security should also address confidential information: "Employees shall also maintain the confidentiality of corporate information. (See Asset Classification policy.)" A discussion on unacceptable conduct is generally included in an employee code of conduct policy; this should include a discussion on unauthorized code and copyright compliance.

4.4.3   Conflict of Interest

Company employees are expected to adhere to the highest standards of conduct. To assure adherence to these standards, employees must have a special sensitivity to conflict-of-interest situations or relationships, as well as the inappropriateness of personal involvement in them. While not always covered by law, these situations can harm the company or its reputation if improperly handled. This is where discussions about due diligence will be addressed. Many organizations restrict conflict-of-interest policy requirements to management levels; all employees should be required to annually review and sign a responsibility statement.

4.4.4   Performance Management

This policy discusses how employee job performance is to be used in determining an employee's appraisal. Information security requirements should be included as an element that affects the level of employee performance. As discussed, having job descriptions for each job assignment will ensure that employees are reviewed fairly and completely at least annually on how they do their job and part of that includes information security.

4.4.5   Employee Discipline

When things go wrong, this policy outlines the steps that are to be taken. As with all policies, it discusses who is responsible for what and leads those individuals to more extensive procedures. This policy is very important for an effective information security program. When an investigation begins, it may eventually lead to a need to implement sanctions on an employee or group of employees. Having a policy that establishes who is responsible for administering these sanctions will ensure that all involved in the investigation are properly protected.

4.4.6 Information Security

The bulk of the remainder of this book addresses writing an effective information security policy. This is the cornerstone of the information security program and works in close harmony with the enterprisewide Asset Classification Policy and the Records Management Policy. This policy established the concept that information is an asset and the property of the organization, and that all employees are required to protect this asset.

4.4.7 Corporate Communications

Instead of individual, topic-specific policies on such items as voice-mail, e-mail, inter-office memos, outside correspondence, a single policy on what is and is not allowed in organization correspondence can be implemented. This policy will support the concepts established in the Employee Standards of Conduct, which address employee conduct and include harassment whether sexual, racial, religious, or ethnic. The policy also discusses libelous and slanderous content and the organization's position on such behavior.

The policy also addresses requests from outside organizations for information. This will include media requests for information as well as representing the organization by speaking at or submitting whitepapers for various business-related conferences or societies.

4.4.8 Workplace Security

This policy addresses the need to provide a safe and secure work environment for the employees. The need to implement sound security practices to protect employees, organization property, and information assets is established here. Included in this policy are the basic security tenets of authorized access to the facility, visitor requirements, property removal, and emergency response plans, which include evacuation procedures.

4.4.9 Business Continuity Plans (BCPs)

For years this process was relegated to the Information Technology department and consisted mainly of the IT disaster recovery plan for the processing environment. The proper focus for this policy is the establishment of business unit procedures to support restoration of critical business processes, applications, and systems in the event of an outage.

Included in the Business Continuity Plan Policy are the needs for business units to:

- Establish effective continuity plans.
- Conduct business impact analyses for all applications, systems, and business processes.
- Identify preventive controls.
- Coordinate the business unit BCP with the IT disaster recovery plan.
- Test the plan and train its employees on the plan.
- Maintain the plan to a current state of readiness.

4.4.10   Procurement and Contracts

This policy establishes the way in which the organization conducts its business with outside firms. This policy addresses those items that must be included in any contract, and this includes language that discusses the need for third parties to comply with organization's policies, procedures, and standards.

This policy is probably one of the most important for information security and other organization policies and standards. We can only write policies and establish standards and procedures for employees; all other third parties must be handled contractually. It is very important that the contract language references any policies, standards, and procedures that are deemed appropriate.

All too often I have reviewed policies that contained language that was something like "the policy applies to all employees, contractors, consultants, per diem, and other third parties." Just because this language appears in a policy does not make it effective. Third parties must be handled contractually. Work with the procurement group and legal staff to ensure that purchase orders and contracts have the necessary language. It would be wise to include a confidentiality or nondisclosure agreement. An example of a confidentiality agreement is included in the Sample Policy and Standards section of this book.

4.4.11   Records Management

This policy was previously referred to as *Records Retention*, but the concept has been refined. Most organizations know that there will be a time when it will be necessary to destroy records. The Records Management

Policy will establish the standards for ensuring information is there as required by regulations and when it is time to properly dispose of the information. This policy normally establishes:

■ The record name
■ A brief description of the record
■ The owning department
■ The required length of time to keep the record

4.4.12 Asset Classification

This policy establishes the need to classify information, the classification categories, and who is responsible for doing so. It normally includes the concepts of employee responsibilities, such as the *Owner, Custodian,* and *User.* It is a companion policy to the Records Management Policy in that it adds the last two elements in information records identification. In addition to the four items identified in the Records Management Policy, the Asset Classification Policy adds:

■ The classification level
■ The owner's job title

4.5 Organizationwide Policy Document

Throughout the enterprisewide policy document, references to information security and the information security program should be incorporated. These concepts should begin with a review of the enterprise's shared beliefs that usually discuss such important concepts as teamwork, accountability, communication, continuous improvement, and benchmarking. Because of the increased emphasis on proper conduct, a formal discussion of the enterprise's support of due diligence concepts should be established.

The use of the term "accountability" when establishing organization goals and beliefs allows the enterprise to commit to the concept that it is willing to accept accountability for the results of decisions made to support the business process or mission of the enterprise. To ensure that appropriate, informed business decisions are made in an open climate of discussion and research, a formal risk analysis process should be implemented to document all management decisions.

By establishing this level of accountability, the enterprise is creating a climate of due diligence throughout the entire organization. A formal business-related risk analysis process will ensure that all decisions are made quickly and efficiently and that the process is recorded. This will allow third parties to examine the process and verify that due diligence was performed.

As a security professional, it is very important that due diligence is established as an enterprise objective and guiding principle. Risk analysis will ensure that all decisions are based on the best needs of the enterprise and that prudent and reasonable controls and safeguards are implemented. With the implementation of more stringent reporting mechanism and laws (*Sarbanes–Oxley*) or international standards such as *British Standards 7799* (*BS 7799*) or *ISO 17799*, the formal adoption of a risk analysis process will assist in proving the enterprise is being managed in a proper manner.

Another important element found in most enterprisewide policy documents is a section on Organizational Responsibilities. This section is where the various mission statements of the enterprise organizations reside, along with any associated responsibilities. For example:

- *Auditing.* Auditing assesses the adequacy of and compliance with management, operating, and financial controls, as well as the administrative and operational effectiveness of organizational units.
- *Information Security.* Information Security (IS) is to direct and support the company and affiliated organizations in the protection of their information assets from intentional or unintentional disclosure, modification, destruction, or denial through the implementation of appropriate information security and business resumption planning policies, procedures, and guidelines.

Other organizations that should be included in the Organizational Responsibilities section include (see Figure 4.2):

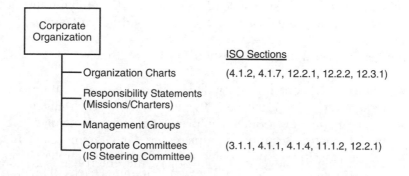

FIGURE 4.2   Corporate Policy Document

- Corporate and Public Affairs
- Finance and Administration
- General Counsel
- Information Security Organization
- Human Resources

Included in the opening section of an enterprisewide policy document is a discussion on enterprise committees. Standing committees are established to develop, to present for executive decision, and, where empowered, to implement recommendations on matters of significant, ongoing concern to the enterprise. Certain committees administer enterprise programs for which two or more organizations share responsibility.

The Information Security Steering Committee identified in ISO 17799 (4.1.1) and discussed as a requirement in the Gramm–Leach–Bliley Act (GLBA) is required to involve the board of directors in the implementation of an enterprisewide information program. The first key responsibility of this committee is the approval and implementation of the Information Security Charter as well as the Information Security Policy and the Asset Classification Policy. In addition to these two enterprisewide policies, the committee is responsible for ensuring that adequate supporting policies, standards, and procedures are implemented to support the information security program.

The Information Security Steering Committee (ISSC) consists of representatives from each of the major business units and is chaired by the Chief Information Security Officer (CISO).

The ISSC is also the group responsible for reviewing and approving the results of the enterprisewide business impact analysis that establishes the relative criticality of each business process, application, and system used in the enterprise. The results of the BIA are then used as input to develop business continuity plans for the enterprise and for the business units. The ISSC is also responsible for reviewing and certifying the BCPs. To ensure adequacy, the BCPs must be exercised at least annually and the exercise reports are presented to the ISSC.

The key responsibilities established for the ISSC include:

- Approve the enterprise's written information security program: required in ISO 17799, BS 7799, and Gramm–Leach–Bliley.
- Oversee the development, implementation, and maintenance of the information security program: required in Gramm–Leach–Bliley.
- Assign specific responsibility for the program implementation: required in ISO 17799, BS 7799, and Gramm–Leach–Bliley.
- Review reports of the state of information security throughout the enterprise: required in Gramm–Leach–Bliley.

4.6 Legal Requirements

Are there legal and business requirements for policies and procedures? The answer to that question is a resounding yes. Not only are there requirements, but the laws and acts define who is responsible and what they must do to meet their obligations. The directors and officers of a corporation are required under the Model Business Corporation Act, which has been adopted in whole or in part by a majority of states, to perform two specific duties: a duty of loyalty and a duty of care.

4.6.1 Duty of Loyalty

By assuming office, senior management commits allegiance to the enterprise and acknowledges that the interest of the enterprise must prevail over any personal or individual interest. The basic principle here is that senior management should not use its position to make a personal profit or gain other personal advantage. The duty of loyalty is evident in certain legal concepts:

- *Conflict of interest:* Individuals must divulge any interest in outside relationships that might conflict with the enterprise's interests.
- *Duty of fairness:* When presented with a conflict of interest, the individual has an obligation to act in the best interest of all parties.
- *Corporate opportunity:* When presented with "material inside information" (advanced notice on mergers, acquisitions, patents, etc.), the individual will not use this information for personal gain.
- *Confidentiality:* All matters involving the corporation should be kept in confidence until they are made public.

4.6.2 Duty of Care

In addition to owing a duty of loyalty to the enterprise, the officers and directors also assume a duty to act carefully in fulfilling the important tasks of monitoring and directing the activities of corporate management. The Model Business Corporation Act established legal standards for compliance. A director shall discharge his or her duties:

- In good faith
- With the care an ordinarily prudent person in a like position would exercise under similar circumstances
- In a manner he or she reasonably believes is in the best interest of the enterprise

LIVERPOOL JOHN MOORES UNIVERSITY
LEARNING SERVICES

4.6.3 Federal Sentencing Guidelines for Criminal Convictions

The Federal Sentencing Guidelines define executive responsibility for fraud, theft, and antitrust violations, and establish a mandatory point system for federal judges to determine appropriate punishment. Because much fraud and falsifying corporate data involves access to computer-held data, liability established under the Guidelines extend to computer-related crime as well. What has caused many executives concern is that the mandatory punishment could apply even when intruders enter a computer system and perpetrate a crime.

While the Guidelines have a mandatory scoring system for punishment, they also have an incentive for proactive crime prevention. The requirement here is for management to show "due diligence" in establishing an effective compliance program. There are seven elements that capture the basic functions inherent in most compliance programs:

1. Establish policies, standards, and procedures to guide the workforce.
2. Appoint a high-level manager to oversee compliance with the policies, standards, and procedures.
3. Exercise due care when granting discretionary authority to employees.
4. Assure compliance policies are being carried out.
5. Communicate the standards and procedures to all employees and others.
6. Enforce the policies, standards, and procedures consistently through appropriate disciplinary measures.
7. Establish procedures for corrections and modifications in case of violations.

These guidelines reward those organizations that make a good-faith effort to prevent unethical activity; this is done by lowering potential fines if, despite the organization's best efforts, unethical or illegal activities are still committed by the organization or its employees. To be judged effective, a compliance program need not prevent all misconduct; however, it must show due diligence in seeking to prevent and detect inappropriate behavior.

4.6.4 The Economic Espionage Act of 1996

The Economic Espionage Act (EEA) of 1996 for the first time makes trade secret theft a federal crime, subject to penalties including fines, forfeiture, and imprisonment. The act reinforces the rules governing trade secrets in that businesses must show that they have taken reasonable measures to protect their proprietary trade secrets in order to seek relief under the EEA.

In "Counterintelligence and Law Enforcement: The Economic Espionage Act of 1996 versus Competitive Intelligence," author Peter F. Kalitka believes that given the penalties companies face under the EEA, that business hiring outside consultants to gather competitive intelligence should establish a policy on this activity. Included in the contract language with the outside consultant should be definitions of:

- What is hard-to-get information?
- How will the information be obtained?
- Do they adhere to the Society of Competitive Intelligence Professionals Code of Ethics?
- Do they have accounts with clients that may be questioned?

4.6.5 The Foreign Corrupt Practices Act (FCPA)

For 20 years, regulators largely ignored the FCPA. This was due in part to an initial amnesty program under which nearly 500 companies admitted violations. Now the federal government has dramatically increased its attention to business activities and is looking to enforce the act with vigor. To avoid liability under the FCPA, companies must implement a due diligence program that includes a set of internal controls and enforcement. A set of policies and procedures that are implemented and audited for compliance are required to meet the test of due diligence.

4.6.5 Sarbanes–Oxley (SOX) Act

The Sarbanes–Oxley (SOX) Act was signed into law on July 30, 2002, and the provisions of the act have a meaningful impact on both public companies and auditors. Two important sections of the act are:

1. Section 302 (Disclosure Controls and Procedures or "DC&P") requires quarterly certification of financial statements by the CEO and CFO. The CEO and CFO must certify the completeness and accuracy of the filings and attest to the effectiveness of internal control.
2. Section 404 (Internal Control Attest) requires annual affirmation of management's responsibility for internal controls over financial reporting. Management must attest to the effectiveness based on an evaluation, and the auditor must attest to and report on management's evaluation.

4.6.6   Health Insurance Portability and Accountability Act (HIPAA)

The Health Insurance Portability and Accountability Act (HIPAA), also known as Kassebaum-Kennedy, after the two senators who spearheaded the bill. Passed in 1996 to help people buy and keep health insurance (portability), even when they have serious health conditions, the law sets basic requirements that health plans must meet. Because states can and have modified and expanded upon these provisions, consumer protections vary from state to state. The law expanded to include strict rules for privacy and security of health information, giving individuals more control over how their health information is used. The privacy and security rules within HIPAA govern the use, disclosure, and handling of any identifiable patient information by "covered" healthcare providers. The law covers the information in whatever form it is seen or heard, and applies to the information in whatever manner it is to be used.

4.6.7   Gramm–Leach–Bliley Act (GLBA)

The Gramm–Leach–Bliley Act (GLBA) was signed into law in 1999. Its primary purpose is to provide privacy of customer information by financial services organizations and comprehensive data protection measures are required. Depending on the financial institutions' supervisory authority, GLBA compliance audits are conducted by either the Office of the Comptroller of the Currency (OCC), the Federal Reserve Systems (Fed), the Federal Deposit Insurance Corporation (FDIC), or the Office of Thrift Supervision (OTS). All financial services organizations must comply with GLBA data protection requirements. These requirements do not pertain only to providers receiving federal funds.

The GLBA requires financial institutions to:

- Insure the security and confidentiality of customer records and information.
- Protect against any anticipated threats or hazards to the security or integrity of such records.
- Protect against unauthorized access.

4.7   Business Requirements

It is a well-accepted fact that it is important to protect the information essential to an organization, in the same way that it is important to protect the financial assets of the organization. Unlike protecting financial assets, which have regulations to support their protection, the protection of information is often left to the individual employee. As with protecting financial assets, everyone knows what the solutions are for protecting information resources. However, identifying these requirements is not good enough; to enforce controls, it is necessary to have a formal written policy that can be used as the basis for all standards and procedures.

4.8 Definitions

4.8.1 Policy

A policy is a high-level statement of enterprise beliefs, goals, and objectives and the general means for their attainment for a specified subject area. When we hear discussions on intrusion detection systems (IDS) monitoring compliance to company policies, these are not the policies we are discussing. The IDS is actually monitoring standards, which we will discuss in more detail later, or rule sets or proxies. We will be creating policies such as the policy on information security shown in Table 4.1.

Later in this chapter we will examine a number of information security policies and then critique them based on an established policy template.

TABLE 4.1 Sample Information Security Policy

Information Security Policy

Business information is an essential asset of the Company. This is true of all business information within the Company, regardless of how it is created, distributed, or stored and whether it is typed, handwritten, printed, filmed, computer-generated, or spoken.

All employees are responsible for protecting corporate information from unauthorized access, modification, duplication, destruction, or disclosure, whether accidental or intentional. This responsibility is essential to Company business. When information is not well protected, the Company can be harmed in various ways, such as significant loss to market share and a damaged reputation.

Details of each employee's responsibilities for protecting Company information are documented in the Information Protection Policies and Standards Manual. Management is responsible for ensuring that all employees understand and adhere to these policies and standards. Management is also responsible for noting variances from established security practices and for initiating corrective actions.

Internal auditors will perform periodic reviews to ensure ongoing compliance with the Company information protection policy. Violations of this policy will be addressed as prescribed in the Human Resource Policy Guide for Management.

TABLE 4.2 Example of Standards

Information Systems Manager/Team Leader

Managers with responsibility for Information Systems must carry out all the appropriate responsibilities as a Manager for their area. In addition, they will act as **Custodian** of information used by those systems but owned by other managers. They must ensure that these owners are identified, appointed, and made aware of their responsibilities.

All managers, supervisors, directors, and other management-level people also have an advisory and assisting role to IS and non-IS managers with respect to:

- Identifying and assessing threats
- Identifying and implementing protective measures (including compliance with these practices)
- Maintaining a satisfactory level of security awareness
- Monitoring the proper operation of security measures within the unit
- Investigating weaknesses and occurrences
- Raising any new issues or circumstances of which they become aware through their specialist role
- Liaising with internal and external audit

4.8.2 Standards

Standards are mandatory requirements that support individual policies. Standards can range from what software or hardware can be used, to what remote access protocol is to be implemented, to who is responsible for approving what. We examine standards in more detail later in this book. When developing an information security policy, it will be necessary to establish a set of supporting standards. Table 4.2 shows an example of what the standards for a specific topic might look like.

4.8.3 Procedures

Procedures are mandatory, step-by-step, detailed actions required to successfully complete a task. Procedures can be very detailed. Recently I was reviewing change management procedures, like the one shown in Table 4.3, and found one that consisted of 42 pages. It was very thorough, but I find it difficult to believe that anyone had ever read the entire document. We discuss procedures in more detail later in this book.

TABLE 4.3   Sample Application Change Management Procedure

General

The System Service Request (SSR) is used to initiate and document all programming activity. It is used to communicate customer needs to Application Development (AD) personnel. An SSR may be initiated and prepared by a customer, a member of the AD staff, or any other individual who has identified a need or requirement, a problem, or an enhancement to an application. No tasks are to be undertaken without a completed SSR.

System Service Request

General

This form, specifying the desired results to be achieved, is completed by the customer and sent, together with supporting documentation, to AD. The request may include the identification of a problem or the documentation of a new request. Customers are encouraged to submit their request in sufficient detail to permit the AD project leader to accurately estimate the effort needed to satisfy the request, but it may be necessary for the project leader to contact the customer and obtain supplementary information. This information should be attached to a copy of the SSR.

After the requested programs have been completed, the agreed-upon Acceptance tests will be conducted. After the customer has verified that the request has been satisfied, the customer will indicate approval on the SSR. This form will also be used to document that the completed project has been placed into production status.

Processing

This section describes the processing of a System Service Request:

1. The customer initiates the process by completing the SSR and forwarding it to the appropriate Project Manager (PM) or the Director of Application Development.
2. The SSR is received in the AD department. Regardless of who in AD actually receives the SSR, it must be delivered to the appropriate PM.
3. If the PM finds the description of requirements on the SSR inadequate or unclear, the PM will directly contact the customer for clarification.

   When the PM fully understands the requirements, the PM will prepare an analysis and an estimate of the effort required to satisfy the request. In some cases, the PM may feel that it is either impossible or impractical to satisfy the request. In this case, the PM will discuss with the customer the reasons why the request should not be implemented. If the customer reaffirms the request, the PM and Director of AD will jointly determine whether to appeal the customer's decision to the Information Systems Steering Committee for a final ruling on the SSR.

TABLE 4.3 (continued) Sample Application Change Management Procedure

4. If the project estimate is forty (40) hours or less, the detailed design should be reviewed with the customer. After design concurrence has been reviewed, the PM will project the tentative target date (TTD) for completion of the SSR. In setting the TTD, the PM will take into consideration the resources available and other project commitments. The TTD will be promptly communicated to the requesting customer.

5. If the project estimate exceeds forty (40) hours, the SSR and any supplemental project documentation will be forwarded to the ISSC for review, priority determination, and authorization to proceed.

    The committee will determine whether the requested change is to be scheduled for immediate implementation, scheduled for future implementation, or disapproved. If the request is disapproved, it is immediately returned to the customer, together with an explanation of the reason(s) for disapproval. If it is approved for implementation, a *priori*ty designation is made and the SSR is returned to AD for implementation scheduling.

    After implementation authorization has been received, the detailed design should be reviewed with the customer. After design concurrence has been received, the PM will project a TTD for completion of the project. In setting a TTD, the PM will take into consideration the resources available and other project commitments. The TTD will be promptly communicated to the customer.

6. The PM will coordinate with AD personnel and other IT management and staff personnel (such as Database Administration, User Support Services, Network Administration, etc.) if their resources will be required to satisfy this request, or if there will be an operational or procedural impact in the other areas.

7. The PM will contact the customer to discuss, in detail, the test(s) that are to be conducted.

8. When Acceptance Testing (AT) has been completed and the customer has verified the accuracy of the results obtained, the customer will indicate their approval to place the project into production by signing the SSR.

9. The Production Control Group (PCG) will place the project into production status. The PM will complete the bottom portion of the SSR, documenting that the project has been placed into production. The PM will log the status of the request as "completed" and file a copy of the SSR. The PM will promptly notify the customer that the project has been completed and placed into production.

Retention of Forms and Documentation
All documentation associated with the processing of each SSR will be retained for at least twelve (12) months.

4.8.4 Guidelines

Guidelines are more general statements designed to achieve the policy's objectives by providing a framework within which to implement procedures. Whereas standards are mandatory, guidelines are recommendations. An everyday example of the difference between a standard and a guideline would be a stop sign, which is a standard, and a "Please Keep Off the Grass" sign, which would be nice but it is not a law.

Some organizations issue overall information security policies and standards documents. These can be a mix of Tier 1, Tier 2, and Tier 3 policies and their supporting standards and guidelines (see Figure 4.3). While it is appropriate to include policies in a document such as this, it is considered impractical to include standards, procedures, or guidelines in Tier 1 policies.

4.9 Policy Key Elements

The information security policy should cover all forms of information. In 1965, the computer industry introduced the concept of the "paperless office." The advent of third-generation computers had many in management believing that all information would be stored and secured electronically and that paper would become obsolete. When talking to management about establishing an information security policy, it will be necessary to discuss with them the need to extend the policy to cover all information wherever it is found and in whatever format. Computer-held information makes up a small percentage of the organization's entire information resources. Make sure the policy meets the needs of the organization.

4.10 Policy Format

The actual physical format (layout) of the policy will depend on what policies look like in your own organization. Policies are generally brief in comparison to procedures and normally consist of one page of text using both sides of the paper. In my classes I stress the concept of brevity. However, it is important to balance brevity with clarity. Utilize all the words you need to complete the thought, but fight the urge to add more information.

Years ago we had a young priest visit our parish and his homily that weekend included a discussion on the concept of imprinting. This concept is normally covered in a basic psychology class and is an early social

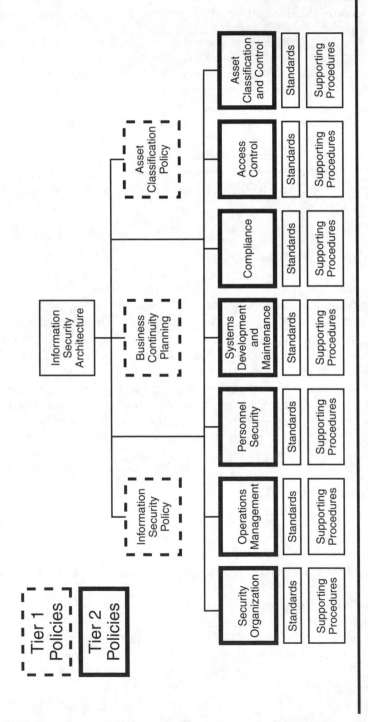

FIGURE 4.3 Overall Information Security Policies and Standards Documents

behavior among birds and is a process that causes the newly hatched birds to become rapidly and strongly attached to social objects such as parents or parental surrogates. While a number of us understood what he was talking about, the majority of the parish just stared at him blankly. So he continued to add explanation after explanation until his homily lasted about 45 minutes. When writing a policy, balance the attention span time limit with what needs to be addressed. Keep it brief but make it understandable.

There are three types of policies and you will use each type at different times in your information security program and throughout the organization to support the business process or mission. The three types of policies are:

1. *Global (Tier 1)*. These are used to create the organization's overall vision and direction.
2. *Topic-specific (Tier 2)*. These address particular subjects of concern.
3. *Application-specific (Tier 3)*. These focus on decisions taken by management to control particular applications (financial reporting, payroll, etc.) or specific systems (budgeting system).

We discuss the information security architecture and each category such as those shown in Figure 4.4.

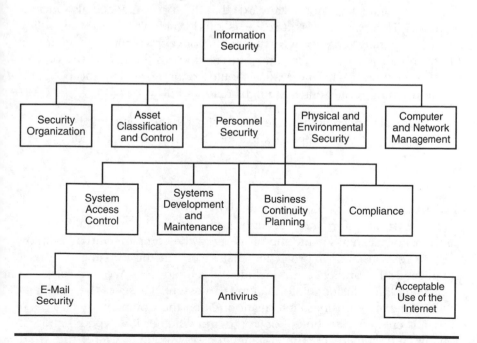

FIGURE 4.4 Topic-Specific (Tier 2) Policies

4.10.1 Global (Tier 1) Policy

Under the Standard of Due Care, and charged with the ultimate responsibility for meeting business objectives or mission requirements, senior management must ensure that necessary resources are effectively applied to develop the capabilities to meet the mission requirements. Senior management must incorporate the results of the risk analysis process into the decision-making process. Senior management is also responsible for issuing global policies to establish the organization's direction in protecting information assets.

An information security policy will define the intent of management and its sponsoring body with regard to protecting the information assets of the organization. It will include the scope of the program — that is, where it will reach and what information is included in this policy. Finally, the policy will establish who is responsible for what.

The components of a global (Tier 1) policy typically include four characteristics: topic, scope, responsibilities, and compliance or consequences.

4.10.1.1 Topic

The topic portion of the policy defines what specifically the policy is going to address. Because the attention span of readers is limited, the topic must appear quickly, say in the opening or topic sentence. I normally suggest (note it is a guideline, not a standard) that the topic sentence also include a "hook." That is, why I as a reader should continue to read this policy. So in the opening sentence we will want to convey two important elements: (1) the topic (it should have something to do with the title of the policy), and (2) the hook (why the reader should continue reading the policy).

An opening topic sentence might read as follows:

> "Information created while employed by the company is the property of the company and must be properly protected."

4.10.1.2 Scope

The scope can be used to broaden or narrow either the topic or the audience. In an information security policy statement, we could say that "information is an asset and the property of the company and all employees are responsible for protecting that asset." In this sentence we have broadened the audience to include all employees. We can also say something like "Business information is an essential asset of the Company. This is true of all business information within the Company, regardless of how it is created, distributed, or stored and whether it is typed, handwritten, printed, filmed, computer-generated, or spoken." Here, the writer broadened the topic to include all types of information assets.

Another example of broadening the scope might be as follows: "Information of the Company, its subsidiaries and affiliates in electronic form, whether being transmitted, or stored, is a key asset of the Company and must be protected according to its sensitivity, criticality, and value." Here, the topic subject is narrowed to "electronic form." However, the audience is broadened to include "subsidiaries and affiliates."

We can also use the scope concept to narrow the topic or audience. In an Employment Agreement Policy, the audience is restricted to a specific group such as the following:

> The parties to this Agreement dated (specify) are (Name of Company), a (specify state and type of company) (the "Company") and (Name of Employee) (the "Executive").
>
> The Company wishes to employ the Executive, and the Executive wishes to accept employment with the Company, on the terms and subject to the conditions set forth in this Agreement. It is therefore agreed as follows:...

Here, the policy is restricted to Executives and will then go on to discuss what can and cannot be done by the executives. A sample Employment Agreement Policy is contained in Section 4.10.2: Topic-Specific (Tier 2) Policy.

4.10.1.3 Responsibilities

Typically, this section of the policy will identify who is responsible for what. When writing, it is better to identify the "who" by job title and not by name. Here again, the Office Administrator's Reference Guide can be of great assistance. The policy will want to identify what is expected from each of the stakeholders.

4.10.1.4 Compliance or Consequences

When business units or employees are found in a noncompliant situation, the policy must spell out the consequences of these actions. For business units or departments, if they are found in noncompliance, they are generally subject to an audit item and will have to prepare a formal compliance response.

For employees, being found in noncompliance with a company policy will mean they are in violation of the organization's Employee Standards of Conduct and will be subject to consequences described in the Employee Discipline Policy.

4.10.1.5 Sample Information Security Global Policies

The next few pages examine sample information security policies and critique them. The written policy should clear up confusion, not generate new problems. When preparing a document for a specific audience, remember that the writer will not have the opportunity to sit down with each reader and explain what each item or sentence means. The writer will not be able to tell every person how the policy will impact the reader's daily assignments. When writing a policy, know the audience. For a global (Tier 1) policy, the audience is the employee base.

Using the general employee population as a base, let us examine a few policies (see Table 4.4, Table 4.5, Table 4.6, and Table 4.7), and see if they have the four key elements we should be looking for. We will want to see if these policies have:

1. Topic (including a topic and a "hook")
2. Scope (whether it broadens or narrows the topic or the audience or both)
3. Responsibilities (based on job titles)
4. Compliance or consequences

Table 4.4 (Example 1) addresses the checklist as follows:

1. *Topic:* "Information is a valuable corporate asset .... As such, steps will be taken to protect information..."
2. *Responsibilities:* "The protection of these assets is a basic management responsibility."
3. *Scope:* "Ensuring that all employees understand their obligation to protect these assets."
4. *Compliance:* "Noting variance from established security practice and for initiating corrective action."

This policy is a good start. However, the topic is vague and that is not acceptable. The most important goal of any writing is to quickly identify the topic. Without the title, we have only a vague idea of where the document is leading us.

When the policy establishes responsibilities, it will work best if you use an active verb. In this example, the writer diminishes the verb and makes it passive by adding the gerund "ing" to the verbs "identify," "ensure," and "note." Try to avoid the passive tense whenever possible.

When identifying levels of management, most organizations have established a scheme for how differing levels are referred to in print. Normally,

TABLE 4.4 A Utility Company's Information Security Policy: Example 1

Information Security Policy

Information is a valuable corporate asset. Business continuity is heavily dependent upon the integrity and continued availability of certain critical information and the means by which that information is gathered, stored, processed, communicated, and reported. As such, steps will be taken to protect information assets from unauthorized use, modification, disclosure, or destruction, whether accidental or intentional. The protection of these assets is a basic management responsibility. Employing officers are responsible for:

- Identifying and protecting computer-related information assets within their assigned area of management control
- Ensuring that these assets are used for management-approved purposes only
- Ensuring that all employees understand their obligation to protect these assets
- Implementing security practices and procedures that are consistent with the Company Information Asset Security Manual and the value of the asset
- Noting variance from established security practice and for initiating corrective action

---

Management with an uppercase M refers to senior management and lowercase *management* refers to line management or supervision.

In the policy in Table 4.4, the writer referred to the "employing officer." For many enterprises, an officer is the most senior level of management. Officers may rank up there with the board of directors. The Chief Executive Officer, Chief Financial Officer, etc. are examples of this management level. It is pretty safe to assume that the writer did not intend for such a high-ranking individual to be involved in this policy.

Table 4.5 (Example 2) addresses the checklist as follows:

1. *Topic.* The policy statement establishes that "company information... that would violate company commitments... or compromise...competitive stance..." must be protected.
2. *Responsibilities.* The policy does establish "Employee responsibilities;" however, if there is to be a reference to another document, there are two standards and one guideline that must be followed:
   - The referenced document must exist.
   - The reader must be able to easily access the referenced document.
   - Referencing other documents should be used judiciously.

TABLE 4.5   A Power Company's Information Security Policy: Example 2

Information Security

Policy Statement
It is the policy of the Power and Light Company to protect all company information from disclosures that would violate company commitments to others or would compromise the competitive stance of the company.

Employee Responsibilities
Employee responsibilities are defined in Company Procedure AUT 15. Violations of these responsibilities are subject to appropriate disciplinary action up to and including discharge, legal action, or having the matter referred to law enforcement agencies.

3. *Scope.* Here, the policy makes a mistake in the first section; the policy actually narrows the scope of the material to be protected by stating that "company information…that would violate company commitments…or compromise…competitive stance….." This statement in fact narrows the overall policy direction to only that information which meets this specific criterion.

4. *Compliance.* Straight out: you violate, you pay the penalty. This may be a bit harsh. Remember that part of policy implementation is acceptance. A better way to state this consequence might be, "Employees found to be in violation of this policy will be subject to the measures described in the Employee Discipline Policy."

Although the policy in Table 4.5 does meet one of the main requirements of a policy — that it be brief — it appears to be too brief. Some very important elements are omitted, especially what role management will play in this policy and how compliance will be monitored. The policy also seems to exclude information about personnel.

The opening sentence discusses the "policy" of the company. The document was drafted as a policy statement, so it is not necessary to add the term "policy" to the text. Let the words establish what the policy is.

Now let us review the policy statement we used as an example earlier in this chapter (see Table 4.6).

For this critique, we examine the policy (Table 4.6) sentence by sentence. Each sentence is numbered, based on where it appears in the policy statement.

1. "Business information is an essential asset of the Company."
   ▪ This starts out as a topic sentence but it leaves out the hook.

TABLE 4.6   A Healthcare Provider's Information Security Policy: Example 3

Information Security Policy

Business information is an essential asset of the Company. This is true of all business information within the Company, regardless of how it is created, distributed, or stored and whether it is typed, handwritten, printed, filmed, computer-generated, or spoken.

All employees are responsible for protecting corporate information from unauthorized access, modification, duplication, destruction, or disclosure, whether accidental or intentional. This responsibility is essential to Company business. When information is not well protected, the Company can be harmed in various ways, such as significant loss to market share and a damaged reputation.

Details of each employee's responsibilities for protecting Company information are documented in the Information Protection Policies and Standards Manual. Management is responsible for ensuring that all employees understand and adhere to these policies and standards. Management is also responsible for noting variances from established security practices and for initiating corrective actions.

Internal auditors will perform periodic reviews to ensure ongoing compliance with the Company information protection policy. Violations of this policy will be addressed as prescribed in the Human Resource Policy Guide for Management.

2. "This is true of all business information within the Company, regardless of how it is created, distributed, or stored and whether it is typed, handwritten, printed, filmed, computer-generated, or spoken."
   - This is scope; it addresses all the various types of information that could be included.
3. "All employees are responsible for protecting corporate information from unauthorized access, modification, duplication, destruction, or disclosure, whether accidental or intentional."
   - Here, finally is the hook. It also has scope in that it includes all employees.
4. "This responsibility is essential to Company business."
   - This is probably additional scope but appears to be part of an explanation. When developing a policy, it is not necessary to include why the policy was created. Explaining the why will be handled in the policy awareness program.
5. "When information is not well protected, the Company can be harmed in various ways, such as significant loss to market share and a damaged reputation."

■ This is definitely why the policy is important. To be clear on this point, the policy needs to be as clear and concise as possible. Try to avoid adding why the policy was created. After the policy has been around for a few years and becomes part of the culture of the organization, it will seem superfluous to have these words in the policy.

6. "Details of each employee's responsibilities for protecting Company information are documented in the Information Protection Policies and Standards Manual."

■ Remember our two standards and one guideline about referencing other works: (1) the document has to exist; (2) it has to be easily accessible to the reader; and (3) use this tactic infrequently. Note in sentence 6 that the author changes information type from "business" information to "company" information. This could add confusion for the reader. Strive to be consistent throughout the policy.

7. "Management is responsible for ensuring that all employees understand and adhere to these policies and standards."

■ Here, the sentence begins with "Management." Is the uppercase "M" for the beginning of the sentence or is it to identify a level of management? When writing a sentence like this, it is better to start with an adjective such as "Company Management." This will reduce the confusion for the reader.

8. "Management is also responsible for noting variances from established security practices and for initiating corrective actions."

■ The same critique as sentence 7. This is a reference to responsibilities and also what to do if a business unit is found to be in a noncompliant condition.

9. "Internal auditors will perform periodic reviews to ensure ongoing compliance with the Company information protection policy."

■ This sentence causes great concern. This is what auditors do, so it is not necessary to include a statement such as this in the policy. Additionally, if this sentence remains, then the policy requires that only internal auditors can conduct reviews of this policy. Remember, when writing anything, to be very careful with what you say. The words will be interpreted by each reader in the manner that best meets their needs.

10. "Violations of this policy will be addressed as prescribed in the Human Resource Policy Guide for Management."

■ As discussed in the review of sentence 7, the rules on other documents apply. This is the final compliance issue as it addresses what occurs when employees are in a noncompliant condition.

We now examine one last sample policy (see Table 4.7). This one appears to have all the elements. I recommend that when you critique something that you read in through completely. Then go back and dissect it sentence by sentence. Look for our four key elements: (1) topic, (2) scope, (3) responsibilities, and (4) compliance.

The opening paragraph is captioned "policy"; this should give us the information we need. It does contain some of the topic sentence we discussed earlier. It has half the requirements we would like to see; it lacks the "hook." The second sentence contains the scope.

Under "Responsibilities" we find the "hook" in the first item. Item numbers two, three, and four seem to be elements that we would normally find in an Asset Classification policy. When I talked to the people who developed this policy, I was told that the company had gone through a paper-reduction process during the past couple of years and had stream-lined its operating documents quite a bit. The new philosophy was that no new policies would be created. After about a year of campaigning and audit comments, the management approval team authorized one new policy. The team took advantage and combined the Information Security Policy and the Asset Classification Policy into the Information Protection Policy. What they did was correct based on the current climate of their organization.

The final section (Compliance) discusses the compliance issues and includes some interesting requirements that management must implement to be compliant with this policy. The Information Protection Group developed a set of policies, standards, and guidelines that could be used by the various departments as a template for their own supporting doc-uments. A sample of this type of document is included in the book under the section "Information Security Reference Guide."

4.10.2 Topic-Specific (Tier 2) Policy

Where the global (Tier 1) policy is intended to address the broad orga-nizationwide issues, the topic-specific (Tier 2) policy is developed to focus on areas of current relevance and concern to the organization. Manage-ment may find it appropriate to issue a policy on how an organization will approach Internet usage or the use of the company-provided e-mail system. Topic-specific policies may also be appropriate when new issues arise, such as when implementing a recently enacted law requiring pro-tection of particular information (GLBA, HIPAA, etc.). The global (Tier 1) policy is usually broad enough that it does not require modification over time, whereas topic-specific (Tier 2) policies are likely to require more frequent revisions as changes in technology and other factors dictate.

Topic-specific policies (see Figure 4.5) will be created most often by an organization. We examine the key elements in the topic-specific policy.

TABLE 4.7   A Utility Company's Information Protection Policy: Example 4

Information Protection

Policy

Information is a company asset and is the property of the Your Company. Your Company information includes information that is electronically generated, printed, filmed, typed, stored, or verbally communicated. Information must be protected according to its sensitivity, criticality, and value, regardless of the media on which it is stored, the manual or automated systems that process it, or the methods by which it is distributed.

Responsibilities

1. Employees are responsible for protecting corporate information from unauthorized access, modification, duplication, destruction, or disclosure.
2. Employees responsible for creating, administering, or using corporate information are identified as information **owners, custodians,** and **users** with responsibilities to protect information under their control.
   a. **Owner:** Employees responsible for the creation or use of the information resource. **Owners** are responsible to define safeguards that assure the confidentiality, availability, and integrity of the information assets. **Owners** are also responsible to place information in the proper classification so that it can be obtained by those who need the information to perform their assigned duties (see Section 4 below).
   b. **Custodian:** Employees responsible for maintaining the safeguards established by the **owner**. The **custodian** is designated by the **owner**.
   c. **Users:** Employees responsible for using and safeguarding information under their control according to the directions of the **owner**. **Users** are authorized access to information assets by the **owner**.
3. Access to information will be granted by the **owner** to those with an approved business need.
4. All corporate information shall be classified by the **owner** into one of three classification categories:
   a. **Confidential:** Information that, if disclosed, could violate the privacy of individuals, reduce the company's competitive advantage, or cause damage to the company.
   b. **Public:** Information that has been made available for public distribution through authorized company channels. (See Corporate Communications Policy.)
   c. **Internal Use:** Information that is intended for use by employees when conducting company business. Information that does not qualify as **Confidential** or **Public** is classified as **Internal Use**.

TABLE 4.7 (continued)   A Utility Company's Information Protection Policy: Example 4

Compliance

1. Each Manager shall:
   a. Develop and administer an information protection program that appropriately classifies and protects corporate information under their control.
   b. Implement an employee awareness program to ensure that all employees are aware of the importance of information and the methods employed for its protection.
   c. Establish an information records retention schedule in compliance with applicable laws and regulations.
2. Employees who fail to comply with the policies will be considered in violation of Your Company's *Employee Standards of Conduct* and will be subject to appropriate corrective action.

When creating an *Information Security Policies and Standards* document, each section in the document will normally begin with a topic-specific policy. The topic-specific policy will narrow the focus to one issue at a time. This will allow the writer to focus on one area and then develop a set of standards to support this particular subject.

Whereas Tier 1 policies are approved by the Information Security Steering Committee, topic-specific (Tier 2) policies can be issued by a single senior manager or director.

As with Tier 1 policies, Tier 2 policies will address management's position on relevant issues. It is necessary to interview management to determine what their concerns are and what is it that they want to have occur. The writer will then take this information and incorporate into the following structure.

4.10.2.1   Thesis Statement

This is similar to the *topic* section discussed in the Tier 1 policies, but it also adds more information to support the goals and objectives of the policy and management's directives. This section will be used to discuss the issue in relevant terms and what conditions are included. If appropriate, it may be useful to specify the goal or justification for the policy. This can be useful in gaining compliance with the policy.

When developing a Workstation Standards document, a topic-specific policy on appropriate software, with supporting standards, would include a discussion of "company-approved" software. This policy would define

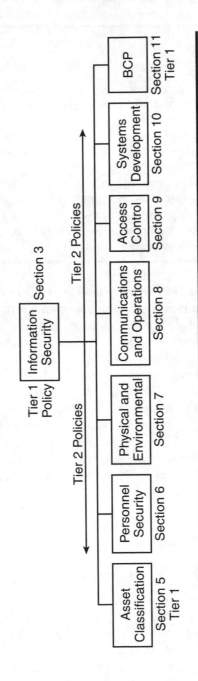

FIGURE 4.5 Topic-Specific Policies by Section

what is meant by "company-approved" software, which might be "any software not approved, purchased, screened, managed, and owned by the organization." The policy would also discuss the conditions required to have software approved.

Once the terms and conditions have been discussed, the remainder of this section would be used to state management's position on the issue.

4.10.2.2 Relevance

The Tier 2 policy also needs to establish to whom the policy applies. In addition to whom, the policy will want to clarify where, how, and when the policy is applicable. Is the policy only enforced when employees are on the work-site campus, or will it extend to off-site activities? It is necessary to identify as many of the conditions and terms as possible.

4.10.2.3 Responsibilities

The assignment of roles and responsibilities is also included in Tier 2 policies. For example, the policy on company-approved software will have to identify the process to get software approved. This would include the authority (by job title) authorized to grant approval and a reference to where this process is documented.

This is a good time to discuss deviations from policy requirements. I have established a personal standard in that I never discuss how an entity can gain a dispensation from the policy. I do *not* like to state that "this is the policy and all employees must comply, except those of you that can find a way around the policy." Most organizations have a process to gain an approved deviation from a policy or standard. This normally requires the petitioner to submit a business case for the deviation, along with alternative controls that would satisfy the spirit of the policy. If some organization or person wants a deviation from the policy, let them discover what the process is.

4.10.2.4 Compliance

For a Tier 2 policy, it may be appropriate to describe, in some detail, the infractions that are unacceptable and the consequences of such behavior. Penalties may be explicitly stated and should be consistent with the Tier 1 Employee Discipline Policy. Remember: when an employee is found in a noncompliant situation, it is management and Human Resources that are responsible for disciplining the individual.

4.10.2.5 Supplementary Information

For any Tier 2 policy, the appropriate individuals in the organization to contact for additional information, guidance, and compliance should be indicated. Typically, the contact information would be specified by job title, not by individual name. It may also be prudent to identify who is the owner of this policy. This information will provide the reader with the appropriate information if he or she has suggestions on how to improve the policy.

To be effective, a policy requires visibility. Visibility aids implementation of the policy by helping to ensure that it is fully communicated throughout the organization. Management presentations, videos, panel discussions, guest speakers, question and answer forums, and newsletters will increase visibility. The organization's Information Security Awareness Program can effectively notify users of new policies. The New Employee Orientation program can also be used to familiarize new employees with the organization's policies.

When introducing policies, it is important to ensure that management's support is clear, especially in areas where employees feel inundated with directives, regulations, or other requirements. Organization policies are the vehicles used to emphasize management's commitment to effective internal controls and their expectations for employee support and compliance.

Table 4.8 provides an example of a Tier 2 (topic-specific) policy.

The Senate Policy discusses what is allowed and what is not allowed. It identifies where a member can go to get additional information on proper usage. In the section indicated by "Scope and Responsibility," item 1 establishes the *topic* or *thesis statement* of this policy.

Item 3 assigns Responsibilities and major headings B and C provide *Supplemental Information*. The only area not apparently covered by this policy is *Compliance*. It also identifies who is responsible for overseeing or monitoring of activities. Item 1 under "Scope and Responsibility" discusses the thesis statement or topic. Under the circumstances, it may be appropriate to omit the compliance or consequences in the policy.

Let us now examine another sample Internet Usage Policy (see Table 4.9). This is an interesting Tier 2 policy in that it adds a "Statement of Compliance" section that the Internet user is to read and sign. I have encountered a number of policies that use this tactic. A word of warning about usage and responsibility statements; they must be revisited annually to ensure employees remember that they signed such a document. It is important that this reminder be part of an annual information security awareness program. This will ensure that the desired effect remains active.

A typical Usage and Responsibility Statement might look like the one in Table 4.10.

TABLE 4.8   Tier 2 Sample Internet Usage Policy: Example 1

U.S. Senate Internet Services Usage Rules and Policies

Policy for Internet Services

A. SCOPE AND RESPONSIBILITY

1. Senate Internet Services ("FTP Server, Gopher, World Wide Web, and Electronic mail") may only be used for official purposes. The use of Senate Internet Services for personal, promotional, commercial, or partisan political or campaign purposes is prohibited.
2. Members of the Senate, as well as Committee Chairmen and Officers of the Senate, may post to the Internet Servers information files that contain matter relating to their official business, activities, and duties. All other offices must request approval from the Committee on Rules and Administration before posting material on the Internet Information Servers.
3. It is the responsibility of each Senator, Committee Chairman, Officer of the Senate, or office head to oversee the use of the Internet Services by his or her office and to ensure that the use of the services is consistent with the requirements established by this policy and applicable laws and regulations.
4. Official records may not be placed on the Internet Servers unless otherwise approved by the Secretary of the Senate and prepared in accordance with Section 501 of Title 44 of the United States Code. Such records include, but are not limited to bills, public laws, committee reports, and other legislative materials.

B. POSTING OR LINKING TO THE FOLLOWING MATTER IS PROHIBITED

1. Political matter:
    a. Matter that specifically solicits political support for the sender or any other person or political party, or a vote or financial assistance for any candidate for any political office is prohibited.
    b. Matter that mentions a Senator or an employee of a Senator as a candidate for political office, or that constitutes electioneering, or that advocates the election or defeat of any individuals, or a political party is prohibited.
2. Personal matter:
    a. Matter that, by its nature, is purely personal and is unrelated to the official business activities and duties of the sender is prohibited.
    b. Matter that constitutes or includes any article, account, sketch, narration, or other text laudatory and complimentary of any Senator on a purely personal or political basis rather than on the basis of performance of official duties as a Senator is prohibited.
    c. Reports of how or when a Senator, the Senator's spouse, or any other member of the Senator's family spends time other than in the performance of, or in connection with, the legislative, representative, and other official functions of such Senator is prohibited.

TABLE 4.8 (continued)   Tier 2 Sample Internet Usage Policy: Example 1

    d. Any transmission expressing holiday greetings from a Senator is prohibited. This prohibition does not preclude an expression of holiday greetings at the commencement or conclusion of an otherwise proper transmission.

5. Promotional matter:
    a. The solicitation of funds for any purpose is prohibited.
    b. The placement of logos or links used for personal, promotional, commercial, or partisan political or campaign purposes is prohibited.

C. RESTRICTIONS ON THE USE OF INTERNET SERVICES

1. During the 60-day period immediately preceding the date of any primary or general election (whether regular, special, or runoff) for any national, state, or local office in which the Senator is a candidate, no Member may place, update, or transmit information using a Senate Internet Server ("FTP Server, Gopher, and World Wide Web), unless the candidacy of the Senator in such election is uncontested.

2. Electronic mail may not be transmitted by a Member during the 60-day period before the date of the Member's primary or general election unless it is in response to a direct inquiry.

3. During the 60-day period immediately before the date of a biennial general federal election, no Member may place or update on the Internet Server any matter on behalf of a Senator who is a candidate for election, unless the candidacy of the Senator in such election is uncontested.

4. An uncontested candidacy is established when the Rules Committee receives written certification from the appropriate state official that the Senator's candidacy may not be contested under state law. Since the candidacy of a Senator who is running for re-election from a state that permits write-in votes on elections day without prior registration or other advance qualification by the candidate may be contested, such a Member is subject to the above restrictions.

5. If a Member is under the restrictions as defined in subtitle C, paragraph (1), above, the following statement must appear on the homepage: ("Pursuant to Senate policy this homepage may not be updated for the 60-day period immediately before the date of a primary or general election"). The words "Senate Policy" must be hypertext linked to the Internet services policy on the Senate Home Page.

6. A Senator's homepage may not refer or be hypertext linked to another Member's site or electronic mail address without authorization from that Member.

7. Any Links to Information not located on a Senate Internet Server must be identified as a link to a non-Senate server.

TABLE 4.9   Sample Internet Usage Policy: Example 2

Internet Usage Policy

Overview

The Brother's Institute will provide access to the information resources of the Internet to assist in supporting teaching and learning, research, and information handling skills. This represents a considerable commitment of Institute resources in the areas of telecommunications, networking, software, storage, and cost.

This Internet Usage Policy is designed to outline for staff and students the conditions of use for these resources.

General

Internet access is provided as an information and learning tool and is to be used for Institute and curriculum related purposes only.

All existing Institute policies and regulations apply to a user's conduct on the Internet, especially (but not exclusively) those that deal with unacceptable behavior, privacy, misuse of Institute resources, sexual harassment, information and data security, and confidentiality.

The Institute has software systems that can monitor and record all Internet usage, and record each chat, newsgroup, or e-mail message. The Institute reserves the right to do this at any time. No user should have any expectation of privacy as to his or her Internet usage.

The Institute reserves the right to inspect any and all files stored on the network in order to ensure compliance with Institute policies.

The Institute will use independently supplied software and data to identify inappropriate or sexually explicit Internet sites. We will block access from within our networks to all such sites that we know of.

If you find yourself connected accidentally to a site that contains sexually explicit or offensive material, you must disconnect from that site immediately, regardless of whether that site had been previously deemed acceptable by any screening or rating program.

No user may use the Institute's Internet facilities to deliberately disable or overload any computer system or network, or to circumvent any system intended to protect the privacy or security of another user.

File Downloading

Any software or files downloaded via the Internet onto the Institute network become the property of the Institute.

Any such files or software may be used only in ways that are consistent with their licenses or copyrights.

No user may use Institute facilities knowingly to download or distribute illegal software or data. The use of Institute resources for illegal activity will be grounds for immediate dismissal.

TABLE 4.9 (continued)   Sample Internet Usage Policy: Example 2

Any file that is downloaded must be scanned for viruses before it is run or accessed.

No user may use the Institute's Internet facilities to deliberately propagate any virus.

Video and audio streaming and downloading represent significant data traffic, which can cause local network congestion. Video and audio downloading are prohibited unless for agreed demonstration purposes.

Chats, Newsgroups, and E-Mail

Each user of the Internet facilities must identify him or herself honestly, accurately, and completely (including Institute status and function if requested) when participating in chats or newsgroups, or when setting up accounts on outside computer systems.

Only those users who are duly authorized to speak to the media on behalf of the Institute may speak or write in the name of the Institute to any newsgroup or Web site.

Other users may participate in newsgroups or chats in the course of information research when relevant to their duties, but they do so as individuals, speaking only for themselves.

The Institute retains the copyright to any material posted to any forum, newsgroup, chat, or World Wide Web page by any employee in the course of his or her duties.

Users are reminded that chats and newsgroups are public forums and it is inappropriate to reveal confidential Institute information.

Offensive material should not be e-mailed. Anyone found doing this will be subject to severe disciplinary action.

Passwords and IDs

Any user who obtains a password or ID for an Internet resource must keep that password confidential.

User IDs and passwords will help maintain individual accountability for Internet resource usage.

The sharing of user IDs or passwords obtained for access to Internet sites is prohibited.

Security

The Institute has installed routers, firewalls, proxies, Internet address screening programs, and other security systems to assure the safety and security of the Institute's networks. Any user who attempts to disable, defeat, or circumvent any Institute security facility will be subject to disciplinary action.

Only those Internet services and functions that have been documented for education purposes within the Institute will be enabled at the Internet firewall.

TABLE 4.9 (continued)   Sample Internet Usage Policy: Example 2

Computers that use their own modems to create independent data connections sidestep our network security mechanisms. Therefore, any computer used for independent dial-up or leased-line connections to any outside computer or network must be physically isolated from the Institute's internal networks.

Any machine used for FTP must not contain any sensitive applications or data, and Java will be disabled for users or networks running mission-critical applications such as the production of core financial and student information.

Statement of Compliance
"I have read the Institute's Internet usage policy. I fully understand the terms of this policy and agree to abide by them. I realize that the Institute's security software may record for management use the Internet address of any site I visit and keep a record of any network activity in which I transmit or receive any kind of file. I acknowledge that any message I send or receive may be recorded and stored in an archive file for management use. I know that any violation of this policy may lead to disciplinary action being taken."

TABLE 4.10   Sample Internet Usage and Responsibility Statement

Internet Usage and Responsibility Statement

I, _____, acknowledge and understand that access to the Internet, as provided by the Company, is for management approved use only. This supports Peltier Associates policies on *Employee Standards of Conduct* and *Information Classification*, and among other things, prohibits the downloading of games, viruses, inappropriate materials or picture files, and unlicensed software from the Internet.

I recognize and accept that while accessing the Internet, I am responsible for maintaining the highest professional and ethical standards, as outlined in the Company policy on *Employee Standards of Conduct*.

I have read and understand the policies mentioned above and accept my responsibility to protect the Company's information and reputation.

Name _____   Date

Another area that requires a Tier 2 policy is the proper use of electronic mail (e-mail). We examine two existing e-mail policies and compare them to the criteria we have established for these types of policies (see Table 4.11 and Table 4.12).

TABLE 4.11   Sample E-Mail Usage Policy: Example 1

Company E-Mail Usage Policy

Policy

Company e-mail services are provided for official Company business use. Personal e-mail is not official Company business, although minimal use of e-mail for personal communication is acceptable. E-mail may be monitored by authorized system administrators. Abuse of the Company e-mail policy, outlined herein, will be brought to the attention of the department director and may result in disciplinary action.

E-Mail Guidelines

1. All users of the Company e-mail system are expected to conduct themselves in a legal, professional, and ethical manner.
2. Users are responsible for their information technology accounts, and may be held accountable if someone uses their account with permission and violates policy.
3. The Company e-mail system shall be used in accordance with Federal and State law and Company policies, and may not be used as a vehicle to harass or intimidate.
4. Company information technology resources are provided to employees for the purpose of business, research, service, and other work-related activities. Access to information technology resources is granted to an individual by the Company for that individual's sole use, and that use must be in furtherance of the mission and purpose of the Company. Information technology resources must be shared among users in an equitable manner. The user may not participate in any behavior that unreasonably interferes with the fair use of information technology resources by another.
5. The Company reserves the right, without notice, to temporarily limit or restrict any individual's use and to inspect, copy, remove, or otherwise alter any data, file, or system resource that may undermine the authorized use of any information technology facility. This is intended to protect the integrity of the Company's information technology facilities and its users against unauthorized or improper use.
6. Users must use only those information technology resources that the Company has authorized for their individual use. Users are authorized to access, use, copy, modify, or delete files and data on their own account. Users are not authorized to perform any of these functions on another user's account or a Company system.
7. User privacy is not to be violated. It is the responsibility of the user to protect their privacy. Users should not leave a password where it can be easily found, give a password to someone else, or leave confidential information on a screen where it could be viewed by an unauthorized person, or leave a public PC or terminal signed on and unattended.

TABLE 4.11 (continued) Sample E-Mail Usage Policy: Example 1

8. Nonbusiness-related chain e-mail messages are not to be forwarded using any Company resource. Chain e-mail is defined as any message sent to one or more people that instructs the recipient to forward it to multiple others and contains some promise of reward for forwarding it or threat of punishment for not doing so. Chain e-mail messages can have technological, social, and legal ramifications. Chain e-mail messages have the ability to clog an entire network and degrade the ability of employees to do their work. Heavy traffic due to chain e-mail messages can disrupt not only the e-mail service but other network activities as well.

9. Users may not intentionally obscure, change, or forge the date, time, physical source, logical source, or other label or header information on electronic mail, files, or reports.

Departments should contact the ISD Help Desk to report all problems with e-mail.

The opening paragraph spells out what this policy is about, what is unacceptable behavior, that activities are subject to monitoring and that noncompliance will be referred to management. This is a good, strong opening statement. The remainder of the policy supports the other objectives of proper e-mail usage.

Items 1, 2, 8, and 9 discuss compliance issues. Item 4 discusses the relevance issues, and items 4, 5, and 7 handle responsibility concerns. I have only one real problem with this policy and that is the use of the term "guideline." Over the years, my research into policy writing has led me to believe that in many instances the term "guideline," when used in a policy like the one above, really means "standard."

When writing policies, it is important to use the language that is accepted in your organization. When I worked for a global manufacturing corporation, we learned that the term "should" meant "must." It was known as a "Company should." That meant that whenever you saw the word "should" in a policy, standard, or procedure, you were to consider it mandatory. The company felt that use of the term "must" was harsh. So it would substitute a less harsh term to make the requirement more palatable. The term "shall" meant that the reader had an option to use or not use whatever was discussed. So for this company, "should" meant "standard" and "shall" meant "guideline."

Research the writing requirements of your organization and make certain you incorporate any idiosyncrasies into your writing. By understanding the form, you will be better able to ensure that the substance is read and accepted.

TABLE 4.12 Sample E-Mail Policy: Example 2

Electronic Mail Policy

1. Every company employee is responsible for ensuring that the electronic mail ("E-Mail") system is used properly and in accordance with this policy. Any questions about this policy should be directed either to the Human Resources Department or to the Company's E-Mail Administrator.

2. The E-Mail system of the Company is part of the business equipment and technology platform and should be used for Company purposes only. Personal business should not be conducted by means of the E-Mail system.

3. Employees should disclose information or messages from the E-Mail system only to authorized employees.

4. Employees do not have a personal privacy right in any matter created on, received through, or sent from the Company E-Mail system. Employees should not enter personal matters into the E-Mail system. The Company, in its discretion, reserves the right to monitor and to access any matter created on, received through, or sent from the E-Mail system.

5. No messages or information should be entered into the Company E-Mail system without a good business reason for doing so. Copies of E-Mail messages should be sent only for good business reasons.

6. Even if you have a password for the E-Mail system, it is impossible to assure the confidentiality of any message created on, received through, or sent from the Company E-Mail system. Any password you use must be known to the Company, as the Company may need to access this information in your absence.

7. The provisions of the Company's no solicitation–no distribution policy (see Employee Handbook) apply fully to the E-Mail system.

8. No E-Mail message should be created or sent that may constitute intimidating, hostile, or offensive material on the basis of sex, race, color, religion, national origin, sexual orientation, or disability. The Company's Policy against sexual or other harassment applies fully to the E-Mail system, and any violation of that policy is grounds for discipline up to and including discharge.

9. The Company expressly reserves the right to access, retrieve, read, and delete any communication that is created on, received through, or sent in the E-Mail system to assure compliance with this or any other Company policy.

10. Any employee who becomes aware of misuse of the E-Mail system should promptly contact either the Human Resources Department or the E-Mail Administrator.

11. Your signature indicates your understanding of this policy and your consent to its contents.

The sample e-mail policy in Table 4.12 has some problems. The opening paragraph is not as strong as the one contained in Example 1 (Table 4.11). Items 1 and 7 discuss the business need for using the e-mail system. I strongly recommend that when writing a policy, try to avoid the term "for company business only." We all know that e-mail and Internet access will be used at times for personal communications or research. The real intent is to prohibit the improper use of these business tools. Look at these forms of communication as you would the use of the company-provided phones. Be consistent in your requirements. If the phone on an employee's desk should be used for company business only and this policy is enforced, then it is safe to use that language for other forms of communication. However, if the phone system policy use allows for limited employee personal use, then the other communication-related policies should reflect this concept. A better term would be "for management-approved activities."

Items 3, 6, and 8 discuss privacy issues for the company and the company's right to monitor activities. When developing this kind of concept, be sure to include the legal staff and human resources in the review of the policy language.

I have to admit that I do not care for item 5. It goes against all that we know about passwords and defeats any attempt to bring individual accountability into the company culture. If employees are to create confidential passwords and then are required to give them to "the Company," then there is no individual accountability. Breaching the confidentiality of the password makes it now public domain.

In the section entitled Sample Topic-Specific Policies, we have assembled draft copies of Tier 2 policies that support the ISO 17799 areas of concern. These sample Tier 2 policies are intended to be used as a guide for language and possible content. As with any policy examples, please read them carefully and make certain that they are appropriate for your organization.

4.10.3 Application-Specific (Tier 3) Policy

Global-level (Tier 1) and topic-specific (Tier 2) policies address policy on a broad level (see Figure 4.6); they usually encompass the entire enterprise. The application-specific (Tier 3) policy focuses on one specific system or application. As the construction of an organization information security architecture takes shape, the final element will be the translation of Tier 1 and Tier 2 policies down to the application and system level.

Many security issue decisions apply only at the application or system level. Some examples of these issues include:

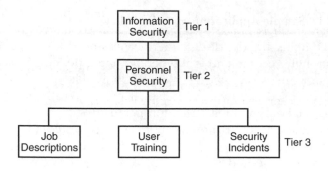

FIGURE 4.6   Tiers 1, 2, and 3

- Who has the authority to read or modify data?
- Under what circumstances can data be read or modified?
- How will remote access be controlled?

To develop a comprehensive set of Tier 3 policies, use a process that determines security requirements from a business or mission objective. Try to avoid implementing requirements based on security issues and concerns. Remember that the security staff has been empowered to support the business process of the organization. Typically, the Tier 3 policy is more free form than Tier 1 and Tier 2 policies. As you prepare to create Tier 3 policies, keep in mind the following concepts:

- Understand the overall business objectives or mission of the enterprise.
- Understand the mission of the application or system.
- Establish requirements that support both sets of objectives.

Typical Tier 3 policies may be as brief as the sample shown in Table 4.13. This Tier 3 policy is brief and to the point. It establishes what is required, who is responsible, and where to go for additional information and help.

We can use the policy in Table 4.14 to point out a few items that typically make for bad reading in a policy. When writing, try to avoid making words stand out. This is particularly true of words that cause people to react negatively. In this policy the writer likes to use uppercase words for emphasis: "MUST," "LATE TIMECARDS," "YOU MUST BE ACCURATE." I find that when words appear like this, the writer was in an agitated state and was taking out his or her personal frustrations on the policy. While what was said in this policy was fairly good, the tone was very negative. The person who wrote this policy probably has a sign posted

TABLE 4.13   Sample Application-Specific Policy

Accounts Payable Policy

Accounts payable checks are issued on Friday only. This will promote efficiency in the accounts payable function. To ensure your check is available, please have your check request or invoice to the Financial Affairs office by close of business on Monday.

For access to the online portion of the Accounts Payable System (APS), please contact the APS System Administrator.

The APS Customer Help Desk is available to answer any additional questions.

We appreciate your cooperation.

in his or her work area that reads "Poor planning on your part does not make it a crisis on my part."

When I do network vulnerability assessments for companies, I like to do a physical walk-through of the work area. I am on the lookout for what I call the "Dilbert factor." This comic strip has given us many a great laugh because we realize that it is our working environment that Scott Adams is identifying. However, be on the lookout for areas that have a high number of Dilbert cartoons posted. This is usually an area of employees who are unhappy with someone or something in the work area. These are the people who might write a policy like the one in Table 4.14.

The policy in Table 4.14 was written in a condescending manner and gives the impression that these highly skilled contractors are dummies. Write in a positive tone and instruct the reader as to what is expected. It is important to identify the consequences of noncompliance, but channel that into a specific subsection that identifies "Noncompliance."

4.11 Summary

In this chapter we discussed that the policy is the cornerstone of an organization's information security architecture; and that a policy was important to establish both internally and externally what an organization's position on a particular topic might be. We define what a policy, standard, procedure, and guideline is and what should be included in each of these documents or statements.

There are three types of policies, and you will use each type at different times in your information security program and throughout the organization to support the business process or mission. The three types of policies are:

TABLE 4.14 Sample Timecard Policy and Instructions

Timecard Policy and Instructions

An original timecard/sheet MUST be turned in before your hours can be processed. Hours MUST be turned in before 10:00 am on Monday to have your paycheck/direct deposit slip available on Thursday. If your timecard is turned in after noon on Wednesday, you will be paid the following week. We can NOT guarantee paycheck availability for LATE TIMECARDS.

The timecard is our invoice; YOU MUST BE ACCURATE!

As with most BOX Group clients, you must work 40 straight time hours in a week before you can get overtime pay. All hours should be listed in the regular hours column until you reach 40. After you have worked 40, all hours should go in the overtime column. Overtime (premium) rates are based upon the terms of BOX Group's purchase order and any applicable tax codes. Because of this, policy may vary from company to company or, depending upon your position, pay rate, etc. Specific overtime rates will be discussed and agreed upon prior to starting your assignment. If you have any questions regarding overtime, contact your branch office.

When you do not work a full 40 hours straight time during the week, Saturday's hours must go toward straight time until you reach the necessary 40 hours.

ONLY write on the timecard the hours you actually work.

When you have a week in which a holiday occurs, you should leave the space blank instead of hours in the regular hours column. The hours for a holiday are not counted toward your total hours worked for that week. If no overtime hours were worked this week, your timecard total would be 32 hours. During a week that a holiday occurs, most BOX Group clients pay overtime over 32 hours in that week.

If you miss a day of work, hours should not be entered for that day.

Copies of timecard: (Client timecard copies differ.)

■ Yellow/White Copies: Payroll/Invoice copies. Return to BOX Group.
■ Pink Copy: Branch copy. Return to BOX Group.
■ Blue Copy: Customer copy Company you are working for/Supervisor.
■ Goldenrod Copy: Employee copy. Keep your copy.

IMPORTANT! Please note that your check will not be generated without the original timecard.

---

1. *Global (Tier 1) policies* are used to create the organization's overall vision and direction.
2. *Topic-specific (Tier 2) policies* address particular subjects of concern. (We discuss the information security architecture and each category such as the one shown in Table 4.15.)

TABLE 4.15 Sample Information Security Policy

Information Security Policy

Policy Statement

Information is a company asset and is the property of the Company. Company information must be protected according to its value, sensitivity, and criticality, regardless of the media on which it is stored, the manual or automated systems that process it, or the methods used to distribute it.

Responsibilities

1. Company officers and senior management are required to make sure that internal controls are adequate to safeguard company assets — including company information.
2. Company line managers are responsible for making sure that all employees are aware of and comply with this information security policy, its supporting policies and standards, and all applicable laws and regulations.
3. All employees, regardless of their status (permanent, part-time, contract, etc.), are responsible for protecting information from unauthorized access, modification, disclosure, and destruction.

Scope

1. Company information includes information that is electronically generated and information that is printed, typed, filmed, or verbally communicated.

Compliance

1. Company management is responsible for monitoring compliance with this information security policy, its supporting policies and standards, and all applicable laws and regulations.
2. Employees, regardless of their status (permanent, part-time, contract, etc.), who fail to comply with this information security policy, its supporting policies and standards, or any applicable law or regulation will be considered in violation of their terms of employment and will be subject to appropriate corrective action.

3. *Application-specific policies* focus on decisions taken by management to control particular applications (financial reporting, payroll, etc.) or systems (budgeting system).

Chapter 5

Asset Classification

5.1 Introduction

With the U.S. Congress on full alert regarding the protection of information assets and the international community certifying organizations to information security standards, the requirement for an asset classification policy is at hand. As a security professional, it is important for you to know that an asset or information classification policy is only one element in the overall information management process. The Information Classification policy should be coupled with a Records Management policy.

Any security standard or best practice should be founded on a solid foundation of an asset classification. To ensure proper protection of our information resources, it is necessary to define what an owner is and how that entity has ultimate responsibility for the information assets within its business unit, and this includes classification and assigning retention requirements. By implementing an asset management scheme and supporting methodology, we are able to determine required controls commensurate with the sensitivity of the information as classified by the owner.

This chapter explores the need for policies, examines the contents of these policies, and then critiques examples of these policies.

5.2 Overview

As discussed in this chapter, information classification is only one of the elements in an effective information management program. Knowing what we have and how important it is to the organization is key to the success for the information security program. The implementation of this program requires that representatives of the organization be charged with exercising the organization's proprietary rights. In addition, a full inventory of these assets must be conducted with a requirement for annual review established.

5.3 Why Classify Information?

Organizations classify information to establish the appropriate levels of protection for these resources. Because resources are limited, it is necessary to prioritize and identify what really needs protection (see Figure 5.1). One of the reasons to classify information is to ensure that scarce resources will go where they will do the most good. The return on investment for implementing an encryption system to protect public domain information would not be considered a sound business decision. All information is created equal, but not all information is of equal value.

Of all the information found within an enterprise, only about ten percent of it is actually competitive advantage, trade secret, or personal information. The biggest portion of organization information is that which must be accessed by employees to do their assigned tasks. The remaining information is that which has been available to the public through authorized channels. Information resources that are classified as "public" would include annual stockholders' reports, press releases, and other authorized public announcements.

An effective way of understanding the difference between internal use information and public information is to picture your organization's connection to the Internet. The Web site and information contained on it that

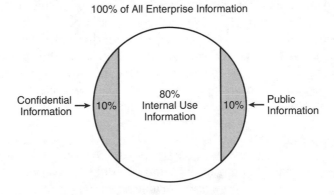

FIGURE 5.1   Information Classification Breakdown

is outside your zone of protection is your public information. Remember that posting information to the public Web site is only done by the Web master and with the approval of the owner of the information. This is your organization's Internet connection.

The portion of Internet access that is behind your zone of protection and contains information for use by employees is your Intranet connection. This area contains information that is unavailable to the outside world but has been made accessible to employees for use while performing their assigned tasks.

For years, the information handling standard was that all information is closed until the owner opens it. This worked well in the mainframe environment when access control packages ruled the single platform of information processing. With the introduction of the client/server environment and the multiple platforms operating situation, no single access control package could handle all of the needs. With decentralized processing and then the move to connect to the Internet, the restrictions on information closure began to weaken. The operating concept during this period was that all information was open until the owner classified it and closed access to it.

Now we have gone full circle. As the decentralized processing environment matured and national and international laws, statutes, and privacy concerns became stronger, the information protection concept has reverted to all information access being closed until the owner opens access. For this to be effective and to allow the organization to demonstrate due diligence, it is incumbent upon the organization to establish an effective information classification policy and supporting handling standards.

Most organizations do not have information that is all the same value or sensitivity. It is necessary to at least develop an initial high-level attempt at classification. This should be done, if for no other reason than to ensure that budgeted resources are not misused in over-protecting nonsensitive, noncritical information assets. Before employees can protect information assets, they must first have a policy that identifies classification levels and then a methodology to implement the policy requirements. An information classification policy that is not overly complex and a methodology that relies on common sense and is facilitated by either information security or records management will make acceptance possible.

5.4 What Is Information Classification?

An information or asset classification process is a business decision process. Information is an asset of the organization, and managers have been charged with protecting and accounting for proper use of all assets. An information classification process will allow managers to meet this fiduciary responsibility. The role of the information security professional — or even information systems personnel — is one of advice and consulting. The final decision is made by the business unit managers or, as we will define soon, the asset owner.

When preparing to develop the information classification policy, it is important to get input from the management team. As discussed in previous chapters, knowing what management really wants will improve the quality of the overall policy. It is important to ask questions to find out what they mean. When my daughter was about seven or eight years old, she came to me and asked, "Pa, where do we come from?" Well I pretended to not hear her so I could research my answer. The next day I sat down with her and discussed the "facts of life" with her. She looked at me and said, "I know all that. What I want to know is where we come from. Terri Lynn comes from Tennessee and Pam comes from Kentucky." So before developing an answer, make sure you understand the question.

When conducting interviews with management and other key personnel, develop a set of questions to ensure a consistency in the direction of the responses. These questions might include some of the following:

- What are the mission-critical or sensitive activities or operations?
- Where is mission-critical or sensitive information stored?
- Where is this information processed?
- Who requires access to this information?

There are no hard and fast rules for determining what constitutes sensitive information. In some instances, it may be that the number of people who require access may affect the classification. The real test of an information classification system is how easy is it for the reader to understand what constitutes sensitive information and what organization-approved label should be affixed to the information asset resource.

5.5 Where to Begin?

With a clearer idea of what management is expecting, it is now time to do some research. I like to contact my fellow information security professionals and find out what they have done to answer problems that I have been assigned. By being a member of the Computer Security Institute (CSI), the Information System Security Association (ISSA), and the Information Systems Audit and Control Association (ISACA), I have ready access to people in my area that are usually willing to share examples of their work.

When developing classification levels, I prefer to discuss the topic with fellow professionals. I recommend that you cultivate contacts in similar business environments and see what your peers are doing. The Internet can generate some examples of classification policies, but many of them are university or government agency related. Be careful of what you uncover in your research; while there are many good ideas and terms out there, they are only good if they are applicable to your specific needs.

Use the information gathered from fellow professionals as a starting point. Your organization will have its own unique variation on the classification policy and categories. We will examine a number of examples of information categories. If you are a government agency, or do work for a government agency, be sure to check with your regulatory affairs group to determine if there are any government-imposed requirements.

5.6 Information Classification Category Examples

5.6.1 Example 1

Using the information in Table 5.1 and Table 5.2, the manager can determine the level of criticality of an information asset.

5.6.2 Example 2

This service provider has established five categories for use by managers in classifying information assets (see Table 5.3). Part of the reason for the use of these categories is that the provider has experience with Department of Defense contracts and has become used to certain classification levels. The concern I have with patterning a policy after a government standard is that there may be confusion as to what is government contact information and what is normal business information. Also, the number of employees exposed to the government standards may impact the drafting of these standards.

5.6.3 Example 3

I recently discussed the classification scheme shown in Table 5.4 with the company that created it to find out how they use the color coding. The sample *Information Security Handbook* included in this book also uses color codes for information classification. The company does not actually use the colors to color-code the documents. Instead, the company identifies the level of classification but requires the footer to contain "Company Red" or whatever color. It gives a good visual for the employees.

LIVERPOOL JOHN MOORES UNIVERSITY
LEARNING SERVICES

TABLE 5.1   Information Classification Category: Example 1

Mega Oil Corporation

- HIGHLY CONFIDENTIAL — Information whose unauthorized disclosure will cause the corporation severe financial, legal, or reputation damage. Examples: acquisitions data, bid details, contract negotiation strategies.
- CONFIDENTIAL — Information whose unauthorized disclosure may cause the corporation financial, legal, or reputation damage. Examples: employee personnel and payroll files, competitive advantage information.
- GENERAL — Information that, because of its personal, technical, or business sensitivity, is restricted for use within the company. Unless otherwise classified, all information within Amoco is in this category.

At this point in the classification scheme, this company has included a mechanism to establish the criticality of the information. It has established its three information classification categories and now adds three impact categories. Using these sets of definitions, the manager of information resources will be able to determine how critical the asset is to the company.

- MAXIMUM — Information whose unauthorized modification and destruction will cause the company severe financial, legal, or reputation damage.
- MEDIUM — Information whose unauthorized modification and destruction may cause the company financial, legal, or reputation damage. Examples: electronic funds transfer, payroll, and commercial checks.
- MINIMUM — Although an error in this data would be of minimal consequence, this is still important company information and therefore will require some minimal controls to ensure a minimal level of assurance that the integrity of the data is maintained. This applies to all data that is not placed in one of the above classifications. Examples: lease production data, expense data, financial data, and exploration data.
- CRITICAL — It is important to assess the availability requirements of data, applications, and systems. A business decision will be required to determine the length of unavailability that can be tolerated prior to expending additional resources to ensure the information availability that is required. Information should be labeled "CRITICAL" if it is determined that special procedures should be used to ensure its availability.

5.6.4   Example 4

The company also requires that specific levels of information contain appropriate markings to identify it as classified information (see Table 5.5). We discuss an Information Handling Matrix later in this chapter. When creating your organization's handling requirements, use the following as thought starters:

TABLE 5.2 Criticality Matrix

Business Impact	Classification Level		
Maximum	1	2	3
Medium	2	2	3
Minimum	2	3	4

1: Availability safeguards must be implemented.
2: Availability safeguards should be implemented.
3: Continue to monitor availability requirements.
4: No additional action required at this time.

TABLE 5.3 Information Classification Category: Example 2

International Service Provider

■ **Top Secret** — Information that, if disclosed, could cause severe impact to the company's competitive advantage or business strategies.
■ **Confidential** — Information that, if disclosed, could violate the privacy of individuals, reduce competitive advantage, or damage the company.
■ **Restricted** — Information that is available to a specific subset of the employee population when conducting company business.
■ **Internal Use**— Information that is intended for use by all employees when conducting company business.
■ **Public** — Information that has been made available to the public through authorized company channels.

■ Make no copies
■ Third-party confidential
■ Attorney–client privileged document
■ Distribution limited to ____
■ Covered by a nonanalysis agreement

5.7 Resist the Urge to Add Categories

Keep the number of information classification categories to as few as possible. If two possible categories do not require substantially different treatment, then combine them. The more categories available, the greater the chance for confusion among managers and employees. Normally, three or four categories should be sufficient to meet your organization's needs.

Additionally, avoid the impulse to classify everything the same. To simplify the classification process, some organizations have flirted with having everything classified as confidential. The problem with this concept

TABLE 5.4   Information Classification Category: Example 3

Global Manufacturer

- *Company Confidential Red* — Provides a significant competitive advantage. Disclosure would cause severe damage to operations. Relates to or describes a long-term strategy or critical business plans. Disclosure would cause regulatory or contractual liability. Disclosure would cause severe damage to our reputation or the public image. Disclosure would cause a severe loss of market share or the ability to be first to market. Disclosure would cause a loss of an important customer, shareholder, or business partner. Disclosure would cause a long-term or severe drop in stock value. Strong likelihood somebody is seeking to acquire this information.
- *Company Confidential Yellow* — Provides a competitive advantage. Disclosure could cause moderate damage to the company or an individual. Relates to or describes an important part of the operational direction of the company over time. Provides important technical or financial aspects of a product line or a business unit. Disclosure could cause a loss of customer or shareholder confidence. Disclosure could cause a temporary drop in stock value. Very likely that some third party would seek to acquire this information.
- *Company Confidential Green* — Might provide a business advantage over those who do not have access to the same information. Might be useful to a competitor. Not easily identifiable by inspection of a product. Not generally known outside the company or available from public sources. Generally available internally. Little competitive interest.
- *Company Public* — Would not provide a business or competitive advantage. Routinely made available to interested members of the general public. Little or no competitive interest.

TABLE 5.5   Information Classification Category: Example 4

- *Company CONFIDENTIAL* — A subset of Company Internal information, the unauthorized disclosure or compromise of which would likely have an adverse impact on the company's competitive position, tarnish its reputation, or embarrass an individual. Examples: customer, financial, pricing, or personnel data; merger/acquisition, product, or marketing plans; new product designs, proprietary processes and systems.
- *Company INTERNAL* — All forms of proprietary information originated or owned by the Company, or entrusted to it by others. Examples: organization charts, policies, procedures, phone directories, some types of training materials.
- *Company PUBLIC* — Information officially released by the Company for widespread public disclosure. Example: press releases, public marketing materials, employment advertising, annual reports, product brochures, the public Web site, etc.

is that confidential information requires special handling. This would violate the concept of placing controls only where they are actually needed. This method would require the organization to waste limited resources protecting assets that do not really require that level of control.

Another pitfall to avoid is to take the information classification categories developed by another enterprise and adopt them verbatim as your own. Use the information created by other organizations to assist in the creation of your organization's unique set of categories and definitions.

In some government sectors there are five categories for information classification (Top-Secret, Secret, Confidential, Restricted, and Unclassified). In addition to these categories, there are additional impact levels of Sensitive and Nonsensitive. Using this scheme, it would be possible to have an information asset of higher concern if it is classified *Restricted/Sensitive* compared to one that is classified *Confidential/Nonsensitive*. In addition, information labeled as *Unclassified* has the classification level of *Unclassified*, so it has actually been classified. Sometimes I think Joseph Heller in *Catch 22* actually established a guideline for government and industry to use when developing standards and policies.

5.8 What Constitutes Confidential Information

There are a number of ways to look at information that can be classified as confidential. We examine a number of statements relating to confidential information. The first is a general statement about sensitive information:

For a general definition of what might constitute confidential information, it may be sufficient to define such information as:

> Information that is disclosed could violate the privacy of individuals, reduce the company's competitive advantage, or could cause damage to the organization.

The Economic Espionage Act of 1996 (EEA) defines "trade secret" information to include "all forms and types of financial, business, scientific, technical, economic, or engineering information," regardless of "how it is stored, complied, or memorialized." The EEA criminalizes the actions of anyone who:

■ Steals, or without authorization, appropriates, takes, carries away, or conceals, or by fraud, artifice, or deception obtains a trade secret
■ Without authorization copies, duplicates, sketches, draws, photographs, downloads, uploads, alters, destroys, photocopies, replicates, transmits, delivers, sends, mails, communicates, or conveys a trade secret

- Receives, buys, or possesses a trade secret, knowing the same to have been stolen or appropriated, obtained, or converted without authorization
- Conspires with one or more other persons to commit any offense described in the EEA under the heading "conspiracy"

There are a number of other information classification types that you may have heard about over the years. Let us take just a minute to review copyright, patent, and trademark.

5.8.1 Copyright

At regular intervals, employees will be creating new work in the form of application programs, transactions, systems, Web sites, etc. To protect the organization from loss of created material, enterprise policies on copyright ownership must be implemented and all employees must be reminded of these policies on a regular basis.

Unlike other forms of intellectual property protection, the basis for copyright occurs at the creation of an original work. Although government copyright offices grant copyrights, every original work has an inherent right to a copyright and is protected by that right even if the work is not published or registered.

All original works of authorship created by employees for a company are the property of the company and are protected by the copyright law. The copyright also applies to consultants doing work for your organization while under a purchase order or other contractual agreement. Unless there is an agreement to the contrary, any work created by a contractor under contract to an organization is owned by the organization, not the contractor.

The types of work that qualify for copyright protection include:

- All types of written works
- Computer databases and software programs (including source code, object code, and micro code)
- Output (including customized screens and printouts)
- Photographs, charts, blueprints, technical drawings, and flowcharts
- Sound recordings

A copyright does not protect:

- Ideas, inventions, processes, and three-dimensional designs (these are covered by *patent law*)
- Brands, products, or slogans (covered by *trademark law*)

The information classification policy you will be developing discusses organization confidential information. Typically, this type of information will consist of either competitive advantage or trade secret information or personal information.

The laws regarding trade secret information were developed from the duty of good faith imposed generally in commercial dealings. A trade secret is commonly defined as information deriving actual or potential economic value by virtue of its not being readily ascertainable through proper means by the public, and which is the subject of reasonable efforts to maintain its secrecy. The legal system protects the owner (in our case, the organization) from someone who uses improper means to learn the trade secret, either directly or indirectly. Therefore, anyone using improper means to learn the trade secret has breached a duty of good faith in dealing with the trade secret owner.

The breach of that duty of good faith usually takes the form of an abuse of a confidence, the use of improper means to ascertain the secret, or a breach of contract. Anyone involved in the breach of that duty is liable for trade secret stealing.

The laws or requirements governing trade secret and competitive advantage information are well established and offer substantial penalties for noncompliance. The area of personal information has become hotter during the past couple years. The passage of the Health Insurance Portability and Accountability Act (HIPAA), Gramm–Leach–Bliley Act (GLBA), European Union privacy laws, and organizations such as Privacy International are working to increase the safeguards required for personal information.

Any policy and supporting standards on information classification levels must take into account not only the trade secret and competitive advantage information, but also include any personal information about employees, customers, clients, and other third parties.

Earlier in this chapter we examined a number of examples of information classification categories. Now we add one other important element: the role of employees in the information classification process.

5.9 Employee Responsibilities

When doing research for this section of the book, I came across the following policy statement:

> The "**Information Owner**" means the party who confides the referenced Confidential Information to the other party, the Confidant. Despite the name, the Information Owner benefits from a Confidentiality Engagement with respect to Confidential Information that it owns or possesses.

These two sentences have five terms that require the reader to get further definitions. As I attempted to determine exactly what it means to "confide," I was sent to a hypertext page that explained that it meant to "entrust" the information to a "confident," which means the "party receiving the information" and at that point I started looking elsewhere for examples.

The two policy sentences above provide a good example of what should be avoided when writing a policy, or writing anything. The document referenced came from an organization with strong roots in the legal and government sectors. If this is your audience, then this is the language for you. If not, try to think like Henry David Thoreau and simplify.

There are typically three areas of employee responsibility: owner, user, and custodian. We discuss each of these concepts and examine how other organizations have defined these responsibilities.

5.9.1   Owner

The information owner is the entity within the organization that has been assigned the responsibility to exercise the organization's proprietary rights and grant access privileges to those with a true business need. This role is normally assigned to the senior level manager within the business unit where the information asset was created or is the primary user of that asset. The managers will have the ultimate responsibility for compliance but will probably delegate the day-to-day activities to some individual who reports to them.

5.9.1.1   Information Owner

The person who creates, or initiates the creation or storage, of the information is the initial owner. In an organization, possibly with divisions, departments, and sections, the owner becomes the unit itself, with the person responsible designated the "head" of the unit.

The information owner is responsible for ensuring that:

- There exists an agreed-upon classification hierarchy, and this hierarchy is appropriate for the types of information processed for that business unit.
- Classify all information stored into the agreed types and create an inventory (listing) of each type.
- For each document or file within each classification category, append its agreed (confidentiality) classification. Its availability should be determined by the respective classification.

■ Ensure that, for each classification type, the appropriate level of information security safeguards is available (e.g., the log-on controls and access permissions applied by the Information Custodian provide the required levels of confidentiality).

■ Periodically check to ensure that information continues to be classified appropriately and that the safeguards remain valid and operative.

I am not certain what being designated "head" actually means, but I do not believe I would want that title. The term "initial owner" may also lead the reader to believe that someone else may come along and become the "final" or "ultimate" leader.

We now review the owner definition from a global media organization.

Owners are authorized employees to whom responsibility has been delegated for the creation or use of specific business data by the *business unit* that "owns" the data. Owners are responsible for defining requirements for safeguards that ensure the confidentiality, availability, and integrity of the information. Owners are also responsible for placing information in the proper classification so that those who need the information to perform their assigned duties can obtain it. The owner provides requirements for security for the information to the custodian. The custodian implements the controls to meet the owner's requirements. This is a fairly good definition. The only element that I might add is the requirement that the Owner monitor the safeguards to ensure Custodian compliance. Let us examine one more example.

> **A. Owner:** Is the company management of an organizational unit, department, etc. where the information is created, or that is the primary user of the information. **Owners** have the responsibility to:

1. Identify the classification level of all corporate information within their organizational unit
2. Define and implement appropriate safeguards to ensure the confidentiality, integrity, and availability of the information resource
3. Monitor safeguards to ensure their compliance and report situations of noncompliance
4. Authorize access to those who have a business need for the information
5. Remove access from those who no longer have a business need for the information

We will see variations on this definition in the following section.

5.9.2 *Custodian*

The next responsibility we must create is that of the information custodian. This entity is responsible for protecting the information asset based on the requirements established by the owner. In an organization that has an information systems organization, the operations group might be considered the custodian of client data and information. They neither have the right to permit anyone access to the information asset, nor can they alter the information in any way without approval from the owner. This would include any programming or system upgrades that would modify the information or the output from applications and transactions.

> An **Information Custodian** is the person responsible for overseeing and implementing the necessary safeguards to protect assets, at the level classified by the information owner.

> This could be the System Administrator, controlling access to a computer network; or a specific application program or even a standard filing cabinet.

This example started out well but finished oddly. Giving examples of what might be considered a custodian is good. Trying to liken a filing cabinet to the opening sentence where the policy identifies the custodian as a "person." When writing, remember to go back and read what you just wrote to make sure the concepts match from beginning to end. Do not try to be cute. Stick to the subject and make sure you say exactly what needs to be said.

> Custodians are authorized system support persons or organizations (employees, contractors, consultants, vendors, etc.) responsible for maintaining the safeguards established by owners. The owner designates the custodian. The custodian is the "steward of the data" for the owner; that is, the Data Center may be the custodian for business application "owned" by a business unit.

The use of the term "steward of the data" brings out a point that needs to be made. Some organizations and cultures prefer other terms than the ones discussed here. When I was younger, I played Pony League baseball for a team called the "Custodians." Our uniforms were the most realistic because we had the name on the front and numbers on the back. The other teams had names such as "Tigers" and "Braves" but had some advertisement about their sponsor on the back. It was not until we played a few games that the other team started calling us the janitors. Custodian to some is a noble name; to others, maybe not so noble. So choose your terms wisely. "Curator," "keeper," and "guardian" are other terms that might work.

Recently we were doing work for HIPAA compliance and developing policies for a hospital. When we discussed the definition for "user," the hospital staff started to chuckle and told us that the term "user" had a totally different meaning there and we needed to find another term.

> B. **Custodian:** Employees designated by the owner to be responsible for maintaining the safeguards established by the owner.

It is important to remember that when using the term "employee," we are actually discussing the virtual employee. We can only write policy for employees; for all third parties, a contract must contain compliance language. Thus, it is perfectly acceptable to identify "employees" even if we know that someone other than an employee might actually perform the function. This is true for all employee responsibilities except "owner." The owner must be an employee; after all, it is the organization's information.

5.9.3   User

The final element is the user. This individual is granted permission by the owner to access the information asset. The user must use the information in the manner agreed upon with the owner. The user has no other rights. When granting access, the owner should use the concept of "least privilege." This means the user is granted only the access he or she specifically needs to perform a business task, and no more.

> An **information user** is the person responsible for viewing, amending, or updating the content of the information assets. This can be any user of the information in the inventory created by the information owner.

The *inventory* discussed here is addressed in both the classification policy and the records management policy, including who has been assigned access needs to be tracked. The custodian is generally responsible for providing the tools to monitor the user list.

> **Users** are authorized system users (employees, contractors, consultants, vendors, etc.) responsible for using and safeguarding information under their control according to the directions of the owner. Users are authorized access to information by the owner.

The final example is similar to the definition used above:

C. **User:** Employees authorized by the owner to access information and use the safeguards established by the owner.

5.10 Classification Examples

This section examines attributes and examples of different classification categories, and presents examples of organization information classification policies.

5.10.1 Classification: Example 1

Critique of Example 1 (Table 5.6) — This is an actual classification policy (very high level) for the executive branch of a national government. There is little here to help the average user. This is an example of a program or general policy statement; however, a topic-specific policy statement may have been more beneficial. Perhaps the next two examples will provide more information.

5.10.2 Classification: Example 2

Critique of Example 2 (Table 5.7) — The policy seems to stress competitive advantage information in its opening paragraphs. It does not appear to address personal information about employees or customers. It does provide for these topics as categories under "Confidential" but it never really

TABLE 5.6   Information Classification Policy: Example 1

Information Classification

- **Policy**: Security classifications should be used to indicate the need and priorities for security protection.

Objective: To ensure that information assets receive an appropriate level of protection.

Statement: Information has varying degrees of sensitivity and criticality. Some items may require an additional level of security protection or special handling. A security classification system should be used to define an appropriate set of security protection levels, and to communicate the need for special handling measures to users.

TABLE 5.7   Information Classification Policy: Example 2

Classification Requirements

Classified data is information developed by the organization with some effort and some expense or investment that provides the organization with a competitive advantage in its relevant industry and that the organization wishes to protect from disclosure.

While defining information protection is a difficult task, four elements serve as the basis for a classification scheme:

1. The information must be of some value to the organization and its competitors so that it provides some demonstrable competitive advantage.
2. The information must be the result of some minimal expense or investment by the organization.
3. The information is somewhat unique in that it is not generally known in the industry or to the public or may not be readily ascertained.
4. The information must be maintained as a relative secret, both within and outside the organization, with reasonable precautions against disclosure of the information. Access to such information could only result from disregarding established standards or from using illegal means.

Top Secret (Secret, Highly Confidential)
Attributes:

- Provides the organization with a very significant competitive edge
- Is of such a nature that unauthorized disclosure would cause severe damage to the organization
- It shows specific business strategies and major directions
- Is essential to the technical or financial success of a product

Examples:

- Specific operating plans, marketing strategies
- Specific descriptions of unique parts or materials, technology intent statements, new technologies and research
- Specific business strategies and major directions

Confidential (Sensitive, Personal, Privileged)
Attributes:

- Provides the organization with a significant competitive edge
- Is of such a nature that unauthorized disclosure would cause damage to the organization
- Shows operational direction over an extended period of time
- Is extremely important to the technical or financial success of a product

TABLE 5.7 (continued) Information Classification Policy: Example 2

Examples:

- Consolidated revenue, cost, profit, or other financial results
- Operating plans, marketing strategies
- Descriptions of unique parts or materials, technology intent statements, new technological studies and research
- Market requirements, technologies, product plans, and revenues

Restricted (Internal Use)
Attributes:

- All business-related information requiring baseline security protection, but failing to meet the specified criteria for higher classification
- Information that is intended for use by employees when conducting company business

Examples:

- Business information
- Organization policies, standards, procedures
- Internal organization announcements

Public (Unclassified)
Attributes:

- Information that, due to its content and context, requires no special protection, or
- Information that has been made available to the public distribution through authorized company channels

Examples:

- Online public information, Web site information
- Internal correspondence, memoranda, and documentation that do not merit special controls
- Public corporate announcements

---

mentions them by name. This appears to be a policy that is somewhat limited in scope. Additionally, it does not establish the scope of the information (is it computer generated only or exactly what information is being addressed?). The employee responsibilities are missing. What is management's responsibility with respect to information classification, and what is expected of the employees? Finally, what are the consequences of noncompliance?

5.10.3   Classification: Example 3

Critique of Example 3 (Table 5.8) — Examples 2 and 3 are very similar. Example 3 does address the role of the owner but fails to define what an owner is. It does not address the issue of noncompliance, and the scope of the policy is vague.

5.10.4   Classification: Example 4

Critique of Example 4 (Table 5.9) — The intent of the policy states that "Information is a corporate asset and is the property of Corporation." The scope of the policy states that "Corporate information includes electronically generated, printed, filmed, typed, or stored." The responsibilities are well-established. The issue of compliance is the only policy element that appears lacking.

5.11 Declassification or Reclassification of Information

Part of an effective information classification program is the ability to combine the requirements with a Records Management Policy. Information assets must be protected, stored, and then destroyed, based on a policy and a set of standards. The Information Classification Policy will ensure that an owner is assigned to each asset, that a proper classification is assigned, and that an information handling set of standards will help maintain control of information copies.

The Records Management Policy requires the owner to provide a brief description of the information record and the record retention requirements. These requirements will be a set of standards that support the Records Management Policy. We briefly examine what typically is part of the Records Management Policy.

5.12 Records Management Policy

An organization's records are one of its most important and valuable assets. Almost every employee is responsible for creating or maintaining organization records of some kind, whether in the form of paper, computer data, optical disk, electronic mail, or voice-mail. Letters, memoranda, and contracts are obviously information records, as are things such as a desk calendar, an appointment book, or an expense record.

TABLE 5.8   Information Classification Policy: Example 3

INFORMATION CLASSIFICATION

Introduction

Information, wherever it is handled or stored (for example, in computers, file cabinets, desktops, fax machines, voice-mail), needs to be protected from unauthorized access, modification, disclosure, and destruction. All information is <u>not</u> created equal. Consequently, segmentation or classification of information into categories is necessary to help identify a framework for evaluating the information's relative value and the appropriate controls required to preserve its value to the company.

Three basic classifications of information have been established. Organizations may define additional subclassifications as necessary to complete their framework for evaluating and preserving information under their control.

When information does require protection, the protection must be consistent. Often, strict access controls are applied to data stored in the mainframe computers but not applied to office workstations. Whether in a mainframe, client/server, workstation, file cabinet, desk drawer, waste basket, or in the mail, information should be subject to appropriate and consistent protection.

The definitions and responsibilities described below represent the minimum level of detail necessary for all organizations across the company. Each organization may decide that additional detail is necessary to adequately implement information classification within their organization.

> *Corporate Policy:* All information must be classified by the **owner** into one of three classifications: **Confidential**, **Internal Use** or **Public**.
>
> (From Company Policy on Information Management)

Confidential

Definition: Information that, if disclosed, could:

- Violate the privacy of individuals,
- Reduce the company's competitive advantage, or
- Cause damage to the company.

Examples: Some examples of **Confidential** information are:

- Personnel records (including name, address, phone, salary, performance rating, social security number, date of birth, marital status, career path, number of dependents, etc.),
- Customer information (including name, address, phone number, energy consumption, credit history, social security number, etc.),
- Shareholder information (including name, address, phone number, number of shares held, social security number, etc.),
- Vendor information (name, address, product pricing specific to the company, etc.),

TABLE 5.8 (continued)   Information Classification Policy: Example 3

■ Health insurance records (including medical, prescription, and psychological records),
■ Specific operating plans, marketing plans, or strategies,
■ Consolidated revenue, cost, profit, or other financial results that are not public record,
■ Descriptions of unique parts or materials, technology intent statements, or new technologies and research that are not public record,
■ Specific business strategies and directions,
■ Major changes in the company's management structure, and
■ Information that requires special skill or training to interpret and employ correctly, such as design or specification files.

If any of these items can be found freely and openly in public records, the company's obligation to protect from disclosure is waived.

Internal Use
Definition: Classify information as **Internal Use** when the information is intended for use by employees when conducting company business.

Examples: Some examples of **Internal Use** information are:

■ Operational business information/reports,
■ Noncompany information that is subject to a nondisclosure agreement with another company,
■ Company phone book,
■ Corporate policies, standards, and procedures, and
■ Internal company announcements.

Public
Definition: Classify information as **Public** if the information has been made available for public distribution through authorized company channels. **Public** information is not sensitive in context or content, and requires no special protection.

Examples: The following are examples of **Public** information:

■ Corporate Annual Report
■ Information specifically generated for public consumption, such as public service bulletins, marketing brochures, and advertisements)

Organizations are required by law to maintain certain types of records, usually for a specified period of time. The failure to retain such documents for these minimum time periods can subject an organization to penalties, fines, or other sanctions, or could put it at a serious disadvantage in

TABLE 5.9   Information Classification Policy: Example 4

Information Management

1. General
   A. Corporate information includes electronically generated, printed, filmed, typed, or stored.
   B. Information is a corporate asset and is the property of Corporation.
2. Information Retention
   A. Each organization shall retain information necessary to the conduct of business.
   B. Each organizational unit shall establish and administer a records management schedule in compliance with applicable laws and regulations, and professional standards and practices, and be compatible with Corporate goals and expectations.
3. Information Protection
   A. Information must be protected according to its sensitivity, criticality, and value, regardless of the media on which it is stored, the manual or automated systems that process it, or the methods by which it is distributed.
   B. Employees are responsible for protecting corporate information from unauthorized access, modification, destruction, or disclosure, whether accidental or intentional. To facilitate the protection of corporate information, employee responsibilities have been established at three levels: **Owner, Custodian,** and **User.**
      1) **Owner:** Company management of the organizational unit where the information is created, or management of the organizational unit that is the primary user of the information. **Owners** are responsible to:
         a) Identify the classification level of all corporate information within their organizational unit,
         b) Define appropriate safeguards to ensure the confidentiality, integrity, and availability of the information resource,
         c) Monitor safeguards to ensure they are properly implemented,
         d) Authorize access to those who have a business need for the information, and
         e) Remove access from those who no longer have a business need for the information.
      2) **Custodian:** Employees designated by the owner to be responsible for maintaining the safeguards established by the owner.
      3) **User:** Employees authorized by the owner to access information and use the safeguards established by the owner.

TABLE 5.9 (continued)   Information Classification Policy: Example 4

    C. Each Vice President shall appoint an Organization Information Protection Coordinator who will administer an information protection program that appropriately classifies and protects corporate information under the Vice President's control and makes employees aware of the importance of information and methods for its protection.

4. Information Classification: To ensure the proper protection of corporate information, the owner shall use a formal review process to classify information into one of the following classifications:

    A. **Public:** Information that has been made available for public distribution through authorized company channels. (Refer to Communication Policy for more information.)

    B. **Confidential:** Information that, if disclosed, could violate the privacy of individuals, reduce the company's competitive advantage, or could cause significant damage to the company.

    C. **Internal Use:** Information that is intended for use by all employees when conducting company business. Most information used in the company would be classified Internal Use.

litigation. Therefore, every organization should implement a Record Management Policy to provide standards for maintaining complete and accurate records to ensure that employees are aware of what records to keep and for how long, what records to dispose of, and how to dispose of them.

The cost of storage and administration problems involved in retaining material beyond its useful life are a few important reasons to establish a Records Management Policy. Consideration should also be given to the impact that a failure to produce subpoenaed records might have on the organization when defending itself against a lawsuit. Determining the proper retention periods for information records is a requirement in today's operating environment. Information records should be kept only as long as they serve a useful purpose or until legal requirements are met. At the end of the retention period, records should be destroyed in a verifiable manner. Implementing effective information classification and records management policies makes sound business sense and shows that management is practicing due diligence.

Before drafting a Records Management Policy, consult with your legal staff to ensure that the policy reflects any relevant statutes. The retention standards that support the policy should be reviewed annually when conducting an organizationwide information asset inventory.

5.12.1 Sample Records Management Policy

See Table 5.10 for a sample Records Management Policy.

5.13 Information Handling Standards Matrix

Later in the book we discuss standards and how they support the implementation of the policy. Because information classification and records management are unique in their standards requirements, it is appropriate to give examples now of what these standards might look like. When developing your standards, use these as a guideline — not a standard.

5.13.1 Printed Material

See Table 5.11 for an information handling matrix for printed material.

5.13.2 Electronically Stored Information

See Table 5.12 for an information handling matrix for electronically stored information.

5.13.3 Electronically Transmitted Information

See Table 5.13 for an information handling matrix for electronically transmitted information.

5.13.4 Record Management Retention Schedule

See Table 5.14 for a sample record retention schedule.

5.14 Information Classification Methodology

The final element in an effective information classification process is to provide management and employees with a method to evaluate information and provide them with an indication of where the information should be classified (see Table 5.15). To accomplish this, it may be necessary to create information classification worksheets. These worksheets can be used by the business units to determine what classifications of information they have within their organization.

TABLE 5.10   Sample Records Management Policy

Records Management Policy

Introduction

It is the policy of the Company to accommodate the timely storage, retrieval, and disposition of records created, utilized, and maintained by the various departments. The period of time that records are maintained is based on the minimum requirements set forth in State and Federal retention schedules.

1.   Role of Retention Center

The role of the Retention Center is to receive, maintain, destroy, and service inactive records that have not met their disposition date. Each business unit is to establish schedules to comply with the minimum amount of time records should be maintained in compliance with State and Federal guidelines. Retention requirements apply whether or not the records are transferred to the Retention Center. Copies of the schedules must be maintained by the business unit and available for inspection.

2.   Role of the Records Manager

The role of the Records Manager is to administer the Records Management program. The Records Manager is well acquainted with all records and record groups within an agency and has expertise in all aspects of records management. The duties of the Records Manager include planning, development, and administration of records management policies. These duties also include the annual organizationwide inventory of all information assets to be conducted by the business unit manager with reports sent to the Records Manager.

3.   Role of Management Personnel

Management Personnel are responsible for records under their control.

4.   Role of Departmental Records Coordinator

The Departmental Records Coordinator is to be a liaison between the department and the Retention Center. It is recommended that each department appoint a Records Coordinator in writing. The letter of appointment should include the Records Coordinator's full name, department, and telephone extension. The letter should be forwarded to the Retention Center and maintained on file.

5.   Type of Documents Maintained in Retention Center

    5.1   Record Retention accepts only public records that are referenced in the State Retention Schedule, except student transcripts. Copies of student transcripts may be obtained from Records and Admissions located at the Student Service Center.

    5.2   Record Retention does not accept personal, active, or nonrecords.

TABLE 5.10 (continued)   Sample Records Management Policy

5.3 Record Retention stores only inactive and permanent records until final disposition according to State and Federal retention schedules. Examples include personnel files, purchase orders, grade books, or surveys.

5.4 Record Retention receives and stores inactive permanent records from TVI departments until final disposition according to State and Federal retention guidelines.

5.5 Record Retention ensures records are classified according to State and Retention guidelines.

5.6 Record Retention ensures records are tracked and entered into an electronic records management software system that tracks record boxes, assigns retention schedules, and records permanent box numbers, destruction dates, and shelf locations.

6. **Services**

6.1 If a department has obsolete records that are deemed confidential or sensitive, or copies of nonrecords, a special request for shredding may be sent to the Record Retention Center. The records can be shredded by the Record Retention Center staff or transferred to the State Record Center for destruction.

6.2 Departments must complete a Request for Destruction form for confidential or nonrecords to be shredded. Departments are required to purchase forms from Central Stores at Shipping & Receiving.

6.3 The Record Retention Center provides consulting services to departments on filing systems and maintenance of records.

7. **Transferring Records**

7.1 Departments should transfer records to Record Retention for storage in January, July, and October.

7.2 Records with a retention period of two years or more should be transferred to Record Retention.

8. **Record Retrieval**

8.1 Records are retrieved and delivered to customers by request, given a 24-hour notice.

8.2 Records can be retrieved for customers on an emergency basis as requested.

8.3 Management personnel, the records coordinator, or the requester will sign for receipt of records. Records are to be checked out for no longer than 30 days. If a longer period is required, a written request should be sent to the Retention Center. If records are checked out for more than a year, the records will be permanently withdrawn from inventory.

TABLE 5.10 (continued)   Sample Records Management Policy

  8.4   Permanent Withdrawal: If a department wishes to withdraw a record permanently from storage, forward a request to Record Retention by phone, fax, or inter-office mail. The department will complete a Withdrawal Request form and the records will be deleted from inventory.

  8.5   Second-Party Withdrawal: If a department requests a record originating from another department, then the requesting department must contact the department of origin to obtain authorization. The department of origin will contact Record Retention for records withdrawal. The department requester must view the requested records at the Record Retention Center.

  8.6   Records should not be returned via inter-office mail due to the confidential nature of the documents.

9. **Record Destruction**

  9.1   Record Retention destroys records according to State guidelines in January, July, and October.

  9.2   Records are destroyed by Record Retention according to State and Federal guidelines when legal requirements are met. A Destruction Request form will be sent to the originating department for review and signature by the Departmental Records Coordinator and by management personnel. Only when the Destruction Request has been reviewed, signed, and returned to Record Retention will the expired records be destroyed. Authorized personnel will shred confidential records. If departments wish to keep the records past their assigned destruction date, management personnel can extend the date no longer than one year unless a litigation, audit, or investigation is pending. Records kept by the department past the retention date of destruction will be permanently withdrawn from inventory.

  9.3   All records scheduled for destruction are reviewed by the Institute's Records Manager and by State Records Analysts for approval.

10. **Supplies**

  10.1 Records must be stored in the appropriate record retention boxes, which are obtained from Central Stores at Shipping & Receiving.

  10.2 Storage Ticket forms and Request for Destruction forms are obtained from Central Stores at Shipping & Receiving.

To complete this worksheet, the employee would fill in the information requested at the top of the worksheet:

- *Organization:* the department designated as the information owner
- *Group:* the reporting group of the individual performing the information classification process

TABLE 5.11   Information Handling Matrix for Printed Material

	Printed Material Handling Standards		
	Confidential	Internal Use	Public
Labeling of documents	Document should identify owner and be marked "CONFIDEN-TIAL" on cover or title page	No special requirements	Document may be marked "PUBLIC" on cover or title page
Duplication of documents	Information owner to determine permissions	Duplication for business purposes only	No special requirements
Mailing of documents	No classification marking on external envelope; "CONFIDENTIAL" marking on cover sheet; confirmation of receipt at discretion of information owner	Mailing requirements determined by information owner	No special requirements
Disposal of documents	Owner observed physical destruction beyond ability to recover	Controlled physical destruction	No special requirements
Storage of documents	Locked up when not in use	Master copy secured against destruction	Master copy secured against destruction
Read access to documents	Owner establishes user access rules; generally highly restricted	Owner establishes user access rules, generally widely available	No special requirements; generally available within and outside company
Review of document classification level	Information owner to establish specific review date (not to exceed one year)	Information owner to review at least annually	No special requirements

- *Review Performed by/Phone:* the name and phone number of the individual performing the review
- *Date:* the date of the review
- *Information Name/Description:* an identifier or description of the information being reviewed

TABLE 5.12   Information Handling Matrix for Electronically Stored Information

	Electronically Stored Information Handling Matrix		
	Confidential	*Internal Use*	*Public*
Storage on fixed media (access controlled)	Unencrypted	Unencrypted	Unencrypted
Storage on fixed media (not access controlled)	Encrypted	Unencrypted	Unencrypted
Storage on removable media	Encrypted	Unencrypted	Unencrypted
Read access to information (includes duplication)	Information owner to authorize individual users	Information owner to define permissions on user, group, or function basis	No special requirements
Update access to information	Information owner to authorize individual users	Information owner to define permissions on user, group, or function basis	Information owners to define permissions
Delete access to information	Information owner to authorize individual users; user confirmation required	Information owner to define permissions on user, group, or function basis; user confirmation required	Information owner to define permissions
Print hard copy report of information	Output to be routed to a predefined, monitored printer	Information owner to define permissions	No special requirements
Internal labeling of information at the application or screen/display level	Notification of "CONFIDENTIAL" to appear at top of display	No special requirements	Notification of "PUBLIC" may optionally appear at top of display
External labeling of exchangeable media	Media must identify owner and be marked CONFIDENTIAL	Marking at discretion of owner	No special requirements

TABLE 5.12 (continued)   Information Handling Matrix for Electronically Stored Information

	Electronically Stored Information Handling Matrix		
	Confidential	*Internal Use*	*Public*
<u>Disposal</u> of electronic media (diskettes, tapes, hard disks, etc.)	Owner observed physical destruction beyond ability to recover	Physical destruction	No special requirements
<u>Disposal</u> of information	Delete by fully writing over information	Delete files through normal platform delete command, option, or facility	No special requirements
<u>Review</u> of classified information for reclassification	Information owner to establish specific review date (not to exceed one year)	Information owner to review annually	Information owner to review annually
<u>Logging</u> access activity	Log all access attempts; information owner to review all access and violation attempts	Log all violation attempts; information owner reviews as appropriate	No special requirements
<u>Access</u> report retention requirements	Information owner to determine retention of access logs (not to exceed one year)	Information owner to determine retention of violation logs (not to exceed six months)	No special requirements

In the section for Information Name/Description, it is necessary to enter the information type. For example:

- Employee Records:
    - Employee performance review records
    - Timecards
    - Employee discipline documents
    - Pay records
    - Medical records

TABLE 5.13 Information Handling Matrix for Electronically Transmitted Information

| | *Electronically Transmitted Information Handling Standards* | | |
	Confidential	*Internal Use*	*Public*
By FAX	Attended at receiving FAX	Information owner to define requirements	No special requirements
By WAN	Confirmation of receipt required; encryption optional	No special requirements; encryption optional	No special requirements
By LAN	Confirmation of receipt required; encryption optional	No special requirements; encryption optional	No special requirements
By inter-office mail	No external labeling on envelope; normal labeling on document	No special requirements	No special requirements
By voice-mail	Confirmation of receipt required (sender); remove message after receipt (recipient)	No special requirements	No special requirements
By electronic messaging (e-mail)	Confirmation of receipt required; encryption optional	No special requirements	No special requirements
By wireless or cellular phone	Do not transmit	No special requirements	No special requirements

- Group Administrative Records:
  - Monthly status reports
  - Yearly status reports
  - Yearly business objectives
- Business Process Records
  - Purchasing contracts
  - Quarterly financial reports
  - Project management tasks, schedules
  - Reference manuals
  - Contract negotiations

TABLE 5.14 Sample Record Retention Schedule

Record	Retain	Record	Retain
Records Management (Retention) Schedule			
Accounts payable schedules	Permanent	General ledgers	Permanent
Accounts receivables schedules	Permanent	Insurance policies	Until expiration
Bank drafts and paid notices	10 Years	Internal repair orders (hardcopy only)	7 Years
Bank statements and reconciliations	10 Years	Internal sales journals	Permanent
Bills of lading	7 Years	Journal vouchers	Permanent
Cancelled checks	10 Years	Miscellaneous schedules	Permanent
Cash disbursements journals	Permanent	New and used vehicle records	7 Years
Cash receipts journals	Permanent	New vehicle sales journals	Permanent
Claims register	7 Years	Office receipts	7 Years
Corporate minutes book	Permanent	Parts, accessories, and service sales journals	Permanent
Correspondence	10 Years	Payroll journals	Permanent
Counter tickets	7 Years	Prepaid and accrued expense schedule	2 Years
CPA audit reports	Permanent	Property tax returns	Permanent
Credit memos	7 Years	Purchase journals	Permanent
Customer files	7 Years	Purchase orders	7 Years
Customer repair orders (both office and hard copy)	7 Years	Receiving reports	7 Years
Documents pertaining to litigation	Permanent	Repair order check sheet	2 Years
Duplicate deposit slips	10 Years	Repair orders — internal (office copy only)	2 Years
Employee earning and history record	Permanent	Sales invoices	7 Years
Employment contracts	Permanent	Salesperson's commission reports	Permanent
Federal revenue agents' reports and related papers	Permanent	Social security tax returns	Permanent
Federal tax returns	Permanent	State and local sales tax returns	Permanent
Financial statements	Permanent	State annual reports	Permanent

TABLE 5.14 (continued) Sample Record Retention Schedule

Records Management (Retention) Schedule			
Record	Retain	Record	Retain
General journals	Permanent	State franchise tax returns	Permanent
		Sundry invoices	7 Years
		Timecards	2 Years
		Federal and state unemployment tax returns	Permanent
		Used and repossessed vehicles journals	Permanent
		Vehicle invoices	7 Years

- Operations Information:
  - Business partner information
  - Asset allocation
  - Trading activities
  - Production formulas
  - Production cost information
  - Customer lists
- Distribution Records:
  - Distribution models
  - Inventory records
  - Parts supplies

Using the definitions, the person(s) performing the review would place a checkmark in the appropriate column; only one checkmark for each item being reviewed. This process would allow the user department to identify all the various types of information found in the department and then be able to determine under which classification they probably fall.

5.15 Authorization for Access

To establish a clear line of authority, some key concepts must be established. As discussed above, there are typically three categories of employee responsibilities. Depending on the specific information being accessed, an individual may fall into more than one category. For example, an employee with a desktop workstation becomes the owner, custodian, and user. To better help understand the concepts, the responsibilities of each category are listed below.

TABLE 5.15   Information Classification Worksheet

Information Classification Review Worksheet

Organization: _____   Group: _____

Review Performed by/Phone: _____   Date: _____

Information Name/Description	Storage Medium	Classifications (Select One)			
		CONFIDENTIAL	RESTRICTED	INTERNAL USE	PUBLIC
		If disclosed, could violate the privacy of individuals, reduce the company's competitive advantage, or cause damage to the company.	Intended for use by a subset of employees when conducting company business (usually regulatory requirement)	Intended for use by all employees when conducting company business.	Made available for public distribution through authorized company channels.

Employee Records

1
2
3
4
5
6

Group Administrative Records

1
2

Business Process Records

5.15.1 Owner

Minimally, the information owner is responsible for:

- Judging the value of the information resource and assigning the proper classification level
- Periodically reviewing the classification level to determine if the status should be changed
- Assessing and defining appropriate controls to ensure that information created is properly safeguarded from unauthorized access, modification, disclosure, or destruction
- Communicating access and safeguard requirements to the information custodian and users
- Providing access to those individuals with a demonstrated business need for access
- Assessing the risk of loss of the information and ensuring that adequate safeguards are in place to mitigate the risk to information integrity, confidentiality, and availability
- Monitoring safeguard requirements to ensure that information is being adequately protected
- Ensuring that a business continuity plan has been implemented and tested to protect information availability

5.15.2 Custodian

At a minimum, the custodian is responsible for:

- Providing proper safeguards for processing equipment, information storage, backup, and recovery
- Providing a secure processing environment that can adequately protect the integrity, confidentiality, and availability of information
- Administering access requests to information properly authorized by the owner

5.15.3 User

The user is responsible for:

- Using the information only for the purpose intended
- Maintaining the integrity, confidentiality, and availability of information accessed

Being granted access to information does not imply or confer authority to grant other users access to that information. This is true whether the information is electronically held, printed, hardcopy, manually prepared, copied, or transmitted.

5.16 Summary

Information classification drives the protection control requirements and this allows information to be protected to a level commensurate to its value to the organization. The cost of over-protection is eliminated and exceptions are minimized. With a policy and methodology, specifications are clear and accountability is established.

There are costs associated with implementing a classification system. The most identifiable costs include labeling classified information, implementing and monitoring controls and safeguards, and proper handling of confidential information.

Information, wherever it is handled or stored, needs to be protected from unauthorized access, modification, disclosure, and destruction. All information is not created equal. Consequently, segmentation or classification of information into categories is necessary to help identify a framework for evaluating the information's relative value. By establishing this relative value, it will be possible to establish cost effective controls that will preserve the information asset for the organization.

The information classification program will require the identification of the record type, the owner, and the classification level. Two thirds of this information may already be gathered by the records management program. Link these two vital processes together to ensure that employee time is not wasted on redundant activities. By combining the effort, the organization will have a better overall information security program.

Chapter 6

Access Control

What is access control? Access control is the technical mechanism that restricts unauthorized users from the system, grants access to authorized users, and limits what authorized users can do on the system. As such, access controls in addition to security policy are the key components of information security. There are several ways in which an organization can implement access control. There are two popular models to follow when it comes to access control: mandatory and discretionary.

6.1   Business Requirements for Access Control

6.1.1   Access Control Policy

In mandatory access control, the permission granted on the system is defined by policy. This is often used in highly secure and government installations. This policy requires a process known as labeling, where each user, file, and system is grouped in security categories. Most private-sector businesses stay away from mandatory access control because of the increased overhead in labeling all users and systems. With mandatory access control, each user is given a label or security clearance, which then governs the amount of access the person will have on the system.

Another popular access control system is discretionary access control. With discretionary access, permissions are not granted by policy but rather granted by the data or system owner. The reduced overhead of discretionary access control makes it more applicable to most private-sector companies. With discretionary access control there is also the possibility that a user will have the ability to grant permissions as well. Think of this as similar to the administrator permission inside Microsoft® operating systems.

Regardless of which access control system is followed — mandatory or discretionary — the organization should always follow another access control principle. This principle is known as least privilege. Least privilege is the absolute minimum amount of permissions necessary for the user to perform his or her job function; it is the amount of access that should be given to the system. This ensures that users will not have additional permissions beyond what is necessary, and allows for a reduced impact on the integrity of system data if a user begins performing malicious acts or accidental errors and omissions.

6.2 User Access Management

6.2.1 Account Authorization

Account authorization is also known as user registration. Whatever you call this process, the function of it will remain the same. This process allows for authorized users to establish initial access to the system and, moreover, what access on the system they will have. Unfortunately, more often than not, organizations tend to use an ad hoc approach to user registration. It is recommended to have defined policies and procedures that govern new account creation and access permissions. This process takes place in most types of access control technologies but has an increased role in access control that uses digital certificates. This is due to the fact that the digital certificate must be generated and distributed to the end user; the process can be somewhat automated using a technology known as a registration authority.

6.2.2 Access Privilege Management

After a user has been with a company for a long period of time, access permissions may no longer align with current job responsibilities. The information security manager should have a procedure in place to review access permissions on a regular basis and make sure that the permissions are appropriate based on the job function of the user. Moreover, the information security manager should also review accounts on the system to make sure that all user accounts have a corresponding user. It is common for users who have left the company to still have valid user accounts on the system. As previously mentioned, there should be a procedure in place when an employee is terminated so that the access is revoked quickly.

6.2.3 Account Authentication Management

In addition to managing the ongoing user permissions and revoking no longer needed accounts, the information security manager should also have a password management scheme in place. Passwords should be changed on a regular basis; the current industry standard is around 30 days. However, the time to change passwords should reflect the security necessary to protect the information on the system. It is not uncommon for an organization to change passwords every 90 days, or longer. In addition to having users change their passwords regularly, passwords should be well selected. A well-selected password will be at least eight characters in length, not based on a dictionary word, and contain at least one unique character. The reason for these criteria is to make it more difficult for an attacker to use a password cracking utility quickly. There are two primary types of password cracking utilities: dictionary and brute force. A dictionary password cracking utility is freely available on the Internet and will a have word list of around 60,000 common words. An attacker will typically begin a password attack using the dictionary cracking tool. This tool, while not guaranteed to succeed in the attack, is much faster than the brute-force password cracking tool. A brute-force password cracking tool, also freely available from the Internet, will try every possible combination of characters until it is successful. In recent tests, we have seen that cracking an 11-character password with a brute-force password cracking tool over a wide area network can take in excess of a month. This means that if you have a good password change policy, you will change the password before the brute-force password cracking utility has adequate time to break the password.

With the common end user having, on average, an eight-character password to remember for information technology resources, it can be difficult for him or her to remember all of the passwords that are sufficiently long and unique while also having the passwords change every 30 days. There is a technology available to help the information security manager and the end user with password management. This technology is single sign-on. The advantage to single sign-on is that each user has only one password to remember for access to all network resources. This allows the administrator to make the password both more complex and changed more frequently without a large increase in the number of calls to the help desk from those who have forgotten to reset their passwords. Single sign-on technology has been beaten about the past few years, and is often still thought of as a mythical technology. In actuality, single sign-on may not be possible but reduced sign-on is a very real possibility.

There are two primary approaches to single sign-on: script-based single sign-on and host-based single sign-on. With script-based single sign-on, the user logs in to the primary network operating system and when this happens, the operating system runs a log-in program, often called a log-in script, that will authenticate the user to other systems on the network. The disadvantage to using this type of single sign-on is that the password stored in the log-in script is often stored in plaintext, which means that no encryption is used to protect the password in the file. Any entity that reads this file will be able to recover the username and password for that user. Also, these username and password combinations are often transmitted on the network in plaintext. This allows any malicious user with a network sniffer to capture the username and password. A network sniffer (see Figure 6.1) is a utility available for free on the Internet that is used to read all the network packets on a network segment. This utility can be used for troubleshooting, but can also be used maliciously to record log-in attempts.

The second type of single sign-on implementation is much more commonly used than the script-based method mentioned previously. This second type is known as host-based single sign-on because it uses a

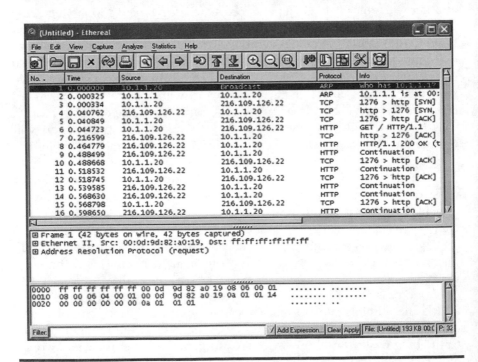

FIGURE 6.1   Network Sniffer

centralized authentication server or host. This implementation requires the user to log into the authentication server and, when the user tries to access other network resources, those applications contact the authentication server to verify the user's access. There are a large number of protocols that can be used for this type of single sign-on. Some of the more common include Kerberos and RADIUS. There are a large number of secondary authentication protocols that are not used as often; these include protocols such as SESAME and RADIUS' successor, DIAMETER. Many of these authentication protocols can be configured to send the username and password encrypted, and this can stop malicious users from intercepting the username and password with a network sniffer.

6.3   System and Network Access Control

6.3.1   Network Access and Security Components

Protecting networking resources is one of the areas of information security that currently receives the most focus. When thinking of security, senior management often envisions firewalls, intrusion detection systems, and other technological solutions, but often overlooks the importance of integrating these with the existing user community. In this section we focus on the technical components of network security and how the technologies can be utilized to improve network security.

Many network devices are left in default or very similar to default configurations. While leaving these devices in this state is often easier, it can be a severe detriment to security. Most devices in this configuration are running many unnecessary services; and while the user community does not use these services, malicious users on the network can exploit the vulnerabilities in these services. To minimize the amount of security holes in the network, the information security manager must disable or remove all the unnecessary services on the devices. This can quickly become a double-edged sword because determining which services are unnecessary can disable functionality of the system. If you ever have a few spare minutes, look in the control panel on your Microsoft Windows system and see how many services are running on that system, but do not disable any service unless you know what the service does. It is very easy to make a nonfunctional system this way.

Normally, a user with the appropriate access control is able to use any PC or workstation on the local area network to run an application or access certain data. However, where such data or system is classified as sensitive or requires restricted physical access, an enforced path may be applied. This is a straightforward configuration setting, performed by the information security manager, whereby access is restricted to a specific workstation or range of workstations. Enforcing the path will provide added security because it reduces the risk of unauthorized access, especially where such a workstation is itself within a secure zone, requiring physical access codes or other physical security mechanisms.

The typical network uses user authentication, wherein a user provides a username for identification and a password for authentication. In some networks the authentication requires not just user authentication but node authentication as well. There are many different ways to get node authentication; it can be from a digital certificate issued to the machine, based on the system's IP address, or from the systems hardware address itself. Using any of these authentication components with the user authentication component is not a good idea. With the exception of the digital certificate, it is very easy to change an IP address or hardware address to "spoof" an address of an authorized machine (see Figure 6.2). Spoofing the user on the rogue machine changes the system or IP address of the system to be that of another system that is trusted or permitted on network. The task of using hardware address node authentication was offered as a security solution to the problems with wireless networks. This authentication was easily bypassed with spoofing, leading to the same security problems that existed previously.

Another key component of network security is to have network monitoring in place. One of the easiest ways to have the security of monitoring the network is to implement remote port protection. This would allow an information security manager to see if a new port becomes active on a switch or hub. "Port" is the term for one of the hardware interfaces on a hub or switch. Most hubs or switches are classified by the number of ports on them. You will often hear of 24 port switches, which means that there are 24 slots for network cables to be connected to the switch. In most environments, there are ports that are not used and left open. If an attacker is able to get physical access to the switch, he can plug a new network device into the open port in the switch. Because this might lead to a security breach, the information security manager should be notified if one of these switch ports that is left open suddenly becomes active. This is where having remote port detection can provide security.

Yet another way to keep your network secure is to minimize the number of devices on a network that interact. To do this, the information security manager may choose to have network segregation. There are many mechanisms for getting segregation in the network. These include using physical distance, virtual local area networks, network address translation, and routing. To use physical distance, the information security manager does not allow the groups of network devices to be connected to the same hubs or switches as the other networks. This seems rather crude, but it can be quite effective. Imagine that, on a multi-floor building,

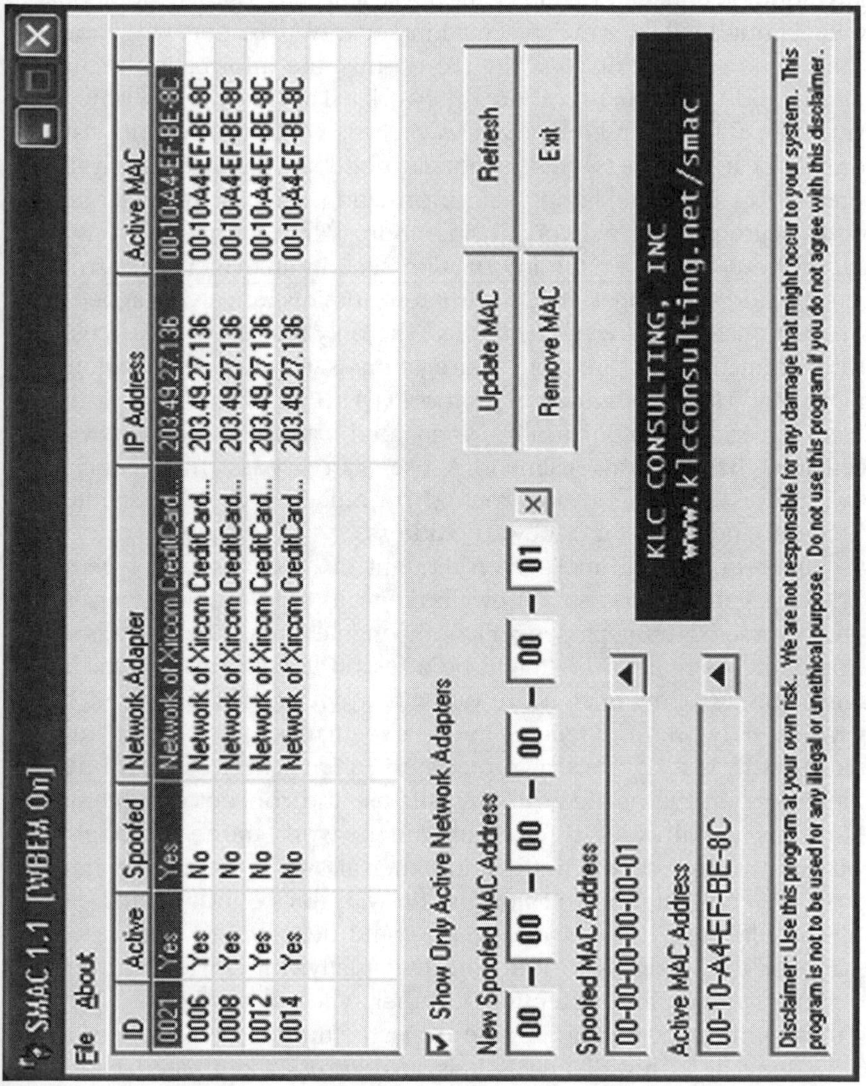

FIGURE 6.2 Spoofing Hardware

the Research & Development department occupies the fourth floor and no other user community needs to access this department. To stop other users from accessing this department, the information security manager can simply choose to not have the Research & Development department share the hub or switch with the other networks. While this method requires additional hardware, it is the easiest to manage. If additional hardware is not available, the information security manager may choose to do the same segregation logically. To do this, the information security manager would use virtual local area networks. This allows one physical switch to be split into multiple logical switches. While the security using the virtual local area networks is not as good as the actual physical network, it can be quite good. The information security manager may choose to segregate the networks using address translation and routing. In both of these examples, the information security manager will use the different IP address ranges that have been administratively assigned to block communication between networks. The only real drawback to using this type of method for network segregation is if your organization is using Dynamic Host Configuration Protocol (DHCP). If your network uses DHCP, a server will automatically assign an IP address for all devices plugged into that network segment. A user can bypass the security of network address translation and routing by plugging the device into a new location and receiving a new IP address.

Of course, one of the most often thought of mechanisms for getting network segregation is to use a firewall. Firewalls were originally an iron wall that protected train passengers from engine fires. These walls did not protect the engineer. This might be a lesson for information security managers. In early networks, a firewall was a device that protected one segment of a network from failures in other segments. However, the more modern firewall is a device that protects an internal network from malicious intruders on the outside. All firewalls use the concept of screening, which means the firewall receives all the network traffic for a given network, and it inspects the traffic and either allows or denies the traffic based on the configuration rules on the firewall device itself. Many early firewalls would have a set of rules that would deny traffic that was not necessary for the business to function. Eventually, this migrated from a list of traffic to deny and accepting all other types of traffic, to a list of traffic to accept and denying all other types of traffic. This is often said to be a "deny all" firewall unless it is an expressly permitted type of firewall. These types of firewalls are currently the most common. There are three primary types of technology currently in use: the packet filter, the stateful inspection, and the proxy-based firewalls.

The packet filter firewall was the first firewall released and is often considered the simplest firewall. It works off a list of static rules and makes the determination based on the source IP address, destination IP address, source port, and destination port. With a packet filter firewall, one of the common rules necessary to permit the network to have Web-based Internet access is a rule that allows all high ports (those above 1024) from all Internet sources into the organization. This allows any hosts on the Internet to send packets into the network over a high port and the firewall will permit it. This creates a rather large security hole in the organization.

The two second-generation firewalls — the stateful inspection and proxy — do not have this security hole. The stateful inspection firewall functions similar to the packet filter firewall but has a small database that allows for the dynamic creation of rules that allow for response traffic to enter back into the firewall. This provides end users with the ability to visit Web pages without creating the rule necessary for the response traffic to be allowed in. The stateful inspection firewall will dynamically allow the response traffic in if the traffic was permitted outbound.

The proxy-based firewall has nothing in common with the packet filter firewall. The proxy-based firewall actually functions by maintaining two separate conversations. One conversation occurs between the client and the proxy firewall, and the other conversation occurs between the destination server and the proxy firewall. The proxy firewall uses more of the IP packet to make the determination of whether or not to permit the traffic. This often causes some performance degradation, but can give increased security.

The information security manager often has to decide between easier administration and increased security. This is the case when it comes to control of the network routing. There are a number of routing protocols (such as RIP, OSPF, and BGP) that can be used. Anytime one of these routing protocols is used, it can make administration easier, but there is the security risk of having an intruder send false information over the router update protocol and corrupting the router's information table.

6.3.2   System Standards

There is difficulty in supporting multiple systems for the information security manager and the support staff. To minimize the differences between systems, it might be in the best interests of your organization to create a standard. This standard would then be a recommended guideline for how the systems should be configured and what software packages should be installed on the systems. This will also help minimize the amount of non-standard applications that will be installed but can have a dangerous security impact on the network.

6.3.3 Remote Access

Remote access is a favorite target of hackers because they are trying to gain remote access to your organization's network. As such, additional security controls must be deployed to protect remote access and remote access services. Some of the more commonly deployed technologies include virtual private networking (VPN) and two-factor authentication. Virtual private networking takes advantage of encryption technologies to help minimize the exposure of allowing outside users to have access to the network.

Two-factor authentication is another technology that can help protect remote access. It uses multiple types of authentication technologies to provide for stronger authentication. Authentication can often be broken down into three categories: something the user has, something the user knows, and something the user is. The most commonly used authentication comes from the "something the user knows" category. This would include things such as:

- Passwords
- PINs
- Passphrases

From the "something the user has" category, we would be looking at authentication components such as:

- Smart cards
- Magnetic cards
- Hardware tokens
- Software tokens

And from the "something the user is" category, we would be looking at biometrics and other behavior-based authentication systems. Biometric devices use unique characteristics of each person, including:

- Fingerprints
- Retina patterns
- Hand geometry
- Palm prints

Two-factor authentication takes an authentication component from two of the groups mentioned above. This requires more than just a username and password to get access. Because remote access connections to the network originate from outside the network, it is a prime location for stronger authentication controls.

6.4 Operating System Access Controls

6.4.1 *Operating Systems Standards*

As discussed previously, standards can minimize the amount of customization of employee workstations and this can minimize the difficulty in performing system and network maintenance. This can be extended further through the use of operating system standards. These standards are provided by a number of sources, including the manufacturer, third-party security organizations, and the government. One of the most common sources of operating system standards is the National Institute of Standards and Technology (NIST). NIST provides standard profiles for varying levels of system security configurations for most common operating systems. In some cases, there are utilities to audit the system against the standard configuration and point out where the system configuration is lacking in meeting the required security profile. These standards cover the complete range of operating system security, from the typical workstation to the highly secure server. These standards allow the information security manager to have a more detailed account of the modifications necessary to appropriately configure system security. The NIST standards are available from http://csrc.nist.gov.

6.4.2 *Change Control Management*

One of the most unglamorous areas of information security is the change control process. In many small organizations, change control is omitted altogether and administration changes are made through an ad hoc process. While not having a change control process reduces administrative overhead, the resulting drawbacks are pretty severe. I know that there were a number of organizations where I was the primary security administrator and spent the first few weeks of the job just running through the existing configurations trying to figure out what the previous administrator had done. This process can be as simple or as complex as your organization requires. In one organization, we implemented a simple change control process wherein a simple paper form was filled out, the changed was discussed at the next staff meeting, and the form was then stored in a folder next to the server on which the change was made. With a small number of servers and a tiny support staff, this process was adequate. With very large companies where the number of information technology support personnel can number in the hundreds or thousands, a process needs to be much more scalable and detailed. A more advanced change control process follows.

- *Step 1: Request of change is formally made.* This requires that the proposed change is documented in written form.
- *Step 2: Analyze request.* After the written request is made, a formal risk assessment may be necessary to determine if the change will have a severe impact on network security.
- *Step 3: Develop the implementation strategy.* During this step, the actual way the change will be made is discussed, responsibilities are defined, and the implementation schedule is devised.
- *Step 4: Calculate the costs of this implementation.* This step will allow for the appropriate budget to be put together to implement the change. A cost analysis may be done to see if the change makes fiscal sense for the organization.
- *Step 5: Review any security implications.* This step determines how the level of risk for the organization will change once the change is made. Often, the change will be made in a development (non-production) environment before the actual change is made to production systems. Having the change made in the development network allows for security testing to be done prior to any changes that would affect the production network.
- *Step 6: Record change request.* In this step, all of the documentation from the previous step is compiled.
- *Step 7: Submit change request for approval.* At this point, all of the documentation is put together and submitted to the information security steering committee for approval.
- *Step 8: Develop change.* If the change requires that code be written or new software be acquired, the basis for the plan is done here.
- *Step 9: Recode segments of the system.* In this step, if the change requires that software be written, then the software is written. This would also be where a new system is developed in the development network and tested.
- *Step 10:* Link these changes to the formal change control request.
- *Step 11:* Submit software for testing and quality approval. Here, the quality control or quality assurance group would review the change for adequacy.
- *Step 12:* Repeat until quality is adequate.
- *Step 13: Implementation.* The code, system, or configuration change is move into production at this point. If your organization has a formal promotion to production sequence, it should be followed.
- *Step 14: Update the version information.* At this point, all the changes have been implemented, so the next phase is to update the documentation and the user training materials, and to inform the user community of the change.
- *Step 15: Report changes to management.* In this step, tell management that the change has been made and is working properly.

The process listed above includes many steps that are not needed for all organizations. Each organization is unique and the change control process should be modified to fit the organization. The most important steps are there to ensure that all changes are submitted, approved, tested, and recorded. This ensures that no changes are made without the change control process.

6.5 Monitoring System Access

6.5.1 Event Logging

Most current systems allow for enabling audit logs, and more and more systems are enabling logging by default. As an information security manager, you need to verify that event logging is enabled and is adequate for the relative security level of the system. In addition to enabling the logging, the log files must be reviewed regularly to detect possible security breaches. With all of the logs coming from all of the different sources, log correlation has become a hot issue during the past few years. If your organization has numerous intrusion detection systems, firewalls, and critical servers, it might be more useful to move to a central log recording system. These systems can also manage one of the more difficult components of log analysis: time synchronization. Many system clocks lose or gain time as the system stays in an operating production environment. A central log reporting system can also function as a network time server to help all system clocks stay synchronized.

6.5.2 Monitoring Standards

In organizations that wish to use information security monitoring, it is a good practice to include a warning banner on the systems before a user is authenticated. These warning banners should have three components:

1. This system is for authorized users only.
2. All activities on this system are monitored
3. By completing the log-on process, you are agreeing to the monitoring.

The warning banner should not include the name of the organization to which the system belongs; that information would be useful for social engineering and other attacks. Also, the warning banner should never include the "welcome" greeting. The best way to avoid legal issues with warning banners is to keep them simple; include only what needs to be included and nothing else.

6.5.3   Intrusion Detection Systems

As previously discussed with single sign-on implementations, some technology has been the target of a bit of bad publicity lately. Intrusion detection systems also fall into this category. Intrusion detection systems (IDS) are designed to function like a burglar alarm on your house — from a technical standpoint, of course. These systems should record suspicious activity against the target system or network, and should alert the information security manager or support staff when an electronic break-in is underway. The biggest downfall with IDS products is the necessary level of customization "of the box." Without significant amounts of customization, the IDS will produce a large number of false-positive alerts. A false positive is created when the IDS alerts the support staff to an event that will not have an impact on the target system. For example, a Code Red attack against and Apache® Web server will not work, but the IDS may still sound the alarm.

Underneath the hood, IDS products function either as a host-based intrusion detection system (HIDS) or a network-based intrusion detection system (NIDS). There are positives and negatives with each type. With an HIDS product, the product protects the system by monitoring a single system. There are a number of different ways that an HIDS can monitor the system. One of the more common ways is for the HIDS product to monitor all network traffic entering or leaving the host. The HIDS product can also function by monitoring the log files on the system itself. The disadvantage of using an HIDS product is that the product, by its very nature, cannot detect common network preamble attacks such as a ping sweep.

A network-based intrusion detection system (NIDS) works by monitoring a network segment to determine if the network traffic matches the pattern of a well-known network attack. This type of system can detect preamble attacks such as a ping sweep, but can be fooled by high network congestion and encryption. Also, the NIDS can have a lag time for new network attacks being written to the intrusion detection system profile. A new network attack may bypass the NIDS device until the attack pattern can be written and the NIDS updated.

In recent years, the IDS have been moving toward a next generation of security technology known as the intrusion prevention system (IPS) (see Figure 6.3). The IPS functions as a traditional IDS system with increased functionality. The IPS also takes on the functionality of a firewall, an antivirus system, and a vulnerability scanner. These components help reduce the number of false positives with the vulnerability scanner functionality. The package can test for the vulnerability before sounding the alarm. In addition to minimizing the number of false positives, the functionality of the other components allows for increased protection.

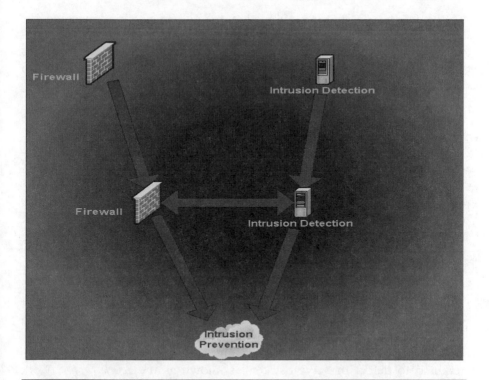

FIGURE 6.3   IDS to IPS Migration

6.6 Cryptography

6.6.1 Definitions

The final powerful weapon we look at in this chapter to assist the information security manager is cryptography. Cryptography is a branch of mathematics that transforms data to keep messages secret. The secrecy in cryptography has its basis in military operations. Cryptography was used to send messages from the central command to the troops on the battlefield without the enemy being able to understand a message if they intercepted it. In the information security battle space of which we are a part, cryptography for us is the denial of access to our messages of unauthorized viewers. In addition to keeping our messages secret, we also want to verify that our messages are coming from our central command. To do this, we use the concept of authenticity. In most information security environments, we can use a username and password combination to verify the authenticity of the sender. However, in sending a message between parties, it can be rather difficult to effectively use the username and password combination to authenticate the message. In addition to verifying that a message actually came from the appropriate person and that only the intended recipient viewed the message, we also want to ensure that the message was not modified along the way. To do this, we use yet another component of cryptography— that of integrity. When we put all these components together, we get *nonrepudiation*. The message will be guaranteed to have come from the sender, gone only to the recipient, and was not modified along the way.

What is cryptography to the information security manager? Cryptography is the implementation of the science of secret writing. This is often called "applied cryptography" by academic sorts. In information security, the cryptosystem is what provides the secrecy of the message. The secrecy our cryptosystem gives us is not absolute secrecy; it does not keep a message secret forever. Rather, the cryptosystem's goal is to keep the message secret for such a period of time that if the cryptosystem were defeated it would take longer than the time the message must be kept secret. The goal of the cryptosystem is twofold: first is the time component just discussed and the second is the cost to defeat the cryptosystem. If it costs our competitor more money to defeat our cryptosystem than the costs of the message if it is read by our competitor, then the cryptosystem has accomplished its goal. The amount of time, effort, and resources required to defeat the cryptosystem is known as the *work factor*. Work factor does not just refer to the amount of CPU time necessary to defeat the cryptosystem, but also the time necessary to develop the system that will go about defeating the cryptosystem.

If a competitor is trying to break into our encrypted message by defeating our cryptosystem, then our competitor is using cryptanalysis. "Cryptanalysis" is the term for trying to defeat the cryptosystem without the appropriate key. What we would be doing with the cryptosystem if we tested our cryptosystem for relative strength is called cryptology.

Our cryptosystem transforms data from one form to another. The form that is able to be read by anyone is called plaintext or cleartext. Once the data has been processed through the cryptosystem, it becomes readable by only the intended recipient. This type of scrambled data is called ciphertext. As we discuss later, there are two primary mechanisms by which the data can be transformed. If it is transformed one character at a time, it is called a stream cipher. If several characters from our message are processed by the cryptosystem at once, the cryptosystem is called a block cipher. We further discuss stream and block ciphers in the following sections. As the cryptosystem transforms our plaintext into ciphertext, it is called enciphering. The reverse process of transforming ciphertext into plaintext is called deciphering. If you have ever tried to read a phone message written by someone with messy handwriting, you have tried to decipher a message.

In 1883, a mathematician named Auguste Kerckhoff published a paper in which he stated that the only secret component of a cryptosystem should be the key. The component of the cryptosystem that actually transforms the data is the algorithm. The algorithm is pretty easy to distinguish from the rest of the cryptosystem; it is the part with all the math involved. Kerckhoff stated that all encryption algorithms should be publicly known because this is the only way that an algorithm can be reviewed for security holes. He also stated that any algorithm that was not publicly known would have more security holes than a publicly known algorithm. This axiom is still true today, most cryptosystems use algorithms that are publicly known. As previously discussed, Kerckhoff stated that the only secret component should be the key. A key is the secret sequence that governs the encipherment and decipherment of the message. It is easiest to think of the key as the password to your cryptosystem. If you do not know the password or key, you cannot read the secret message.

Due to the fact that the encryption key should always be kept secret, it can present a problem distributing keys to a user community. Many users lose their encryption keys, and the data often must still be recovered. One of the many components that allows for this data to be recovered is key clustering. With key clustering, another key can be used to encrypt and decrypt the data. Another term that works along with key clustering is "key escrow." Key escrow occurs when a key, often used in emergency purposes, is distributed to different individuals. This allows for the recovery of data only when two people are working together. This stops an administrator from using his key for malicious purposes.

The cryptosystem that you use to protect confidential messages in your organization can use many different types of encryption systems. Encryption systems are how the cryptosystem and its algorithm can go about transforming the data. There are many different types of encryption systems and most algorithms can combine multiple types.

The first type of encryption system that we will look at is the classical substitution cipher. If you have ever pulled a secret decoder ring out of a cereal box, then you have possessed a classical substitution cipher. A classical substitution cipher will replace one letter from the plaintext message with another character to make the message encrypted. One of the first cryptosystems used an algorithm known as the Caesar cipher. The Caesar cipher substituted characters by shifting the alphabet three spaces off a certain letter. For example, if we pick the letter "A," the cipher would move it forward three characters to the letter "D." We could then substitute all the letters "A" in our original message with the letter "D."

Here is an example our original message:

This is a plaintext message

Once we have processed the messages through the Caesar cipher using "C" as our key, the encrypted message becomes:

Wklv lv d sodlqwhaw phvvdjh

As opposed to classical substitution ciphers, an algorithm could use a transposition or permutation cipher. This cipher does not change one letter for another; rather, it changes the sequence of the letters in the message. A simple way to perform this operation is to write all the letters of a word in reverse order.

Here is an example of the original message:

This is a plaintext message

Once we have processed the message through our transposition cipher, we would end up with a message like this:

sihT si a txetnialp egassem

There are many other encryption systems available. Another type of cipher is the poly-alphabetic cipher. The Caesar cipher that previously discussed is also an example of a poly-alphabetic cipher in that the message was switched from one alphabet (the one starting with the letter "A") to a new alphabet (the one starting with the letter "D"). Another cipher is the running key cipher. With a running key cipher, all communications come from a preagreed-upon set of characters. For example, I give you the encrypted message 1234. It probably would not seem like a very well-encrypted message. But what if we had previously agreed that "1" would mean "building one," "2" would mean "floor two," "3" would mean "room three," and "4" would mean "room four"? And on the whiteboard of room four there was a message written; then we would have a secret message. Concealment is another type of encryption system. If you skip every third word in a message, there may be a secret message hidden in it.

Steganography is not exactly a form of cryptography; it is actually hiding in plain sight. The advantage of steganography is that no one can tell that a secret message is being sent. With cryptography, anytime a message is sent, someone could look at the message with a packet sniffer and determine that the message was encrypted. With steganography, the same person with a packet sniffer would only see a photo or a music file go by. Steganography hides hidden messages in pictures or music files. This technology is currently being used in more organizations, and the fear is that terrorist organizations are using similar technology. There was an Internet rumor spreading around rapidly in 2002 that terrorists were posting hidden messages in steganographed picture files on Internet auction sites. After some research, the rumor was found to be false.

Do you remember your days of using pig Latin to speak in messages in front of your parents? Pig Latin was an example of a code. A code is just a generic term for agreeing on a system to hide messages.

There are also encryption machines. A machine that was most popular was called the enigma machine. It had numerous rotors and switches that were attached to a typewriter keyboard. When the wheels and switches were turned by the Nazis in World War II, the machine would change the keys pressed on the typewriter keyboard into another character on the paper.

6.6.2 Public Key and Private Key

The two primary types of algorithms are private key and public key algorithms. Private key algorithms are easier to set up for a small number of users. All of the secrecy from private key algorithms comes from keeping the key secure. The key, if exposed, will allow any person who has the key to decrypt the message. Private key cryptography is also known as symmetric cryptography because whatever process is done to encrypt the message, the reverse process is done to decrypt the message.

In public key cryptography, there are two keys that are related. The two keys in public key cryptography are known as the private key and the public key. These keys are related so that anything encrypted with the public key can be decrypted with the private key, and anything encrypted with the private key can be decrypted with the public key. The security in public key cryptography is in keeping the private key secure. The public key is called the public key because anyone can have access to it. Public key cryptography is also known as asymmetric cryptography because the process done to encrypt the message is not done in reverse to decrypt the message. The private key in public key cryptography acts as a trap door that decrypts a message encrypted with the public key.

There can be many components to implement public key cryptography. The technical structures necessary to implement public key cryptography are collectively known as public key infrastructure (PKI). With PKI, public keys are published as certificates on a certificate authority. PKI may have all of the following components:

- Certification Authority (CA)
- Registration Authority (RA)
- Certificate Repository
- Certificate Revocation List

6.6.3 *Block Mode, Cipher Block, and Stream Ciphers*

As previously discussed, ciphers can either encrypt data a single character at a time (stream ciphers) or a number of characters at a time (block ciphers). Figure 6.4 illustrates a block cipher encrypting a block of text at a time.

As opposed to a block cipher, a stream cipher encrypts the message a bit of text at a time. This means that a stream cipher breaks a message down into 1's and 0's before the message is encrypted. To encrypt the stream of 1's and 0's from the message, the stream cipher uses a component known as a key stream generator. The key is then input into the key stream generator to generate a stream of random 1's and 0's. The original message is then put through a mathematical process known as exclusive ORing (X-OR) where the two bits are compared. If the bit from the original message is a 1 and the bit from the key stream generator is a 1, then the encrypted message would send out a 0 or the first bit. If the two bits are the same, the X-OR process yields 0; if the two bits are different, the process yields a 1.

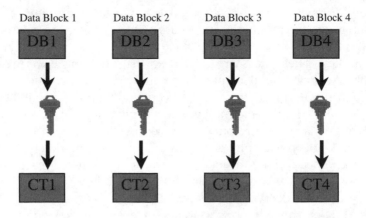

ï   Block Ciphers

FIGURE 6.4   Block Cipher

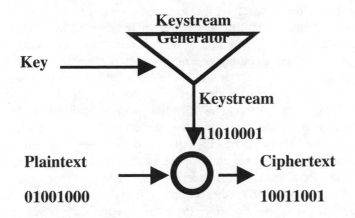

FIGURE 6.5 **Stream Cipher**

Consider the following example:

Original message: 1 0 1 0 1 0 1 0 1
Key stream: 0 1 0 1 1 0 1 0 0
                ─ ─ ─ ─ ─ ─ ─ ─ ─
Encrypted Message: 1 1 1 1 0 0 0 0 1

Because a stream cipher is generally less complex in terms of lines of code necessary to implement it, a stream cipher is often used in hardware (see Figure 6.5). The encryption protocol Wired Equivalent Privacy (WEP), which is used by wireless networks, uses a stream cipher called RC4.

Because the randomness of the 1's and 0's coming from the key stream generator is critical to the security of a stream cipher, there are rules that must apply to a key stream generator. A key stream generator must have long periods where the key stream does not repeat. The key stream must be functionally complex, which means that the key stream cannot be the key and then the key in reverse and then the key. The key stream must be statistically unpredictable, which means there are no patterns to the key stream. The key stream must be unbiased, which means there are as many 1's as 0's. The key stream cannot be easily related to the key. All of these rules increase the security and secrecy of a stream cipher.

6.6.4 Cryptanalysis

Bad guys do cryptanalysis. Well ..., not just guys and not all of them are bad; but cryptanalysis is the process of trying to defeat cryptography without the secret key. The most common type of cryptanalysis is the ciphertext-only attack. This occurs when an attacker looks at the encrypted messages with a utility such as a network sniffer and looks at the stream of ciphertext to see if patterns emerge. A twist on the ciphertext-only attack is known as a birthday attack. With a birthday attack, an attacker looks at the stream of messages to find two or more messages that are the same being transmitted. This is much more efficient than the attacker encrypting his own message and then watching the stream of encrypted messages for one that matches his encrypted message. The birthday attack takes advantage of the nonrandomness of the English language. Because some words are used more frequently than others, those words will be encrypted more often than the others, and will show up more often in the stream of encrypted words. There are many other types of attack a cryptanalyst can attempt. Following are some of the types of attack and a brief summary of what the attack entails:

- *Known plaintext attack:* sample of ciphertext and the corresponding plaintext is available as well.
- *Chosen plaintext attack:* cryptosystem is loaded with hidden key provided and input of any plaintext. The attacker can then see the output to determine how the algorithm functions.
- *Adaptive chosen plaintext attack:* same as above except you are able to choose plaintext samples dynamically, and alter your choice based on results of previous encryptions.
- *Chosen ciphertext attack:* the cryptanalyst may choose a piece of ciphertext and attempt to obtain the corresponding decrypted plaintext.
- *Man-in-the-middle attack:* the attacker inserts himself during the key exchange between parties and intercepts the encryption keys.
- *Timing attacks:* repeatedly measuring exact execution times of cryptographic operations.
- *Brute-force attack:* trying all keys until correct key is identified.
- *Rubber hose cryptanalysis:* includes beating, threatening, and extorting to get the secret key.

6.7 Sample Access Control Policy

See Table 6.1 for a sample access control policy.

TABLE 6.1   Sample Access Control Policy

Access Control Policy

Policy

COMPANY management and employees must implement effective controls to prevent unauthorized access to information held in information systems. Users of applications, systems, and business processes, including support staff, should be provided with access to information and application systems based on individual business need requirements. All access is granted on a least-privilege model. That is, access is restricted to only most restrictive privileges granted based on need of a specific job task.

Standards

Access tools must be used to control access within application systems. Access to software and information is allowed only for authorized users. Only the least amount of access to software and information — necessary to carry out the tasks for which the access is needed — will be granted. Application systems shall:

- Ensure only the information owner and those people and processes authorized by the information owner have access to the application system
- Provide protection against using software utilities that bypass the system or application controls
- Control the use of other systems with which our information is shared, to change or delete the information

Responsibilities

- Information resource owners must ensure compliance with this policy and only they are authorized to grant access.
- All employees of COMPANY, or any other third parties who access the COMPANY's applications and information, are to use the information based on owner approval and do not have authority to grant access to other entities.

Scope

This policy applies to all COMPANY employees.

Contract language for all third-party personnel (full-time, part-time, or contract) shall identify specific COMPANY requirements for compliance. Failure to meet the terms and conditions of the contract could lead to the termination of the contract and possible legal reparation.

Compliance

Employees who fail to comply with the policies will be considered to be in violation of the COMPANY's *Employee Standards of Conduct* and will be subject to appropriate corrective action.

6.8 Summary

In this chapter we discussed many of the technologies available to the information security manager to help protect the network. We discussed access control systems and the models for access control. We then discussed single sign-on technologies and the positives and negatives of each. We also discussed common protocols used for host-based single sign-on. We then covered authentication and other mechanisms for authentication, including two-factor authentication. We then moved on to access and audit logs and how to use them, and this became the discussion on intrusion detection systems. We discussed the types of intrusion detection systems and then the positives and negatives of each. After IDS, we discussed firewalls and the types of firewalls, and finally moved on to a discussion about encryption. All the topics discussed here were covered at a very high level, and several books have been written on each of the technologies. Refer to the reference section at the back of this book for further reading on any of these topics.

Chapter 7

Physical Security

7.1 Data Center Requirements

The nature of physical security for a data center should be one of concentric rings of defense — with requirements for entry getting more difficult the closer we get to the center of the rings. While company employees, authorized visitors, and vendors might be allowed inside the outermost ring, for example, only data center employees and accompanied vendors might be allowed within the innermost ring (see Figure 7.1 for illustration).

The reason for this is obvious. If we take a number of precautions to protect information accessed at devices throughout the organization, then we must at least make sure that no damage or tampering can happen to the hardware on which the information is stored and processed.

To take this idea of concentric rings of protection a little further, we should start by considering the data center itself. Is the building that houses the data center standing by itself, or is the data center in a building that houses other functions? If the data center is in a dedicated building, what approaches are open to the building, and how well-protected are staff members as they enter and leave the building? We may want to start building a picture of the exterior of the building to show the "outer ring" of protection, including entrances and exits, car parking facilities, and lighting. This picture of the outer ring might look like the example in Figure 7.2.

Having said all that, the principle of consistency must still be applied. There is no point in building physical access controls at a cost of several

FIGURE 7.1   Concentric Rings of Protection

million dollars if the potential damage that could be done to a data center is less than several tens of millions of dollars. Remember that the cost of controls must be consistent with the value of the asset being protected, and the definition of "consistent" depends on what risks your organization's management decides to accept.

7.2   Physical Access Controls

When considering the physical access controls that are appropriate for (and consistent with) your organization, we must take into account a number of variables, including the assets to be protected, the potential threat to those assets, and your organization's attitude toward risk.

7.2.1   Assets to be Protected

Some organizations may decide to centralize operations and, in the course of doing so, build large, expensive "server farms" on their premises. On the other end of the scale, an organization might decide to take a decentralized approach and distribute its computers and computing equipment around the organization's many buildings.

The amount of effort put into protecting physical assets in both of the above scenarios might well come to the same total amount but would be

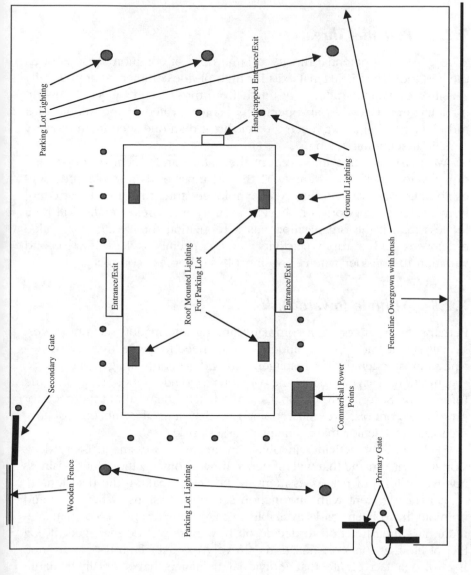

FIGURE 7.2 Outer Ring of Protection

spent on different forms of protection. For a large server farm, several concentric rings of technology-based protection and access control might be appropriate whereas, for the distributed version, simply keeping individual servers in locked rooms might be sufficient. This is one variation to consider when choosing appropriate physical access controls.

7.2.2 Potential Threats

When assessing potential threats, a large dose of common sense is often the best tool. The threats that exist for high-profile commercial or politically sensitive operations differ very much from those faced by, say, a biscuit manufacturer. Likewise, an operations center located in the middle of a turbulent city will face a much greater threat than one sited in an industry park in a semirural setting.

We must also take into account the nature and recent history of the organization itself. For example, if the organization is a stable and long-established one with no history of employee strife, then the threat countermeasures (in the form of physical security measures) to take will be a lot less than if the organization has a reputation for having disgruntled employees and disruptive activity on the premises. This is a second variation to consider when choosing physical access controls.

7.2.3 Attitude toward Risk

Perhaps the most common complaint among information security professionals is that "they" do not understand the need for protective controls — "they" most often being management and senior management of the organization. Leaving aside the obvious rejoinder about it being the Information Security Professional's job to teach "them" about the need for protective controls, we must point out that it is the function of any organization's senior management to assess risk.

Daily business activities involve constant risk assessment. Every decision that is taken and that will influence how an organization does business involves a form of risk assessment in the act of making the decision.

It is no different with information security decisions. When facts and opinions have been made available to management and senior management, it is their function to decide on how risks will be managed. It is a fact of life that some organizations are very risk-averse and some are not. It is also a fact of life that individual managers have equally variable attitudes toward risk. These constitute the third set of variations to consider when choosing physical access controls.

7.2.4 Sample Controls

Having looked at the complications involved in choosing appropriate physical access controls, it becomes clear that no "one-size-fits-all" solution exists. Each organization must examine its own particular assets, risks, and attitudes toward risk before deciding on appropriate physical access controls. When that examination has been performed, the organization will want to consider the following list of items when designing controls over physical access:

- Physical security protection for IT equipment and systems should be established, based on defined perimeters through strategically located barriers throughout the organization (already discussed at the start of this chapter).
- The security of the protection given must be consistent with the value of the assets or services being protected (already discussed at the start of this chapter).
- Support functions and equipment are sited to minimize the risks of unauthorized access to secure areas or compromising sensitive information; for example, network engineers who will be called on often to enter the data center should not have their workplace located away from the data center.
- Physical barriers, where they are necessary, are extended from floor to ceiling to prevent unauthorized entry and environmental contamination. That is, walls that are meant to prevent access, slow the spread of fire, or exclude dusty or polluted air must go all the way from the actual ceiling of the building to the solid floor of the building and not just from a false ceiling to the raised floor.
- Personnel other than those working in a secure area are not informed of the activities within the secure area. While no one expects a cloak of secrecy to be hung over the existence of a data center or other sensitive operation, details of the business conducted inside a protected perimeter need not be known to anyone who does not have access inside the perimeter.
- Unsupervised lone working in sensitive areas must be prohibited (both for safety and to prevent opportunities for malicious activities).
- Computer equipment managed by the organization is housed in dedicated areas separate from third-party-managed computer equipment. Where a process or part of the organization's computing activity is carried out by a third party, that third party's equipment should be housed in an area that lets their engineers access the equipment without having access to the organization's computer

equipment. Keeping the two entities' equipment in separate cages in the same room can usually satisfy this.

■ Secure areas, when vacated, must be physically locked and periodically checked.

■ Personnel supplying or maintaining support services are granted access to secure areas only when required and authorized, and their access is restricted and their activities are monitored.

■ Unauthorized photography, recording, or video equipment must be prohibited within the security perimeters.

■ Entry controls over secure areas must be established to ensure that only authorized personnel can gain access; and a rigorous, auditable procedure for authorizing access must be put in place.

■ Visitors to secure areas must be supervised, and their date and time of entry and departure will be recorded.

■ Visitors to secure areas are granted access only for specific, authorized purposes.

■ All personnel must be required to wear visible identification within the secure area. The necessary addition to this is that we must foster a culture in which employees feel comfortable in challenging anyone who is in a secure area without visible identification.

■ Access rights to secure areas will be revoked immediately for staff who leave employment.

7.3 Fire Prevention and Detection

Fire prevention and detection standards vary according to the premises — whether or not the premises also house materials or processes that increase the risk of fire and whether or not the premises themselves are located in an area where fire risk is higher or lower.

Generally, the local fire authority (Fire Marshall in the United States) can be consulted for advice on fire prevention and detection measures, and architects and vendors of data center equipment are also ready to give advice.

There are, however, some fire prevention and detection precautions that should be judged as standard and minimum requirements for premises that house computers and critical information.

7.3.1 Fire Prevention

No smoking is the first rule. Although this is a common requirement throughout the United States at the time of writing, it is neither a federal law nor a universally implemented state law. However, the use of smoking materials anywhere within a building that houses or processes critical information must be prohibited.

All flammable material — such as printer paper, plastic wrapping, and tapes — should be stored in an area separated from the main server or computer room by a fire-rated wall. Supplies for one day's processing can be kept in the server or computer room, but larger supplies must be stored separately.

Flammable or highly combustible materials must also be kept out of such premises. Where an organization produces, uses, or transports hazardous materials, all such materials must be stored away from premises where critical information is stored or processed. Where janitorial staff use flammable or combustible cleaning solvents, they should also be stored offsite. If that is not possible, they should be stored in an area that is behind a fireproof door and has its own smoke detecting equipment.

Many organizations now find it prudent to limit the amount of electrical power used in each cabinet and cage in the data center. High use of electrical power creates a build-up of heat and also creates the potential for the build-up of static electricity — both fire hazards. Ventilation and grounding are the keys, of course, to limiting the risk from these; but limiting the amount of electrical power used in any physical area also reduces the chance of a heat or static electricity build-up. Most designers of data centers recommend that the ambient temperature in data centers should not exceed 74 degrees Fahrenheit (23 Centigrade) because that reduces the risk of such build-ups and also eases the control of humidity within the room.

Of course, when controlling the temperature and humidity in an enclosed space, it is necessary to monitor them, and the system used to monitor temperature and humidity in a data center must have the following characteristics:

- The data gathered must be representative of the room being monitored. That is, if only one sensor is used in the room, it is unlikely that a true picture of temperature and humidity will be available. Fluctuations from one part of the room to the next will not be detected and "hotspots" — unless they happen to occur under the sensor — will go unnoticed.
- The monitoring system must be capable of storing and presenting historical data. Seasonal and event-based fluctuations provide important indicators of how to manage temperature and humidity.
- The monitoring system must be able to provide alarms when temperature and humidity fall outside acceptable parameters. Fire, flood, or any failure of the heating or cooling systems are all critical events, and the monitoring system must be able to alert staff to their occurrence.

7.3.2 Fire Detection

The most common sources of fires in data centers include the electrical system and the hardware. Breakdowns in insulation and the resultant short-circuiting can lead to intense heat that can melt materials or cause a fire. Data center fires are often small or smoldering, with little effect on the temperature in the room. Because the smoke itself can impact the computer hardware, it is necessary to employ a detection system that is sensitive to smoke and other products of combustion rather than the temperature. The specific detection and extinguishing system depends on the specific design and exposures of the individual data center area. In the United States, NFPA 75 states that automatic detection equipment must be installed to provide early warning of fire. The equipment used must be a listed smoke detection type, and every installation of smoke detection equipment must be engineered for the specific area to be protected (giving due consideration to air currents and patterns within the space to be monitored).

Smoke and fire detectors should be wired to a central alarm panel that is continuously monitored and ideally is constructed so that any alarm given is repeated instantly at the nearest firehouse. Where permanent connection to the firehouse is not possible, an external alarm should be installed to allow people outside the building to be notified and to raise the alarm with the emergency services.

7.3.3 Fire Fighting

In data centers, as much damage can be done by the fire suppression equipment as by the fire itself. Nonetheless, effective fire suppression systems must be installed in data centers.

A passive system reacts to smoke and fire without manual intervention. The most common forms of passive suppression are sprinkler systems or chemical suppression systems. Sprinkler systems can be flooded (wet pipe) or pre-action (dry pipe). A flooded system means that the pipes are full at all times, which allows the system to discharge immediately upon detection. A pre-action system will fill the sprinkler pipes upon an initial detection, but will delay discharging until a second detection criteria has been met. Chemical total flooding systems work by suffocating the fire within the controlled zone. The suppression chemical most often found in data centers is Halon 1301. Halon is being eliminated in favor of the more environmentally friendly FM200 or various forms of water suppression. Carbon dioxide suppression systems are also used but can be a concern due to operator safety issues in the instance of a discharge. These can be used independently or in combination, depending on the exposures in the room, local ordinances, and insurance requirements.

The ideal system would incorporate both a gas system and a pre-action water sprinkler system. The gas suppression systems are friendlier to computing equipment. Water sprinklers often cause catastrophic and irreparable damage to the hardware, whereas the hardware in a room subjected to a gas discharge can often be brought back online soon after the room is purged.

Gas systems are, however, "one-shot" designs. If the fire is not put out in the initial discharge, there is no second chance. The gas system cannot be reused until it is recharged or connected to a backup source. Water systems can continue to address the fire until it has been brought under control. While this is more likely to damage the hardware, it is also a more secure means of protecting the building structure.

Water suppression systems are often preferred or mandated by building owners or insurance companies. Water systems are also highly recommended in areas containing a high level of combustible materials use or storage. The decision of what means of fire suppression to utilize must incorporate numerous factors, including the mission and criticality of the data center operations.

7.4 Verified Disposal of Documents

While security precautions and fire prevention and suppression systems can ensure the safety of information within data centers, often little is done to protect information when it leaves the data center. Printed documents and documents on electronic media all leave the data center and, hopefully, fall under policies and standards for the protection of data throughout the workplace. But when documents are disposed of, all too often the commonsense rules for protecting information are left behind.

We see documents clearly marked "Confidential" (or which, according to the content of the documents, should be clearly marked as such but are not) tossed into garbage cans and set out with the rest of the office rubbish. Where paper documents are collected, they are often left unattended — a convenient place for a wrong-doer to browse through a company's paper output. In one facility I visited, the facility owners thoughtfully provided containers in which to dispose of confidential documents — large garbage cans clearly marked "Confidential Documents Only". Once again, a convenient receptacle for wrong-doers to search.

It makes sense, does it not, that if we are to spend any money or effort to protect information, then the "circle of protection" ought to surround the information all the way to its destruction — and yet it so often does not.

7.4.1 Collection of Documents

The procedures for the collection of documents prior to their disposal should be documented and taught to all employees — and should avoid using large receptacles clearly marked "Confidential Documents Only."

Every single department in the organization must have easy access to the containers used to dispose of documents. Where it involves more than a minute of time to properly dispose of a document, confidential documents will be put in garbage cans next to desks. Documents should be collected at fixed points in receptacles lined with opaque bags so that when the bags are taken away for disposal, the documents cannot be read through the bags themselves.

Where documents are collected in bins, we have to make a decision on whether or not to lock the bins. For locked bins, the advantages are that paper is secure (relatively) once deposited in the bin and we can demonstrate — to clients and auditors — that our information security circle of protection encompasses documents ready for disposal. Disadvantages include the procedures necessary to track keys, the extra expense, and the added attraction (for wrong-doers) of a locked (versus unlocked) document bin.

Clearly, every organization must make its own decisions on how to collect information destined for disposal, and those decisions will be based on criteria already discussed in this book. One thing is certain, however, and that is: if a secure document disposal process does not exist, then sooner or later confidential documents will end up in the hands of someone who can use them to cause trouble for the company.

7.4.2 Document Destruction Options

There are three basic options for destruction of documents: recycling (commonly called pulping), shredding, and burning; some organizations use a combination of one or more of these.

When considering recycling or pulping as an option, the following factors must be taken into account:

■ Recycling with a bonded service usually means contracting with a service to have the paper hauled to a bonded recycler or directly to a bonded paper mill. All of the paper sent to the recycler should be documented with shipping information. and a Certificate of Destruction should be received to certify that the paper was sent directly to a specified location on a specific date and was destroyed on a specific date.

■ Where bonded recycling service is not available or is prohibitively expensive to use, we can perform an assessment of the recycler's procedures and facilities. If we find that recyclers handle and process paper in a manner that meets confidentiality standards for security, then we may use them instead of the more expensive, bonded alternative.

Shredding paper increases its volume and sometimes produces a false sense of security. Less expensive shredders, in fact, only cut paper into ribbons that can be easily pieced together again and read. Even when we opt for a more expensive shredding option, we must consider the following points:

■ While shredding can be an effective way of disposing of documents, it is also expensive and labor intensive; and if other options are available, it might not be necessary. Some organizations do their own shredding with small, departmental shredders while others choose to do it in a centralized fashion using a large, industrial centralized shredder.

■ Some organizations also decide to minimize on-site shredding by working with a recycling hauler that provides secure services such as off-site shredding. These hauler companies pick up the paper from a central point and either shred it on site in mobile units or transport it to a bulk shredding facility. These firms come under the category of destruction firms, and they should always be able to provide a Certificate of Destruction.

7.4.3   Choosing Services

Document disposal and recycling functions are most often contracted services. However, the organization's responsibility for security of the documents does not end when they are removed from the facility. Making sure that the documents are subject to secure and reasonable processes until the information is destroyed is still the organization's facility's responsibility.

7.5 Agreements

Everyone outside the organization that owns the documents who is involved in the destruction of the documents (including waste haulers, recycling facilities, and landfill and incinerator owners) should sign an agreement that states that they know they will be handling confidential information from the organization, and they agree to maintain the confidentiality of that information. The agreement must limit the vendor to use and disclosure of documents and the information contained in the documents to those uses stated in a contract.

Contractual language protecting the confidentiality of the waste should be built into all contracts with solid waste and recycling haulers and include the following elements:

- Specify the method of destruction or disposal.
- Specify the time that will elapse between acquisition and destruction or disposal of documents (or electronic media, if that is also to be disposed of).
- Establish safeguards against breaches in confidentiality.
- Indemnify the organization from loss due to unauthorized disclosure.
- Require that the vendor maintain liability insurance in specified amounts at all times the contract is in effect.
- Provide proof of destruction or disposal.

One final point to consider when deciding how to dispose of documents is their collection in a loading dock area. We must secure our solid waste compactors and containers by locking all accessible openings to the compactor. Metal doors can be welded onto the compactors to allow them to be easily locked. Ensure the loading dock is secure at all times. The container for the documents and the loading dock itself must be designed to minimize or eliminate the risk of documents blowing around in the wind before or while they are being collected for disposal.

7.5.1 Duress Alarms

In many facilities, certain operations are carried out that place staff in positions of heightened vulnerability. For example, in a bank, tellers are at risk from criminals who rob the bank during business hours. In data centers, employees who handle negotiable instruments (checks, stock certificates, etc.) may also be at risk.

Where employees are performing jobs that increase the risk of their being vulnerable to coercion or attack, each employee's workspace must be provided with a duress alarm. The alarm activator (button or switch) should be placed so that it can be used without its use being noticed by others (a footswitch, for example, can be used without anyone watching being aware of its use).

The choice of whether the alarm should sound locally or not will be based on an assessment of the type of risk the alarm is meant to indicate. That is, if sounding the alarm locally is likely to increase the risk to the employee setting off the alarm, then the alarm should not sound locally. By the same token, if a local alarm might bring help more quickly or alleviate the situation, then one should be installed.

Whether local or remote, all employees who might be called upon to respond to the alarm must be trained in response techniques, and the response procedures must be kept up to date and stored at the place where responding employees normally work.

7.6 Intrusion Detection Systems

In the context of physical security, intrusion detection systems mean tools used to detect activity on the boundaries of a protected facility. When we commit to physically protecting the premises on which our staff work and which house our information processing equipment, we should carry out an exhaustive risk analysis and, where the threat requires, consider installing a perimeter intrusion detection system (IDS).

The simplest IDS is a guard patrol. Guards who walk the corridors and perimeter of a facility are very effective at identifying attempts to break into the facility and either raising the alarm or ending the attempt by challenging the intruder. Of course, the most obvious shortcoming of a guard patrol is that the patrol cannot be at all points of the facility at the same time.

This leads to the next simplest IDS and that is video monitoring. We can place video cameras at locations in the facility where all points in the perimeter can be monitored simultaneously and, when an intrusion attempt is detected, the person charged with monitoring the video surveillance can raise an alarm.

7.6.1 *Purpose*

Our first task in defining the requirements of an IDS is to define what is to be protected and what is the level and nature of the threat. For general threats we might ask: How does anything from the outside get to the inside? Are parking lots secure? What is the mail delivery system? What is the environmental system exposure? What are the loading dock procedures? What building access controls exist?

Other questions to ask in defining the purpose of the IDS relate to the history of the facility. For example, has there been a specific parking lot incident, grounds incident, or a property/facility trespassing incident? Are there general vulnerability concerns that may include trespass, assault, or intimidation? When was the last occurrence, and what were the circumstances? Are the authorities aware and involved? Is there documentation available for review?

Answering these questions will help define the purpose of the IDS (and what it needs to achieve). The next task is planning the system itself.

7.6.2   Planning

Of course, both of the examples given above should have been chosen as the result of a need identified by a risk assessment plus careful planning. The planning should have been carried out with an objective to provide a solution that addresses:

- Surveillance
- Control
- Maintenance
- Training

During the planning, the nature of the facility and the contents of the facility themselves should be taken into account. For example, the IDS requirements for a dedicated data center campus, situated on its own grounds and surrounded by a perimeter fence, differ greatly from those for a data center housed on the warehouse floor of a multi-story building in a city center.

7.6.3   Elements

The planning should produce a draft design that addresses the requirements of the premises. The elements of intrusion detection required will depend on the facilities; for example, the dedicated data center might require a perimeter fence, lighting on that fence and in the space between the fence and the walls of the facility, video cameras, and then the perimeter system for the building itself. On the other hand, a facility contained in a multi-use building will require intrusion detection systems on the doors, windows, floors, walls, and ceilings of only the part of the facility that contains the data center.

Elements to consider when installing an IDS include:

- Video surveillance
- Illumination

- Motion detection sensors
- Heat sensors
- Alarm systems for windows and doors
- "Break-glass" sensors (noise sensors that can detect the sound made by broken glass)
- Pressure sensors for floors and stairs

7.6.4 Procedures

Whatever tools or technologies are used in the IDS, the system will fail to provide security unless adequate procedures are put in place and training on those procedures is given to staff expected to monitor and react to alarms created by the IDS.

Staff should be trained twice a year on what IDS alarms mean and how to respond to them. Those staff responsible for monitoring the IDS must be taught to recognize intrusion attempts and how to respond according to a response scale (i.e., when it is appropriate to respond in person, when to respond with assistance from facility personnel, and when law enforcement should be called for assistance).

Procedures should also include logging procedures that allow for all events — not just events requiring responses — to be logged for audit purposes or for purposes of follow-up.

7.7 Sample Physical Security Policy

See Table 7.1 for a sample physical security policy.

7.8 Summary

The nature of physical security for a data center should be one of concentric rings of defense — with requirements for entry getting more difficult the closer we get to the center of the rings. The reason for this is obvious: if we take a number of precautions to protect information accessed at devices throughout the organization, then we must make at least as sure that no damage or tampering can happen to the hardware on which the information is stored and processed. Having said that, the principle of consistency must still be applied. There is no point in building physical access controls at a cost of several million dollars if the potential damage that could be done to a data center is less than several tens of millions of dollars.

TABLE 7.1   Sample Physical Security Policy

Physical Security

Policy
It is the responsibility of The Company management to provide a safe and secure workplace for all employees.

Standards

- The Company offices will be protected from unauthorized access.
- Areas within buildings that house sensitive information or high-risk equipment will be protected against unauthorized access, fire, water, and other hazards.
- Devices that are critical to the operation of company business processes will be identified in the Company Business Impact Analysis (BIA) process and will be protected against power failure.

Responsibilities

- Senior management and the officers of The Company are required to maintain accurate records and to employ internal controls designed to safeguard company assets and property against unauthorized use or disposition.
- The Company assets include but are not limited to physical property, intellectual property, patents, trade secrets, copyrights, and trademarks.
- Additionally, it is the responsibility of Company line management to ensure that staff is aware of and fully complies with the company's security guidelines and all relevant laws and regulations.

Compliance

- Management is responsible for conducting periodic reviews and audits to assure compliance with all policies, procedures, practices, standards, and guidelines.
- Employees who fail to comply with the policies will be treated as being in violation of the *Employee Standards of Conduct* and will be subject to appropriate corrective action.

Chapter 8

Risk Analysis and Risk Management

8.1 Introduction

Risk management is the process that allows business managers to balance operational and economic costs of protective measures and achieve gains in mission capability by protecting business processes that support the business objectives or mission of the enterprise.

Senior management must ensure that the enterprise has the capabilities needed to accomplish its mission.

Most organizations have tight budgets for security. To get the best bang for the security buck, management needs a process to determine spending.

8.2 Frequently Asked Questions on Risk Analysis

8.2.1 Why Conduct a Risk Analysis?

Management is charged with showing that "due diligence" is performed during decision-making processes for any enterprise. A formal risk analysis provides the documentation that due diligence is performed.

A risk analysis also lets an enterprise take control of its own destiny. With an effective risk analysis process in place, only those controls and safeguards that are actually needed will be implemented. An enterprise will never again face having to implement a mandated control to "be in compliance with audit requirements."

8.2.2   When to Conduct a Risk Analysis?

A risk analysis should be conducted whenever money or resources are to be spent. Before starting a task, project, or development cycle, an enterprise should conduct an analysis of the need for the project. Understanding the concepts of risk analysis and applying them to the business needs of the enterprise will ensure that only necessary spending is done.

8.2.3   Who Should Conduct the Risk Analysis?

Most risk analysis projects fail because the internal experts and subject matter experts are not included in the process. A process such as the Facilitated Risk Analysis Process (FRAP) takes advantage of the internal experts. No one knows your systems and applications better than the people who develop and run them.

8.2.4   How Long Should a Risk Analysis Take?

It should be completed in days, not weeks or months. To meet the needs of an enterprise, the risk analysis process must be completed quickly with a minimum impact on the employees' already busy schedule.

8.2.5   What a Risk Analysis Analyzes

Risk analysis can be used to review any task, project, or idea. By learning the basic concepts of risk analysis, an organization can use it to determine if a project should be undertaken, if a specific product should be purchased, if a new control should be implemented, or if the enterprise is at risk from some threat.

8.2.6   What Can the Results of a Risk Analysis Tell an Organization?

The greatest benefit of a risk analysis is determining whether or not it is prudent to proceed. It allows management to examine all currently identified concerns, prioritize the level of vulnerability, and then select an appropriate level of control or accept the risk.

The goal of risk analysis is not to eliminate all risk. It is a tool used by management to reduce risk to an acceptable level.

8.2.7   Who Should Review the Results of a Risk Analysis?

A risk analysis is rarely conducted without a senior management sponsor. The results are geared to provide management with the information it needs to make informed business decisions. The results of a risk analysis are normally classified as confidential and are provided to only the sponsor and to those deemed appropriate by the sponsor.

8.2.8   How Is the Success of the Risk Analysis Measured?

The tangible way to measure success is to see a lower bottom line for cost. Risk analysis can assist in this process by identifying only those controls that need implementation.

Another way that the success of a risk analysis is measured is if there is a time when management decisions are called into review. By having a formal process in place that demonstrates the due diligence of management in the decision-making process, this kind of inquiring will be dealt with quickly and successfully.

Effective risk management must be totally integrated into the organization's system development life cycle (SDLC). The typical SDLC has five phases and they can be termed almost anything. Regardless of what the phases are labeled, they all have the same key concepts:

- Analysis
- Design
- Construction
- Test
- Maintenance

The National Institute of Standards and Technology (NIST) uses the following terms: Initiation, Development or Acquisition, Implementation, Operation or Maintenance, and Disposal.

As Figure 8.1 illustrates, risk analysis is mapped throughout the SDLC. The first time risk analysis is required occurs when there is a discussion on whether or not a new system application of a business process is required.

The SDLC phases include:

- *Analysis:* the need for a new system, application or process and its scope are documented.
- *Design:* the system or process is designed and requirements are gathered.

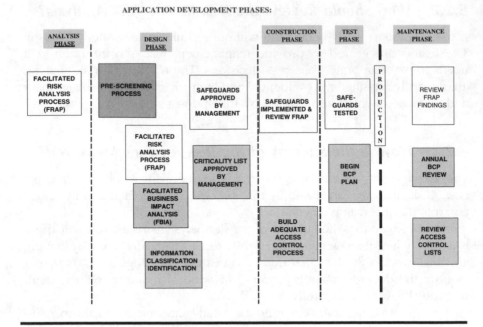

FIGURE 8.1 System Development Life Cycle

■ *Development:* the system or process is purchased, developed, or otherwise constructed.

■ *Test:* system security features should be configured, enabled, tested, and verified.

■ *Maintenance:* when changes or updates are made to the system, the changes to hardware and software are noted and the risk analysis process is revisited.

Risk management activities include:

■ *Analysis:* identified risks are used to support the development of system requirements, including security needs.

■ *Design:* security needs lead to architecture and design trade-offs.

■ *Development:* the security controls and safeguards are created or implemented as part of the development process.

■ *Test:* safeguards and controls are tested to ensure that decisions regarding risks identified are reduced to acceptable levels prior to movement to production.

■ *Maintenance:* controls and safeguards are reexamined when changes or updates occur, or at regularly scheduled intervals.

Risk management is an enterprise management responsibility. Each group has a different role and these roles support the activities of the other roles and responsibilities. Let us examine the typical roles found in an organization and what they are responsible for with regard to risk analysis and risk management.

- *Senior management.* Under the Standard of Due Care, senior management is charged with the ultimate responsibility for meeting business objectives or mission requirements. Senior management must ensure that necessary resources are effectively applied to develop the capabilities to meet the mission requirements. Senior management must incorporate the results of the risk analysis process into the decision-making process.
- *Chief Information Security Officer (CISO).* The CISO is responsible for the organization's planning, budgeting, and performance, including its information security components. Decisions made in this area should be based on an effective risk management program.
- *System and Information Owners.* These are the business unit managers assigned as functional owners of organization assets and are responsible for ensuring that proper controls are in place to address integrity, confidentiality, and availability of the information resources that they are assigned ownership. The term "owner" must be established in the Asset Classification Policy.
- *Business Managers.* The managers (aka owners) are the individuals with the authority and responsibility for making cost/benefit decisions essential to ensure accomplishment of organization mission objectives. Their involvement in the risk management process enables the selection of business-orientated controls. The charge of being an owner supports the objective of fulfilling the fiduciary responsibility of management to protect the assets of the enterprise.
- *Information Security Administrator (ISA; formerly ISSO).* This is the security program manager responsible for the organization's security programs, including risk management. The ISA has changed its designation because the "officer" designation is normally restricted to senior executives. The officers can be held personally liable if internal controls are not adequate.

8.3 Information Security Life Cycle

When implementing risk management, it will be necessary to view this process as part of the ongoing information security life cycle (see Figure 8.2). As with any business process, the information security life cycle starts

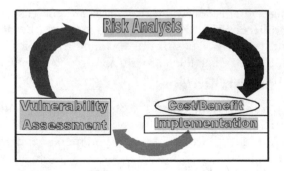

FIGURE 8.2   Information Security Life Cycle

with a risk analysis. Management is charged with showing that "due diligence" is performed during decision-making processes for any enterprise. A formal risk analysis provides the documentation that due diligence is performed. Typically, risk analysis results will be used on two occasions: (1) when a decision needs to be made and (2) when there arises a need to examine the decision-making process.

A risk analysis also lets an enterprise take control of its own destiny. With an effective risk analysis process in place, only those controls and safeguards that are actually needed will be implemented. An enterprise will never again face having to implement a mandated control to "be in compliance with audit requirements."

A risk analysis should be conducted whenever money or resources are to be spent. Before starting a task, project, or development cycle, an enterprise should conduct an analysis of the need for the project. Understanding the concepts of risk analysis and applying them to the business needs of the enterprise will ensure that only necessary spending is done.

Once a risk analysis has been conducted, it will be necessary to conduct a cost and benefit analysis to determine which controls will help mitigate the risk to an acceptable level at a cost the enterprise can afford. It is unwise to implement controls or safeguards just because they seem to be the right thing to do or because other enterprises are doing so. Each organization is unique, and the levels of revenue and exposure are different. By conducting a proper risk analysis, the controls or safeguards will meet the enterprise's specific needs.

Once the controls or safeguards have been implemented, it is appropriate to conduct an assessment to determine if the controls are working. In the information security profession, the term "vulnerability" has been defined as a condition of a missing or ineffectively administered safeguard or control that allows a threat to occur with a greater impact or frequency, or both. When conducting an NVA (network vulnerability assessment), the team will be assessing existing controls, safeguards, and processes that are part of the network. This process, the assessment, will ensure that controls are effective and that they will remain so.

8.4 Risk Analysis Process

Risk analysis has three deliverables: (1) identify threats; (2) establish a risk level by determining probability that a threat will occur and the impact if the threat does occur; and finally, (3) identification of controls and safeguards that can reduce the risk to an acceptable level. As we examine the risk analysis portion of the risk management process, we will discuss six steps that will provide the three deliverables we need. Risk is a function of the probability that an identified threat will occur and then the impact that the threat will have on the business process or mission of the asset under review. We now examine the six steps necessary to perform the risk analysis portion of the risk management process.

8.4.1   Asset Definition

The first step in the risk analysis process is to define the process, application, system, or asset that is going to have the risk analysis performed upon it. The key here is to establish the boundaries of what is to be reviewed. Most failed projects come to grief because the scope of the project was poorly defined to begin with, or because the scope was not managed well and was allowed to "creep" until it was out of control. If we are going to manage risk analysis as a project, then the asset definition must be looked upon as a scope statement. All of the elements that go into writing a successful scope statement should be used to define the asset and what will be expected from the risk analysis process.

To gather relevant information about the asset or process under review, the risk management team can use a number of techniques. These include questionnaires, on-site interviews, documentation review, and scanning tools. It will be necessary to describe in words exactly what the risk analysis is going to review. Once it has been identified, it will be necessary to determine what resources will be needed to support the asset (platforms, operating systems, personnel, etc.) and what business processes this asset will impact.

8.4.2   Threat Identification

We define a threat as an undesirable event that could impact the business objectives or mission of the business unit or enterprise. Some threats come from existing controls that were either implemented incorrectly or have passed their usefulness and now provide a weakness to the system or platform that can be exploited to circumvent the intended behavior of the control. This process is known as exploiting a *vulnerability*.

We will want to create as complete a list of threats as possible. Typically, there are three major categories of threats:

1. *Natural threats:* floods, earthquakes, tornadoes, landslides, avalanches, electrical storms, and other such events.
2. *Human threats:* events that are either enabled by or caused by human beings, such as unintentional acts (errors and omissions) or deliberate acts (fraud, malicious software, unauthorized access). Statistically, the threat that causes the largest loss to information resources remains human errors and omissions.
3. *Environmental threats:* long-term power outages, pollution, chemical spills, or liquid leakage.

To create a complete list of threats, there are a number of different methods that can be used. These include developing checklists. While I think checklists are important and should be used, I must caution you that if used improperly, a checklist will impact the free flow of ideas and information. So use them to ensure that everything gets covered or identified, but do not make them available at the beginning of the process.

Another method of gathering threats is to examine historical data. Research what types of events have occurred as well as how often they have occurred. Once you have the threat, it may be necessary to determine the annual rate of occurrence (ARO). This data can be obtained from a number of sources. For natural threats, the National Weather Center is a good place to obtain these rates of occurrence. For accidental human threats, an insurance underwriter will have the figures. For deliberate threats, contact local law enforcement or the organization's security force. For environmental threats, facilities management and the local power companies will have the relevant information.

The method I like best is *brainstorming*. I like to get a number of people (stakeholders) together and give them a structure to focus their thoughts on, and then let them identify all the threats they can think of. When we brainstorm, there are no wrong answers. We want to ensure that all threats get identified. Once we have completed the information gathering, then we will clean up duplicates and combine like threats.

8.4.3 Determine Probability of Occurrence

Once a list of threats has been finalized, it is necessary to determine how likely that threat is to occur. The risk management team will want to derive an overall likelihood that indicates the probability that a potential threat may be exercised against the risk analysis asset under review. It will be necessary to establish definitions on probability and a number of other key terms. We will discuss sample definitions as soon as we finish addressing the six steps of risk analysis.

8.4.4 Determine the Impact of the Threat

Having determined the probability that a threat might occur, it will then be necessary to determine the impact that the threat will have on the organization. Before determining the impact value, it is necessary to ensure that the scope of the risk analysis has been properly defined. It will be necessary to ensure that the risk management team understands the objectives or mission of the asset under review and how it impacts the organization's overall mission or objectives.

When determining the risk level (probability and impact), it will be necessary to establish the framework from which the evaluation is to occur. That is, how will existing controls impact the results? Typically, during the initial review, the threats are examined as if there are no controls in place. This will provide the risk management team with a baseline risk level from which you can identify the controls and safeguards and measure their effectiveness.

Although we make the assertion that no controls are in place, in the scope statement we will identify assumptions and constraints. These assumptions might include the concepts that a risk analysis has been performed on the supporting infrastructure elements and that appropriate controls have been implemented. This will mean that such an activity must have taken place or is scheduled to take place as soon as possible. By establishing these assumptions, the risk management team can focus on the threats and impacts related directly to the asset under review.

The results of the review of probability and impact is the determination of a risk level that can be assigned to each threat. Once the risk level is established, then the team can identify appropriate actions. Steps two and three determine the likelihood that a given threat might occur, the magnitude of the impact should the threat occur, and the adequacy of controls already in place. The final element will be to identify controls for those high-level threats that have no control or whose control is inadequate.

The risk level process will require the use of definitions for probability and impact, as well as definitions of levels. The following are sample definitions and how they might be used by the risk management team (see Table 8.1):

TABLE 8.1   Probability Impact Matrix

Probability	Impact		
High	A	B	C
Medium	B	B	C
Low	B	C	D

A: Corrective action must be implemented.
B: Corrective action should be implemented.
C: Requires monitor.
D: No action required at this time.

■ *Probability:* the likelihood that a threat event will occur.
  ■ *High probability:* very likely that the threat will occur within the next year.
  ■ *Medium probability:* possible that the threat will occur during the next year.
  ■ *Low probability:* highly unlikely that the threat will occur during the next year.
■ *Impact:* the measure of the magnitude of loss or harm to the value of an asset.
  ■ *High impact:* shutdown of critical business unit that leads to a significant loss of business, corporate image, or profit.
  ■ *Medium impact:* short interruption of critical process or system that results in a limited financial loss to a single business unit.
  ■ *Low impact:* interruption with no financial loss.

8.4.5   Controls Recommended

After assigning the risk level, the team will identify controls or safeguards that could possibly eliminate the risk or at least reduce the risk to an acceptable level. Remember that one of the goals of risk analysis is to document the organization's due diligence when making business decisions. Therefore, it is important to identify as many controls and safeguards as possible. By doing this the team will be able to document all the options that were considered.

The are a number of factors that need to be considered when recommending controls and alternative solutions. For example, how effective is the recommended control? One way to determine the relative effectiveness is to perform the risk level process (probability and impact) to the threat with the control in place. If the risk level is not reduced to an acceptable point, then the team may want to examine another option.

There may also be legal and regulatory requirements to implement specific controls. With so many new and expanding requirements mandated by government agencies, controlling boards, and laws, it will be necessary for the risk management team to be current on these requirements.

When selecting any type of control, it will be necessary to measure the operational impact on the organization. Every control will have an impact in some manner. It could be the expenditure for the control itself. It could be the impact of productivity and turn-around time. Even if the control is a new procedure, the effect on the employees must be reviewed and used in the determination on whether to implement or not.

A final consideration is the safety and reliability of the control or safeguard. Does the control have a track record that demonstrates that it will allow the organization to operate in a safe and secure mode? The overall safety of the organization's intellectual property is at stake. The last thing that the risk management team wants to do is implement a control that puts the enterprise at a greater risk.

The expenditure on controls must be balanced against the actual business harm. A good rule of thumb is that if the control costs more than the asset it is designed to protect, then the return on investment will probably be low. One way to identify a good "bang for the buck" is to identify each control and cross-reference it to all of the threats that could be mitigated by the implementation of that specific control. This process will provide the team with an initial idea of which control is most cost effective.

To be effective, the risk analysis process should be applied across the entire organization. That is, all of the elements and methodology that make up the risk analysis process should be standard and all business units trained in its use. The output from the risk analysis will lead the organization to identify controls that should reduce the level of threat occurrence.

8.4.6   Documentation

Once the risk analysis is complete, the results should be documented in a standard format and a report issued to the asset owner. This report will help senior management, the business owner, make decisions on policy, procedures, budget, and systems and management changes. The risk analysis report should be presented in a systematic and analytical manner that assesses risk so that senior management will understand the risks and allocate resources to reduce the risk to an acceptable level.

8.5   Risk Mitigation

Risk mitigation is a systematic methodology used by senior management to reduce organizational risk. The process of risk mitigation can be achieved through a number of different methods. We will take a few minutes and discuss the six most common methods of risk mitigation.

1. *Risk assumption.* After examining the threats and determining the risk level, the team's findings lead management to determine that it is the best business decision to accept the potential risk and continue operating. This is an acceptable outcome of the risk analysis process. If, after completing the risk analysis process, management decides to accept the risk, then it has performed its due diligence.
2. *Risk alleviation.* Senior management approves the implementation of the controls recommended by the risk management team that will lower the risk to an acceptable level.
3. *Risk avoidance.* This is where after performing the risk analysis, management chooses to avoid the risks by eliminating the process that could cause the risks; for example, foregoing certain functions or enhancements of a system or application that would place too great an exposure on the organization.
4. *Risk limitation.* To limit the risk by implementing controls that minimize the adverse impact of a threat that would exercise a vulnerability. Typically, the controls would come from the security architecture of controls that include the areas of avoidance, assurance, detective, or recovery controls.
5. *Risk planning.* This is a process where it is decided to manage risk by developing an architecture that prioritizes, implements, and maintains controls.
6. *Risk transference.* Here, management transfers the risk using other options to compensate for a loss such as purchasing an insurance policy.

Whichever risk mitigation technique is used, the business objectives or mission of an organization must be considered when selecting any of these techniques.

8.6 Control Categories

In the information security architecture there are four layers of controls. These layers begin with Avoidance, then Assurance, then Detection, and finally Recovery. Or you can create a set of controls that map to the enterprise, such as Operations, Applications, Systems, Security, etc. Mapping to some standard such as ISO 17799 is another option. When identifying possible controls, it could be beneficial to categorize controls into logical groupings. We examine two such groupings in Table 8.2 and Table 8.3.

Another way to map controls is by using some standard, such as ISO 17799 (see Table 8.3).

The new regulations of HIPAA, GLBA, and SOX will require all of us to include these controls in our risk analysis controls selection process. Table 8.4 provides a HIPAA controls list example. The numbers in parentheses are the matching section number found in ISO 17799. ISO17799 is actually "a comprehensive set of controls comprising best practices in information security." It is essentially, in part (extended), an internationally recognized generic information security standard.

Its predecessor, titled BS7799-1, has existed in various forms for a number of years, although the standard only really gained widespread recognition following publication by ISO (the International Standards Organization) in December 2000. Formal certification and accreditation were also introduced around the same time.

The object of the controls list is to identify categories of controls that will lead the team to determine the specific control required. When developing your list, be sure to be thorough but do not be so pedantic that the list of controls is similar to reading *War and Peace*.

8.7 Cost/Benefit Analysis

To allocate resources and implement cost-effective controls, organizations, after identifying all possible controls and evaluating their feasibility and effectiveness, should conduct a cost/benefit analysis. This process should be conducted for each new or enhanced control to determine if the control recommended is appropriate for the organization. A cost/benefit analysis should determine the impact of implementing the new or enhanced control and then determine the impact of not implementing the control.

Remember that one of the long-term costs of any control is the requirement to maintain its effectiveness. It is therefore necessary to factor this cost into the benefit requirement of any control. When performing a cost/benefit analysis, it is necessary to consider the cost of implementation based on some of the following:

■ Costs of implementation, including initial outlay for hardware and software
■ Reduction in operational effectiveness
■ Implementation of additional policies and procedures to support the new controls

TABLE 8.2   Controls List by IT Group

Application Controls	Application Control	Design and implement application controls (data entry edit checking, fields requiring validation, alarm indicators, password expiration capabilities, checksums) to ensure the integrity, confidentiality, and availability of application information.
Application Controls	Acceptance Testing	Develop testing procedures to be followed during applications development and during modifications to the existing application that include user participation and acceptance.
Application Controls	Training	Implement user programs (user performance evaluations) designed to encourage compliance with policies and procedures in place to ensure the appropriate utilization of the application.
Application Controls	Training	Application developers will provide documentation, guidance, and support to the operations staff (Operations) in implementing mechanisms to ensure that the transfer of information between applications is secure.
Application Controls	Corrective Strategies	The Development Team will develop corrective strategies such as reworked processes, revised application logic, etc.
Operations Controls	Backup	Backup requirements will be determined and communicated to Operations, including a request that an electronic notification that backups were completed be sent to the application System Administrator. Operations will be requested to test the backup procedures.
Operations Controls	Recovery Plan	Develop, document, and test recovery procedures designed to ensure that the application and information can be recovered, using the backups created, in the event of loss.
Operations Controls	Risk Analysis	Conduct a risk analysis to determine the level of exposure to identified threats and identify possible safeguards or controls.
Operations Controls	Anti-Virus	(1) Ensure LAN Administrator installs the corporate standard antiviral software on all computers. (2) Training and awareness of virus prevention techniques will be incorporated in the organization intrusion prevention program.

TABLE 8.2 (continued)   Controls List by IT Group

Operations Controls	Interface Dependencies	Systems that feed information will be identified and communicated to Operations to stress the impact to the functionality if these feeder applications are unavailable.
Operations Controls	Maintenance	Time requirements for technical maintenance will be tracked and a request for adjustment will be communicated to management if experience warrants.
Operations Controls	Service Level Agreement	Acquire service level agreements to establish level of customer expectations and assurances from supporting operations.
Operations Controls	Maintenance	Acquire maintenance and supplier agreements to facilitate the continued operational status of the application.
Operations Controls	Change Management	Production migration controls such as search and remove processes to ensure data stores are clean.
Operations Controls	Business Impact Analysis	A formal business impact analysis will be conducted to determine the asset's relative criticality with other enterprise assets.
Operations Controls	Backup	Training for a backup to the System Administrator will be provided and duties rotated between them to ensure the adequacy of the training program.
Operations Controls	Backup	A formal employee security awareness program has been implemented and is updated and presented to the employees at least on an annual basis.
Operations Controls	Recovery Plan	Access Sourced: Implement a mechanism to limit access to confidential information to specific network paths or physical locations.
Operations Controls	Risk Analysis	Implement user authentication mechanisms (such as firewalls, dial-in controls, Secure ID) to limit access to authorized personnel.
Physical Security	Physical Security	Conduct a risk analysis to determine the level of exposure to identified threats and identify possible safeguards or controls.
Security Controls	Security Awareness	Implement an access control mechanism to prevent unauthorized access to information. This mechanism will include the capability of detecting, logging and reporting attempts to breach the security of this information.

LIVERPOOL
JOHN MOORES UNIVERSITY
AVRIL ROBARTS LRC
TEL. 0151 231 4022

TABLE 8.2 (continued)   Controls List by IT Group

Security Controls	Access Control	Implement encryption mechanisms (data, end-to-end) to prevent unauthorized access to protect the integrity and confidentiality of information.
Security Controls	Access Control	Adhere to a change management process designed to facilitate a structured approach to modifications of the application, to ensure appropriate steps, and that precautions are followed. "Emergency" modifications should be included in this process.
Security Controls	Access Control	Control procedures are in place to ensure that appropriate system logs are reviewed by independent third parties to review system update activities.
Security Controls	Access Control	In consultation with Facilities Management, facilitate the implementation of physical security controls designed to protect the information, software, and hardware required of the system.
Security Controls	Policy	Develop policies and procedures to limit access and operating privileges to those with a business need.
Security Controls	Training	User training will include instruction and documentation on the proper use of the application. The importance of maintaining the confidentiality of user accounts, passwords, and the confidential and competitive nature of information will be stressed.
Security Controls	Review	Implement mechanisms to monitor, report, and audit activities identified as requiring independent reviews, including periodic reviews of user IDs to ascertain and verify the business need.
Security Controls	Asset Classification	The asset under review will be classified using enterprise policies, standards, and procedures on asset classification.
Security Controls	Access Control	Mechanisms to protect the database against unauthorized access, and modifications made from outside the application, will be determined and implemented.

TABLE 8.2 (continued)   Controls List by IT Group

Security Controls	Management Support	Request management support to ensure the cooperation and coordination of various business units.
Security Controls	Proprietary	Processes are in place to ensure that company proprietary assets are protected and that the company is in compliance with all third-party license agreements.
Systems Controls	Change Management	Backup requirements will be determined and communicated to Operations, including a request that an electronic notification that backups were completed be sent to the application System Administrator. Operations will be requested to test the backup procedures.
Systems Controls	Monitor System Logs	Develop, document, and test all recovery procedures designed to ensure that the application and information can be recovered, using the backups created, in the event of loss.

- Cost of possibly hiring additional staff or, at a minimum, training existing staff in the new controls
- Cost of educating support personnel to maintain the effectiveness of the control

8.8 Summary

Practically no system or activity is risk-free, and not all implemented controls can eliminate the risk they intend to address. The purpose of risk management is to analyze the business risks of a process, application, system, or other asset to determine the most prudent method for safe operation. The risk analysis team reviews these assets with the business objectives as their primary consideration. We neither want, nor can we use a control mechanism that reduces risk to zero. A security program that has as its goal one-hundred percent security will cause the organization to have zero percent productivity.

The risk analysis process has two key objectives: (1) to implement only those controls necessary and (2) to document management's due diligence. As security professionals we are aware that our goal is to provide support for the organization and to ensure that management objectives are met. By implementing an effective risk management and risk analysis process, this objective will be met and embraced by our user community.

LIVERPOOL JOHN MOORES UNIVERSITY
LEARNING SERVICES

TABLE 8.3   Control List using ISO 17799

ISO 17799 Section	Category	Control Description
Security Policy	Policy (3.1)	Develop and implement an Information Security Policy.
Organizational Security	Management Information Security Forum (4.1)	Establish a corporate committee to oversee information security. Develop and implement an Information Security Organization mission statement.
Organizational Security	Security of Third-Party Access (4.2)	Implement a process to analyze third-party connection risks and implement specific security standards to combat third-party connection risks.
Organizational Security	Security Requirements in Outsourcing Contracts (4.3)	Implement standards and user training to ensure that virus detection and prevention measures are adequate.
Asset Classification and Control	Accounting of Assets (5.1)	Establish an inventory of major assets associated with each information system.
Asset Classification and Control	Information Classification (5.2)	Implement standards for security classification of the level of protection required for information assets.
Asset Classification and Control	Information Labeling and Handling (5.2)	Implement standards to ensure the proper handling of information assets.
Personnel Security	Security in Job Descriptions (6.1)	Ensure that security responsibilities are included in employee job descriptions.
Personnel Security	User Training ((6.2)	Implement training standards to ensure that users are trained in information security policies and procedures, security requirements, business controls, and correct use of IT facilities.
Personnel Security	Responding to Security Incidents and Malfunctions (6.3)	Implement procedures and standards for formal reporting and incident response action to be taken on receipt of an incident report.

TABLE 8.3 (continued)   Control List using ISO 17799

ISO 17799 Section	Category	Control Description
Physical and Environmental Security	Secure Areas (7.1)	Implement standards to ensure that physical security protection exists, based on defined perimeters through strategically located barriers throughout the organization.
Physical & Environmental Security	Equipment Security (7.2)	Implement standards to ensure that equipment is located properly to reduce risks of environmental hazards and unauthorized access.
Physical & Environmental Security	General Controls (7.3)	Implement a clear desk/clear screen policy for sensitive material to reduce risks of unauthorized access, loss, or damage outside normal working hours.
Communications and Operations Management	Documented Operating Procedures (8.1)	Implement operating procedures to clearly document that all operational computer systems are being operated in a correct, secure manner.
Communications and Operations Management	System Planning and Acceptance (8.2)	Implement standards to ensure that capacity requirements are monitored, and future requirements projected, to reduce the risk of system overload.
Communications and Operations Management	Protection from Malicious Software (8.3)	Implement standards and user training to ensure that virus detection and prevention measures are adequate.
Communications and Operations Management	Housekeeping (8.4)	Establish procedures for making regular backup copies of essential business data and software to ensure that it can be recovered following a computer disaster or media failure.
Communications and Operations Management	Network Management (8.5)	Implement appropriate standards to ensure the security of data in networks and the protection of connected services from unauthorized access.
Communications and Operations Management	Media Handling and Security (8.6)	Implement procedures for the management of removable computer media such as tapes, disks, cassettes, and printed reports.

TABLE 8.3 (continued)   Control List using ISO 17799

ISO 17799 Section	Category	Control Description
Communications and Operations Management	Exchanges of Information and Software (8.7)	Implement procedures to establish that formal agreements exist, including software escrow agreements when appropriate, for exchanging data and software (whether electronically or manually) between organizations.
Access Control	Business requirement for System Access (9.1)	Implement a risk analysis process to gather business requirements to document access control levels.
Access Control	User Access Management (9.2)	Implement procedures for user registration and deregistration access to all multiuse IT services.
Access Control	User Responsibility (9.3)	Implement user training to ensure that users have been taught good security practices in the selection and use of passwords.
Access Control	Network Access Control (9.4)	Implement procedures to ensure that network and computer services that can be accessed by an individual user or from a particular terminal are consistent with business access control policy.
Access Control	Operating System Access Control (9.5)	Implement standards for automatic terminal identification to authenticate connections to specific locations.
Access Control	Application Access Control (9.6)	Implement procedures to restrict access to applications system data and functions in accordance with defined access policy and based on individual requirements.
Access Control	Monitoring System Access and Use (9.7)	Implement standards to have audit trails record exceptions and other security-relevant information, and that they are maintained to assist in future investigations and in access control monitoring.
Access Control	Remote Access and Telecommuting (9.8)	Implement a formal policy and supporting standards that address the risks of working with mobile computing facilities, including requirements for physical protection, access controls, cryptographic techniques, backup, and virus protection.

TABLE 8.3 (continued)   Control List using ISO 17799

ISO 17799 Section	Category	Control Description
Systems Development and Maintenance	Security Requirements of Systems (10.1)	Implement standards to ensure that analysis of security requirements is part of the requirement analysis stage of each development project.
Systems Development and Maintenance	Security in Application Systems (10.2)	Implement standards to ensure that data input into applications systems is validated to ensure that it is correct and appropriate.
Systems Development and Maintenance	Cryptography (10.3)	Implement policies and standards on the use of cryptographic controls, including management of encryption keys, and effective implementation.
Systems Development and Maintenance	Security of System Files (10.4)	Implement standards. Is there strict control exercised over the implementation of software on operational systems?
Systems Development and Maintenance	Security in Development and Support Environments (10.5)	Implement standards and procedures for formal change control procedures.
Business Continuity Management	Aspects of Business Continuity Planning (11.1)	Implement procedures for the development and maintenance of business continuity plans across the organization.
Compliance	Compliance with Legal Requirements (12.1)	Implement standards to ensure that all relevant statutory, regulatory, and contractual requirements are specifically defined and documented for each information system.
Compliance	Reviews of Security Policy and Technical Compliances (12.2)	Implement standards to ensure that all areas within the organization are considered for regular review to ensure compliance with security policies and standards.

TABLE 8.4   HIPAA Controls List

Control Number	HIPAA Section	Category	Control Description
Administrative			
1	Risk Analysis	Security Management Process	Conduct an accurate and thorough assessment of the potential risks and vulnerabilities to the confidentiality, integrity, and availability of Electronically Protected Health Information (EPHI).
2	Risk Management	Security Management Process	Implement security measures sufficient to reduce risks and vulnerabilities to a reasonable and appropriate level.
3	Sanction Policy	Security Management Process	Apply appropriate sanctions against workforce members who fail to comply with the security policies and procedures of the covered entity.
4	Information System Activity Review	Security Management Process	Implement procedures to regularly review records of information systems activity.
5	Privacy Officer	Assigned Security Responsibility	Identify a single person responsible for the development and implementation of the policies and procedures supporting HIPAA compliance.
6	Authorization/ Supervision	Workforce Security	Implement procedures for the authorization and supervision of workforce members who work with EPHI or in locations where it might be accessed.
7	Workforce Clearance Procedure	Workforce Security	Implement procedures to determine that the access of a workforce member to EPHI is appropriate.
8	Termination Procedure	Workforce Security	Implement procedures for terminating access to EPHI when the employment of a workforce member ends or as required by access authorization policies.

TABLE 8.4 (continued)   HIPAA Controls List

Control Number	HIPAA Section	Category	Control Description
9	Isolate Healthcare Clearinghouse Functions	Information Access Management	If a Covered Entity (CE) operates a healthcare clearinghouse, it must implement policies and procedures to protect the EPHI maintained by the clearinghouse from unauthorized access by the larger organization.
10	Access Authorization	Information Access Management	Implement policies and procedures for granting access to EPHI, for example, through access to a workstation, transaction, program, process, or other mechanism.
11	Access Establishment and Modification	Information Access Management	Implement policies and procedures that, based on the entity's access authorization policies, establish, document, review, and modify a user's right of access to a workstation, transaction, program, or process.
12	Security Reminders	Security Awareness and Training	Implement a security awareness and training program for all members of the workforce, including management.
13	Protection from Malicious Software	Security Awareness and Training	Periodic security reminders.
14	Log-in Monitoring	Security Awareness and Training	Procedures guarding against, detecting, and reporting malicious software.
15	Password Management	Security Awareness and Training	Procedures to monitor log-in attempts and report discrepancies.

TABLE 8.4 (continued)   HIPAA Controls List

Control Number	HIPAA Section	Category	Control Description
16	Response and Reporting	Security Incident Procedures	Identify and respond to suspected or known security incidents; mitigate, to the extent practicable, harmful effects of the security incidents that are known to the CE; and document security incidents and their outcomes.
17	Data Backup	Contingency Plan	Establish and implement procedures to create and maintain retrievable exact copies of EPHI.
18	Disaster Recovery Plan	Contingency Plan	Establish (and implement as needed) procedures to restore any loss of data.
19	Emergency Mode Operations Plan	Contingency Plan	Establish (and implement as needed) procedures to enable continuation of critical business processes to assure access to EPHI and to provide for adequate protection of EPHI while operating in emergency mode.
20	Testing and Revision Procedures	Contingency Plan	Implement procedures for periodic testing and revision of contingency plans.
21	Applications and Data Criticality	Contingency Plan	Assess the relative criticality of specific applications and data in support of other contingency plan components.

Physical Safeguards

Control Number	HIPAA Section	Category	Control Description
22	Contingency Operations	Facility Access Control	Establish (and implement as needed) procedures that allow facility access in support of restoration of lost data under the disaster recovery plan and emergency mode operations plan in the event of an emergency.

TABLE 8.4 (continued)   HIPAA Controls List

Control Number	HIPAA Section	Category	Control Description
23	Facility Security Plan	Facility Access Control	Implement policies and procedures to safeguard the facility and the equipment therein from unauthorized physical access, tampering, and theft.
24	Access Control and Validation Procedures	Facility Access Control	Implement procedures to control and validate a person's access to facilities based on their role or function, including visitor control, and control of access to software programs for testing and revision.
25	Maintenance Records	Facility Access Control	Implement policies and procedures to document repairs and modifications to the physical components of a facility that are related to security.
26	Workstation Security	Workstation Use	Implement physical safeguards for all workstations that access EPHI to restrict access to authorized users.
27	Disposal	Device and Media Control	Implement policies and procedures to address the final disposition of EPHI and the hardware or electronic media on which it is stored.
28	Media Re-use	Device and Media Control	Implement procedures for removal of EPHI from electronic media prior to re-use.
29	Accountability	Device and Media Control	Maintain a record of the movement of hardware and software and any person responsible for movement.
30	Data Backup and Storage	Device and Media Control	Create a retrievable, exact copy of EPHI, when needed, prior to moving equipment.

TABLE 8.4 (continued)   HIPAA Controls List

Control Number	HIPAA Section	Category	Control Description
Technical Safeguards			
31	Unique User Identification	Access Control	Assign a unique name and number for identifying and tracking user identity.
32	Emergency Access Procedure	Access Control	Establish (and implement as needed) procedures for obtaining necessary EPHI during an emergency.
33	Automatic Logoff	Access Control	Implement electronic procedures that terminate an electronic session after a predetermined time of inactivity.
34	Encryption and Decryption	Access Control	Implement a mechanism to encrypt and decrypt EPHI.
35	Integrity	Audit Controls	Implement policies and procedures to protect EPHI from improper alteration or destruction.
36	Business Associate Contracts	Transmission Security	The contract between the CE and its BA must meet the [following] requirements, as applicable: A CE is not in compliance if it knew of a pattern of activity or practice of the BA that constituted a material breach or violation of the BA's obligation under the contract, unless the CE took reasonable steps to cure the breach or end the violation and, if such steps were unsuccessful, to: (A) terminate the contract, if feasible; or (B) report the problem to the Secretary of HHS, if not.

TABLE 8.4 (continued)   HIPAA Controls List

Control Number	HIPAA Section	Category	Control Description
37	Documentation	Policies and Procedures	Maintain the policies and procedures required by the security rule in writing which may be electronic; and if an action, activity, or assessment is required to be documented, maintain a written record, which may be electronic.
38	Time Limit	Policies and Procedures	Retain the documentation required by the Security Rule for six years from the date of its creation or the date when it was last in effect, whichever is later.
39	Availability	Policies and Procedures	Make documentation available to those persons responsible for implementing the procedures to which the documentation pertains.
40	Updates		Review documentation periodically, and update as needed, in response to environmental and operational changes affecting the security of the EPHI.

Chapter 9

Business Continuity Planning

9.1 Overview

Business continuity planning is the process of ensuring that your organization can continue doing business even when its normal facilities or place of business is unavailable. In earlier years, many companies undertook what they called "disaster recovery planning" — which was nothing more than making sure that their computer operations could be resumed as quickly as necessary when the data center was unavailable. When companies tested their "disaster recovery plans," some of them realized that being able to recover data center operations was all very well but pointless if the organization's offices and other places of business — where the functions provided by the data center were used — were also unavailable.

Business continuity plans should certainly contain plans for recovering the functionality of the data center, but the focus of a business continuity plan must be to return the organization to a "business as usual" state (or as close to it as possible) as quickly as possible after a disruptive event. Disruptive events can indeed be catastrophic — as indicated by the old title of "disaster recovery plan" or in such instances as what occurred at the World Trade Center in 2001 — but are more frequently mundane in character. For example, one company I know of had its front-office (as opposed to data center) operations interrupted by a lightning strike on an electricity transformer on the corner of the block. Hardly a "disaster" in itself, but it did interrupt the electricity supply to the building, which the local fire marshal promptly evacuated, requiring the company to enact its business continuity plan.

Business continuity plans are notoriously difficult to sell to senior management, and that is a cause for frustration among information security professionals. Creating and testing a business continuity plan (BCP) is a very significant commitment of resources, and many executives take a wait-and-see approach to dealing with the risk of business interruption. Some organization managers (in some cases quite rightly) take the position that the organization's insurance coverage will provide in the event of an interruption of normal business processes; but in most cases, no amount of insurance payment will compensate for the loss of a business that was slow to or failed to recover after a business interruption.

An approach to convincing reluctant organization managers to undertake business continuity planning is to break the process into components and "sell" each component on its own values. This chapter examines the components of a business continuity plan. It should be noted here that this chapter is not an exhaustive guide to business continuity planning. There are many fine organizations and publications dedicated to this activity, and this chapter is meant only as a guide to the most common and necessary components of the business continuity planning process.

9.2 Business Continuity Planning Policy

All components of an information security program depend for their legitimacy on a policy statement that says, in effect, that "the organization will do this and will do it because...." Business continuity planning policy must serve the same purpose and must conform to the same requirements as every other information security policy.

A policy is a high-level statement of beliefs and objectives for the enterprise. Because it is high level, it must be brief; and being brief increases its readability. When writing a policy, it is as dangerous to say too much as it is to say too little. An organization's policy will almost certainly go through a rigorous process of review and comment by the organization's senior management. That process is time consuming and therefore costly, and it drives us to make sure that the process is invoked as seldom as possible. The implication is that a policy must be as close to timeless as possible. In other words, the contents of the policy should remain unchanged for as long as possible. This contributes a reason for the policy to be brief — the more content included in a policy, the more likely it is that the policy will need change.

A business continuity planning policy should be easy to understand (it is sometimes suggested that our audience's comprehension level is sixth grade) and should be applicable to the organization for which it is written — it should describe the needs of the organization and not simply be a generic statement of BCP requirements. The BCP policy should be enforceable; it should not contain only statements of "motherhood and apple pie" sentimentality but should use language that allows measurement of compliance. The policy should also clearly support the business objectives of the organization.

The actual format of the policy will depend on what policies normally look like in your organization. This is important because the policy must be reviewed, and those who are reviewing it will have a problem if it does not immediately look like other policies in the enterprise.

In general, a policy should contain four sections:

1. Policy statement
2. Scope
3. Responsibilities
4. Compliance

9.2.1   Policy Statement

This is where we say what our policy is regarding business continuity planning. It may seem too obvious to be worth explaining, but a remarkable number of organizations do publish "policies" that lack any discernable statement of what the policy actually is.

9.2.2   Scope

The scope establishes to whom the policy applies. Very often, the scope says nothing more than "all employees" but some policies require more detail — for example, when the policy applies in different ways depending on whether employees are full-time, contract, or temporary.

9.2.3   Responsibilities

Here the policy states "who does what" in relation to applying the policy throughout the organization. It is advisable that, when talking about responsibilities, we stay away from naming individuals and stick to talking about positions — Senior Management, Information Security, etc.

9.2.4 Compliance

This is a statement of how compliance with the policy is going to be measured and, equally important, a statement of what will happen when noncompliance or willful breach of a policy is discovered.

Taking all of the above, a business continuity planning policy for your organization might look like that one in Table 9.1.

9.3 Conducting a Business Impact Analysis (BIA)

Having said that there are many excellent sources of information on business continuity planning, business impact analysis (BIA) is such an important part of "getting it right" in continuity planning that we should look at it in detail here.

We conduct BIAs to find out the "maximum tolerable outage" for each of our organization's business processes. That is, we need to know — for each business process — the maximum length of time the organization can tolerate being without the process before its absence has a significant impact on our ability to continue to do business. Establishing the "maximum tolerable outage" for a business process is the same as establishing the recovery time objective — which, in turn, will be an input when we start to choose what our continuity planning strategy will be. (Continuity planning strategy, while not discussed in this book, is the process of using the output of the BIA to determine whether we will base our continuity plans on a "hot" — or fully equipped and ready to go — site or some other, less fully equipped version.)

The methods for conducting a BIA can be many and varied; thus, in this book we discuss the most basic method: individual interviewing and information collation. There are some prerequisites for the interview process, however; steps we must take to make sure that the process goes smoothly and that the information produced by the interviews is accepted as valid.

9.3.1 Identify Sponsor(s)

We need a sponsor for the BIA as we will be taking up time with members of staff in every business department (or a number of departments in a limited-scope BIA). The sponsor must carry some authority over the organization (or the part of the organization we will examine) so that he or she can require cooperation with the BIA process. The sponsor is also involved in reviewing the results of the BIA and in testing the results for "sanity."

TABLE 9.1   Sample BCP Policy

Policy:

It is the policy of the (organization name) that it will create and maintain a Business Continuity Plan that will ensure the ability to continue to operate in the event that access to normal business facilities is denied for any reason other than lawful intervention. The following measures will support those plans:

- A process to develop and maintain business continuity plans across the organization is in place.
- (Organization name) will maintain a single business continuity plan framework to ensure that all levels of the plan are consistent, and to identify priorities for testing and maintenance.
- (Organization name) will carry out regular tests of business continuity plans — as defined in the standards that support this policy — to ensure that they are effective.
- Regular updates to the business continuity plan will be carried out to protect the investment in developing the initial plan, and to ensure its continuing effectiveness.

Scope:

This policy applies to all business operations of (organization name). It is intended that each business unit — defined at the level of those units managed by a Vice President — create and maintain its own business continuity plan and make sure it is compatible with the overall business continuity plan of (organization name).

Responsibilities:

(Organization name) officers and senior management have the responsibility to ensure that the measures listed in the policy statement are implemented effectively.

Compliance:

(Organization name) officers and senior management are required to ensure that internal audit mechanisms exist to monitor and measure compliance with this policy.

(Organization name) line management has the responsibility to communicate the content of this policy, to measure compliance with this policy, and to take appropriate action in areas of noncompliance.

All (organization name) employees, regardless of their status (permanent, part-time, contract, etc.), are required to comply with this policy. Failure to comply with this policy will lead to disciplinary measures that may include dismissal.

9.3.2 Scope

Many organizations are too large to conduct a BIA for every unit in the enterprise at roughly the same time. Where that is the case, we must identify which business units are going to participate in the BIA and — having acquired a sponsor with authority over those business units — clearly define the boundaries of the units and, by doing so, define the boundaries of the BIA. The boundaries can be defined by physical limits such as a specific location, by points in the business process (for example, when an invoice leaves a unit where it has been approved and goes to a unit where it can be processed for payment), or by organizational authority — perhaps all of the business units that report to a specific manager or officer of the organization.

9.3.3 Information Meeting

Having defined the scope of the BIA, the next step is to prepare and deliver information about the BIA to the management of the business unit(s) that will be participating. The information meeting should tell managers — in detail — what is going to happen (how the BIA will be conducted), what is required (the kind of information that will be gathered), what will be done with the information gathered and what the managers need to do — which is passed on to their staff — with what they have learned in the information meeting and to nominate appropriate staff to participate in the BIA.

9.3.4 Information Gathering

The success of the BIA depends on gathering accurate information about the business processes in the organization. To gather accurate information, we must learn as much about the organization as we can before beginning the BIA. This means gathering as much of the following as possible:

- *Organization and people:* organization charts and other information that identifies people and what they do; telephone directories can be helpful.
- *Locations and numbers:* maps of physical locations and the number of people working at each location.
- *Constraints:* an understanding of any constraints on the BIA, such as times of the day or week when it is not convenient to schedule interviews.

9.3.5 Questionnaire Design

Once the sponsor and scope of the BIA have been identified and the initial information meeting held, we can begin to design the questionnaire that we will use during the BIA. The use of a questionnaire is critical because it ensures that everyone participating will be answering the same set of questions about their business; and if we prepare questionnaire support documents correctly, everyone will receive the same set of help and instructions on how to answer the questions.

A simple BIA questionnaire is included in this chapter. In this questionnaire, respondents are asked to complete information about themselves, the department in which they work, and the business function they are about to describe. It follows then that a separate questionnaire must be completed for each business function included in the scope of the BIA.

The next part of the questionnaire deals with business processes — again implying that a form must be completed for each business process in each department in the scope. The questionnaire asks the respondent to describe each business process, how often the process is performed (hourly, daily, etc.), and what critical time periods exist for each process. This last section requires that the respondent complete information on times that are particularly important to the completion of each process, such as closing dates for payroll entry, lead times for check printing, etc.

The questionnaire asks the respondent to give an indication of the length of time the organization could continue to function without this business process. Here, the respondent is being asked to judge what would happen if the process did not execute for given periods of time (four hours, twelve hours, etc.). It is important that the respondent is encouraged to think about the process from end-to-end — that is, the impact on the organization if the process did not happen at all — as we do not intend to do the BIA on a lower lever of granularity than the process as a whole.

Finally, the questionnaire requires the respondent to list resources required to carry out the process in normal business circumstances and those required to carry out the process in a recovery situation. While these two entries may often be the same, they are sometimes not; and identifying the times when they are different can be a difficult process. This process is discussed more fully in the section entitled "Conducting Interviews" (Section 9.3.7).

More complex BIA questionnaires can be used to gather more information and produce more detailed information on the criticality of business processes. For example, a complex BIA questionnaire — in addition to the information gathered on the simple one — might ask for information on:

- Service level agreements to which the process in question must be performed
- The financial impact of the failure to perform the process
- The financial contribution made to the organization by the performance of the process
- The nonfinancial impacts (organization image, customer confidence, etc.) of the failure to perform the process
- The dependencies that exist between the process in question and other processes or functions
- The IT applications used in the process

9.3.6 Scheduling the Interviews

When preparatory steps are being completed, we need to consider a few things about scheduling the interviews themselves. The first thing to consider is the impact on the staff. A comprehensive BIA will rely on responses from a large number of staff members and, because BIA interviews can take a significant amount of time, careful scheduling is required to avoid compromising the ability of a business unit to carry out its business while interviews are going on.

At this point, the remainder of the BIA consists of conducting interviews, tabulating the results of those interviews, and presenting those results; thus, it might be worthwhile pausing to take a look at a graphic that represents the process so far. The graphic is shown in Figure 9.1.

FIGURE 9.1   BIA Partial Process

9.3.7 Conducting Interviews

Prior to scheduling and conducting BIA interviews, we should have identified the sponsor of the BIA and, through information meetings, equipped business unit managers to inform all who will be involved in the BIA of what will happen and what is expected of them.

In addition, it is important that we equip ourselves with a meaningful questionnaire for the BIA — along with supporting documents that explain the purpose of the BIA and how to answer the questions. We should have provided a copy of the BIA questionnaire and instructions — in advance of the interview — to everyone who will be asked to complete a questionnaire.

The purpose of the interview is to complete the questionnaire. During the interview, it may be necessary to take notes in addition to the information gathered on the questionnaire — as the perfect questionnaire has yet to be designed. The notes might comment on such things as peak processing times, critical periods in the process, and the resources needed to recover the process.

The subject of resources may be the most difficult part of the interview. When asked to count the number of people, for example, who are necessary to conduct the process in normal business circumstances and then to estimate the number necessary to conduct the process in a recovery situation, the interview subject might be tempted to give the same number. Reasons for this might include an unwillingness to give the impression that the process is currently overstaffed. It is helpful, at this stage in the interview, to ask the interview subject to imagine that a recovery situation would require less interaction with staff from other departments or having their staff work a slightly longer day than is necessary.

9.3.8 Tabulating the Information

It is important that the information gathered from the interview be tabulated as soon as possible after concluding the interview. It is human nature to decide to take a note of some detail, believing that we will surely remember it, and then forget it if we allow too much time to elapse between the interview and tabulating the results of the interview.

Tabulating the information from the interviews should include producing summary sheets showing a list of the processes analyzed and the relative criticality of each. How to show the relative criticality is a matter of choice (ranked by maximum allowable outage, ranked in ABC order, assigned a numerical value) and is less important than explaining the meaning of the rankings to all involved.

Results must be tabulated in a number of different ways for different purposes during the remainder of the continuity planning process. For

TABLE 9.2   Business Processes by Maximum Tolerable Outage

Business Unit	Maximum Tolerable Outage	Business Process	IT Service
Wire transfer	0 hours	Retail account funds transfer	Wide area network SWIFT terminal Account maintenance
	0 hours	Reconciliation	Account balance
Account enquiries	8 hours	Account enquiries	Wide area network Account balance

example, at some point in the process of deciding on a continuity strategy, we will have to tabulate the resources required for each process. However, the two most common needs for tabulated data are to show the business processes ranked by maximum tolerable outage and to show the business processes supported by each IT service. An example of each of these tables is shown in Table 9.2.

9.3.9   Presenting the Results

The tabulated results (see Table 9.3) of the interviews should be reported back to each interview participant, and participants should be asked to verify that the results fairly show the information they gave.

TABLE 9.3   Tabulated Results — Business Processes by IT Service

IT Service	Business Unit	Time-Critical Business Function	Maximum Tolerable Downtime
Wide area network	Wire Transfer	Retail account funds transfer	0 hours
		Reconciliation	0 hours
	Account enquiries	Account enquiries	8 hours
SWIFT terminal	Wire Transfer	Retail account funds transfer	0 hours
Account maintenance	Wire Transfer	Retail account funds transfer	0 hours
Account balance	Wire Transfer	Reconciliation	0 hours
	Account enquiries	Account enquiries	8 hours

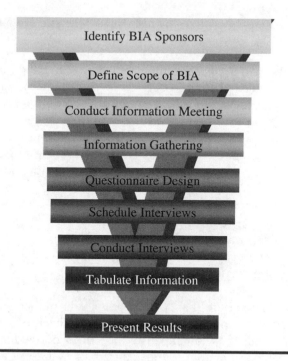

FIGURE 9.2 The BIA Process

When the results have been verified by the interview subjects, the entire tabulation should be presented to the BIA sponsor, who will be invited to review the results in light of his or her knowledge of the business carried out by the departments analyzed. It is not uncommon for this review to result in a revisitation of some parts of the interview process, as the sponsor may be able to lend a better perspective to the relative importance of the various business processes involved and the resources estimated in the BIA.

When the results have been reviewed, revisited if necessary, and then retabulated, they can be presented to the sponsor once again and used as input to the next step of the BCP process — the strategy selection. Once again, there are many excellent works discussing strategy selection and therefore that detail of BCP will not be discussed here.

To revisit, when the interviews have been concluded and the results tabulated and presented, the entire BIA process can be represented by the graphic shown in Figure 9.2.

9.4 Preventive Controls

Another fundamental part of business continuity planning is preventive controls. Every organization should do some kind of business continuity planning; but for some, that will take no other form of examining their preventive controls and, having deemed them to be sufficient, do nothing else.

Having performed a business impact analysis (BIA), the next major step in business continuity planning (BCP) is to use the information from the BIA as input to our selection of a strategy for recovering critical business processes. Along the way, and before we select our strategy, it is necessary to recognize what preventive controls exist in our organization — controls that might save us money and effort when we pursue our BCP strategy.

The types of preventive controls we are looking for include:

- Information security controls
- Environmental security
- Physical security
- Disaster recovery plans (i.e., existing plans to recovery IT capabilities)
- Information security awareness programs

It should be noted here that some works list insurance as a preventive control. Strictly speaking, insurance is not a preventive control but a compensatory control, as having insurance does not reduce the risk of anything happening; it simply reduces the financial impact after an event.

In examining preventive controls, we will have to gather evidence of the existence and nature of the controls and to do that we will be looking for documents and talking to key people. Table 9.4 sets out the kind of data we are looking for and the key people to whom we should be talking.

Information about preventive controls (and, indeed, the compensatory control insurance), like the information from the BIA, must be presented to the interview subjects and used as input to the next step in the planning process — strategy selection.

9.5 Recovery Strategies

Development of a recovery strategy is the last stage before developing the recovery plan itself. Developing a recovery strategy lends itself well to the workshop format because it requires a very effective, real-time sharing of information and views. The purpose of the workshop is to determine which recovery strategy is most appropriate for our organization and document that (and the path to our decision) so that the strategy can be approved by senior management (if they are not present at the workshop) and our recovery planners can begin to construct the BCP.

Attendance at the workshop should be mandatory for every department for which a recovery plan is to be built. It is also desirable that the senior

TABLE 9.4   Preventive Control Information

Preventive Control	Data Sought	Interview Subjects
Information security	Information security policies, standards, and procedures	Information security management, internal audit, IT management, selected business unit management
Environmental security	Facilities plans and environmental controls diagrams	Facilities management, risk management, physical security management, data center management, internal audit
Physical security	Facilities diagrams, physical security policies	Facilities management, physical security management (if different than facilities management), internal audit
Disaster recovery plans	Existing recovery plans, plan test reports	Recovery plan management, data center management, internal audit
Information security awareness	Information security awareness plans and status reports, awareness materials	Information security management, internal audit, IT management, selected business unit management

management member(s) who will approve the selected recovery strategy also attend the workshop but we recognize the real-word difficulty in making this happen.

9.5.1   Hot Site, Cold Site, Warm Site, Mobile Site

As the purpose of the recovery strategy workshop is to determine the most appropriate recovery strategy for our organization, before discussing the process for selecting that strategy we should discuss some key terms.

Part of selecting the recovery strategy will be to determine what type of facility we will need to use while executing our recovery plan. Some of that determination will be based on our need to recover IT facilities, and that need will be dictated by the results of our BIA. Where the BIA indicates that certain IT facilities must be available within four hours of a business interruption, for example, we may be looking at a need for a hot site. By the same token, if the first IT system is not needed until 24 hours after a business interruption, then a warm site may suffice.

To explain the differences in these terms and the terms in the heading to this section, we will have to look at three aspects of the terms: (1) what

TABLE 9.5 Recovery Site Characteristics

Recovery Site Type	Characteristics
Hot site	A site equipped with everything necessary to "walk in and resume business immediately." Typically has all the equipment needed for the enterprise to continue operation, including office space and furniture, telephones, and computer equipment. In the case of a data center hot site, generally equipped with computer equipment in a specialized environment, system software, and applications. Data may be "mirrored" to the hot site or brought in from a backup storage area.
Warm site	A site equipped with basic necessities such as office space, furniture, and telephone jacks. In the case of a data center warm site, generally equipped with computer equipment but not system software, applications, or data.
Cold site	A site that is a bare workspace, generally providing heat, light, and power — but little or nothing else.

the terms mean in relation to the services provided by each; (2) what each type of site costs; and (3) what BIA requirements might demand each type of site. For the purposes of these figures, two recovery-site terms are combined into the terms listed. A "mirror" site is an example of a hot site where data and transactions processed at the original site are also processed, in real-time, at the recovery site. A "mobile" site can be an example of any one of the three sites — depending on how the mobile facility is equipped — and thus will also not be listed separately.

Table 9.5 shows characteristics of the three types of sites being considered in our recovery strategy selection workshop.

In terms of cost — as might be expected — hot site recovery facilities are much more expensive than cold site facilities. The ability to walk into a recovery facility and immediately begin exercising the recovery plan requires an investment in equipment and time that will be recouped by the fees charged to users of the site.

The cost of recovery facilities can vary, depending on the type of agreement used to secure the site. A purely commercial agreement, in which our organization (the client) agrees to pay for a recovery site operated by a vendor of recovery services, will generally require an up-front fee plus a monthly "subscription" fee, and, in many cases, a fee to access the site when necessary. (Some vendors of recovery site services allow a fixed number of "free" accesses for testing recovery plans.)

Another type of agreement is a reciprocal agreement: one in which our company and a company with similar requirements and facilities agree

TABLE 9.6   Recovery Timescales

Recovery Site	Must Recover Critical Systems In
Hot site	2–12 hours
Warm site	12–24 hours
Cold site	24 hours or more

to provide each other with space and facilities in which to recover business or data processing operations in the event that one company's facilities become inaccessible. Of course, this type of agreement is much less expensive than the previous example offered, but consideration must be given to the practicalities of the recovery situation and testing of recovery plans. Many companies enter reciprocal agreements and then find that maintaining their site to accommodate their agreement partners' recovery requirements is costly and inconvenient. Another inconvenience to consider is the agreement partner's need to access our site to test their recovery plans (and what disruption that might cause to our "normal" operations of the time).

Whatever the prices of the various options available for recovery facilities, the choice will largely be driven by the results of the BIA. For example, there is little point in choosing the least expensive option for recovery sites (cold site) if the BIA indicates that business operations or data center operations must be resumed within four hours of interruption — four hours is clearly not long enough to equip a cold site with the furniture, equipment, and systems necessary to resume operations for even a small company. Table 9.6 gives an indication of the thresholds of time that can be met by each type of recovery site. For each entry in the table, we are assuming that the recovery requirement is to recover data center operations (because these are generally more complex and time consuming than other business operations) and that a good standard of backup has been operated so that up-to-date applications and data are available for recovery.

9.5.2   Key Considerations

The objective of the recovery strategy selection workshop is to translate the results of the BIA into requirements for recovery strategy. Whether these are requirements for recovering computing resources or for recovering other business processes, the purpose is to determine the technical and human requirements for recovering the ability to carry out the process.

In general, there are four areas to consider when choosing a recovery strategy.

9.5.2.1 People

For each critical business process identified in the BIA, we should also identify the number of people necessary to restore that business function, the skill sets that these people should have, and, by default, what people or skill sets might not be necessary in a recovery situation. Not all departments or staff will be necessary to recover most business processes.

9.5.2.2 Communications

- *Voice*. Phone service is very often a critical resource needed to restore normal business operations. We must know (from the BIA) what provisions we have to make to not only set up voice communications at the recovery site, but also to divert our normal phone services from the affected site to the recovery site (so that customers calling our normal phone numbers are automatically diverted to the phones at the recovery site).
- *Data*. As with phone service, the BIA should provide us with an estimate of what is needed — at a recovery site — in terms of data communications. When we determine our recovery strategy and select a recovery site, this information will provide specifications for the data network that must exist at the recovery site.

9.5.2.3 Computing Equipment

- Mainframe hardware resources (also includes midrange)
- Mainframe data storage requirements, usually expressed in gigabytes
- Unique (i.e., nonstandard) hardware resources
- Departmental computing needs (e.g., PCs, LANs, WANs)
- Distributed systems
- IT systems supporting E-commerce activities

9.5.2.4 Facilities

Once the above — and the physical furniture and equipment requirements — from the BIA have been calculated, we can use them to define the physical facility requirements.

The availability of all these resources must be considered when choosing a recovery strategy. If we are choosing a vendor for a recovery site (as opposed to a reciprocal agreement), we must communicate our requirements to selected vendors in a Request for Proposal (RFP) to allow the vendors to compete for the business of providing a recovery facility. In the event that we opt for a reciprocal agreement, we will use the requirements we have defined in our recovery strategy selection workshop to define the facilities our agreement partner must make available.

9.6. Plan Construction, Testing, and Maintenance

9.6.1 Plan Construction

When a recovery strategy has been selected, work can begin on creating the recovery plan itself. To be more accurate, work will begin on creating all the individual recovery plans that go into making up the complete recovery plan.

The overall recovery plan for our organization — or the part of the organization that was within the scope of the BIA — is a shell or template in which we fit the recovery plans of component parts of the organization. The overall recovery plan is managed by the plan manager, who trains individuals in business units to contribute recovery plans for their business units and those recovery plans are in a format that fits the overall recovery plan.

Each business unit's recovery plan will contain the procedures and documentation needed for that business unit to resume operations in a recovery facility. With the exception of Facilities Management and IT, each business unit's plans will assume that the recovery facility will be available when needed and that IT services will be available when needed. It is Facilities Management's and IT's recovery plans that will ensure that those facilities and services will be available.

Each recovery plan will be based on elements of information gathered during the BIA:

- Information about the availability of the recovery facility
- List of critical processes and the maximum tolerable downtime for each
- Resources (equipment, IT applications, people, supplies, etc.) needed to recover each process

We should note here that creating the recovery plan is an activity that has had a high failure rate in the past. This is a staff-intensive, time-consuming process and one that causes some organizations to "lose their nerve" before a tested plan has been produced. The best way to prevent this from happening is through successful management that guides the process and separates it into small, measurable pieces so that progress is clearly visible at frequent points.

The plan manager should begin the process by holding workshops to introduce all business unit planners to each other, to the planning process and to the help available. Table 9.7 shows a summary of activities necessary to begin to build recovery plans (and Crisis Management Plans, discussed later).

The components of each plan should include the following, where appropriate:

- Plan overview and assumptions
- Responsibilities for development, testing, and maintaining the plans
- Continuity team structure and reporting requirements
- Detailed procedures for recovery of time-critical business processes, computer applications, networks, systems, facilities, etc.
- Recovery locations and emergency operations centers
- Emergency operations communications procedures
- Recovery timeframes
- Supporting inventory information:
  - Hardware
  - Software
  - Networks
  - Data
  - People
  - Space
  - Furniture
  - Supplies
  - Transportation
  - External agents
  - Documentation
  - Data

In the workshop, the recovery plan manager should explain what is required as content for each section of the plan from each business unit planner.

9.6.1.1 Crisis Management Plan

A special subset of the recovery plan is called the Crisis Management plan and this refers to the management activity that must be performed when a recovery is required. In an emergency or recovery situation, the organization's management becomes the crisis management team and is responsible for the following:

- Contact emergency services and liaise with them
- Set up communications center

TABLE 9.7   Summary Planning Activities

Business Processes	IT Systems	Crisis Management
Workshop: Business unit management develops continuity team structures for each BU involved in the effort. Develops activities and tasks to recover time-critical BU processes, including resources (workstations, facilities, space, vital records, people, telephones, etc.). Assigns activities and tasks to BU recovery planning team members.	Workshop: IT management develops continuity team structures and activities and tasks to recover time-critical IT resources (apps, nets, systems, etc.). Assigns activities and tasks to IT recovery planning team members.	Meet with senior management and facilitate development of Crisis Management team structures.
BU recovery planning team establishes communications processes and reporting timeframes.	IT recovery planning team establishes communications processes and reporting timeframes.	Assist senior management in development of activities and tasks to facilitate management of the organization through an emergency/crisis event.
BU recovery planning team gathers and documents all inventory information for those resources that support time-critical resources.	IT recovery planning team gathers and documents all inventory information for those resources that support time-critical resources.	Identify and establish Crisis Management Emergency Operations Center location(s).
BU recovery planning team develops recovery plan as described in workshop.	IT recovery planning team develops recovery plan as described in workshop.	Establish communications processes and reporting timeframes with IT and business unit recovery planning teams, as well as with external communities (i.e., shareholders, civil authorities, customers/clients, employee families, press, etc.).

TABLE 9.7 (continued) Summary Planning Activities

Business Processes	IT Systems	Crisis Management
		Develop procedures for site management (damage limitation, forensics, damage assessment, return planning, etc.).

- Damage limitation at the original site
- Damage assessment when the original site is accessible
- Original site forensics
- Recovery activity management
- Site restoration plans
- Plans to return processing to original site

9.6.1.2 Plan Distribution

When the initial draft of the business unit and IT recovery plans and the crisis management plan have been developed, the drafts should be assembled into one plan and then distributed to all members of the recovery teams.

There is a school of thought that says that only the relevant parts of each plan should be distributed to teams (crisis management plan to senior management, IT plan to IT, etc.), but more good can be created if all members of all recovery planning teams can see the plans made by others. This is especially important in the early stages of testing, as we shall see later.

Copies of recovery plans should be kept in three places. Each member of each recovery team should have two copies: one to keep at the normal place of work and one to be kept off site (usually at home). A third, complete copy of the entire recovery plan should be stored at an off-site facility — usually the same facility used to store backup copies of data.

9.6.2 Plan Testing

When draft plans have been prepared, each must be tested. This is another part of the recovery planning process that is resource-intensive and time consuming but is entirely necessary because no recovery plan was ever prepared right the first time. (Indeed, given the changing nature of the processes to be recovered, it might be said that no recovery plan is ever "right" in the sense that it perfectly reflects everything needed to recover a process at the time recovery is needed. Therefore, repeated testing is needed to keep plans up-to-date and as close to complete as possible.)

9.6.2.1   Line Testing

Line testing is performed when business unit and IT recovery plans and crisis management plans are first drafted. Line testing is nothing more than a review of the draft plans — line by line — by members of the recovery planning teams.

Each draft plan is read by every member of each recovery planning team and notes are made on inconsistencies and omissions. It makes sense, after the first read-through, for all members of the recovery teams to gather in a workshop setting to review the notes they have made.

In the workshop, whiteboards and flipcharts are used to note the comments made by each team member. The workshop process is that each member, in turn, reads aloud their remarks and a scribe — appointed by the recovery plan manager — tabulates the comments on whiteboards and flipcharts. The scribe takes responsibility for eliminating duplication and takes note of the comments of the person who drafted the plan. For each remark offered by a plan reviewer (recovery team member), the author is required to add an action (such as "amend plan accordingly"). Table 9.8 provides an example of how the workshop notes might look.

At the end of the line testing workshop (or series of workshops if it is found necessary to split them up due to time constraints), each recovery plan team amends its plan to incorporate the remarks made in the workshop. The second level of testing will be performed on the next draft version of the plans.

9.6.2.2   Walk-Through Testing

When an initial draft of the plan has been reviewed and amended, a second type of test — walk-through testing — can be performed.

Like line testing, walk-through testing is conducted in a workshop setting and will most likely require a series of workshops because this type of testing is time consuming. Each business unit's (or IT or crisis management) recovery plan is "acted out" around a workshop. The purpose of this type of testing is to locate and resolve timing issues in plans and requires each recovery planning team to simultaneously review their plans' timing requirements. For example, it may be found that a business process' recovery depends on the availability of IT systems that have not had time to be recovered by the time they are required by the business process.

TABLE 9.8   Line Testing Review Table

Back-Office Process Recovery Plan

Plan Section	Remark	Author's Comment	Author's Action
Recovery timeframes	Process #3 does not reflect the recovery timeframe listed in the BIA	Recovery timeframe has been reviewed since the BIA	Amend original BIA data
People	Process #5 requires the participation of members of staff who will be required at that time to recover process #3	Lack of adequate skills	Review recovery timeframe or initiate training for additional member of staff
Transportation	No plan has been made to transport staff from original site to recovery site	Omission	Add to second draft of plan
External agents	Process #5 requires the participation of check stock suppliers	Intention is to rely on current stocks	Review current stock levels and likely recovery times and amend plan if necessary

Like the line testing workshop, the walk-through testing workshop should produce a table of remarks and actions that can be used by planners to refine and improve their draft plans.

9.6.2.3   Single Process Testing

The next step in the testing process is testing the ability to recover a single process (or in an IT test to test the recovery of the operating system or single application). Some organizations forego this step and, instead, go to multiple process testing — perhaps testing the recovery of a small number of processes or applications.

This test is an actual test of relocating to a recovery site. The test should be scheduled with care and should involve the actual execution of the test plans.

In this, as in more complex tests of the recovery plans, audit is invaluable. In every test of the plans from this point on, people should be available for no other purpose than to audit the test (Internal Audit often fulfills this duty) and to provide notes and observations at a meeting after the test is over (often referred to as the post-mortem). The notes and observations are used in the same way that the Line Testing Review Table (Table 9.8) is used — to provide the input for correcting errors and omissions in the recovery plans that have been tested.

9.6.2.4   Full Testing

When a number of single process tests have been conducted and confidence has grown about the ability to test, then the organization is ready to schedule and carry out a test of the entire recovery plan. In practice, organizations that have large, complex recovery plans tend to test groups of processes or applications recovery as testing the complete recovery plan can be extremely disruptive to normal operations. However, it is necessary to test the complete plan at least once a year.

Full tests, like single process testing, are carried out at the recovery facility and try as far as possible to replicate the conditions that will be found in an actual recovery situation.

9.6.2.5   Plan Testing Summary

Table 9.9 shows a summary of the considerations and actions that must be taken to plan and conduct single process and full recovery tests.

9.6.3   Plan Maintenance

Recovery plans should be tested in some form twice each year. Whether that form is a walk-through test or a full test depends on the resources available to the organization, but a full test (once the plan is fully developed and has gone through the line, walk-through, and single process tests) should be performed once per year because testing is the most effective way to perform plan maintenance.

However, business processes and IT configurations change more frequently than once or twice per year, and each change makes the recovery plan out of date. Therefore, a method must be found to update plans between tests.

The plan manager, each month, should poll every recovery planner for updates to their individual plans and incorporate those updates in the overall recovery plan. Once per month, the plan manager should send out a notice to each recovery planner and ask for updates. Generally, the updates will contain the following sections:

TABLE 9.9 Test Considerations and Actions

Testing Process Component	Considerations and Actions
Test plan preparation	Meeting of recovery planners scope the test and prepare test schedule, objectives, timing, resources required, personnel involved, follow-up, and reporting requirements
Test logistics preparation	Notify off-site workspace locations, transportation, off-site storage, and other internal and external participants as appropriate and brief them on test plan schedules and activities
Test execution	Activate Emergency Operations Center (EOC) location and execute Test Plan
Post-test debrief	Meeting of recovery planners and recovery teams to review test objectives met and document test results
Continuity plan update	Update recovery plans with lessons learned from test
Test scheduling	Prepare follow-on and long-term recovery plan test schedules
Management update	Prepare and escalate written results of recovery plan test for management review and approval

- Detailed procedures for recovery of time-critical business processes, computer applications, networks, systems, facilities, etc.
- Recovery timeframes
- Supporting inventory information:
  - Hardware
  - Software
  - Networks
  - Data
  - People

It should be noted that the plan manager should not allow nonresponse to the request for updates. Nonresponse may mean that the request was not received or that the recovery planner has simply been too busy to prepare the response. Each recovery planner must be required to send a response — even if the response is "No update."

When all responses have been received, the plan manager updates the master copy of the plan and the copy kept at the off-site location, and sends the updated pages to each recovery planner (two copies: one for the workplace and one for their off-site facility).

The recovery planner then produces a report for management that shows the updates made.

TABLE 9.10 Sample Business Continuity Plan Policy

Business Continuity Planning

Policy

The continued operations of COMPANY business activities in the event of an emergency must be addressed by each business unit in a Business Continuity Plan (BCP). The business unit BCPs must be coordinated with the COMPANY BCP and the COMPANY **Emergency Response Plan**.

Standards

- Every business unit will have a documented and tested BCP.
- Each business unit will conduct a Business Impact Analysis (BIA) to determine their critical business processes, applications, systems, and platforms. The BIA results are to be presented to the Management Committee for review and approval.
- The BIA results are to be reviewed by the business unit annually to ensure results are still appropriate.
- The business unit BCPs must be coordinated with the COMPANY-wide BCP.

Responsibilities

- The Management Committee of COMPANY is required to review and approve business unit BCPs as well as the COMPANY BCP.
- Additionally, it is the responsibility of COMPANY managers to ensure that the business unit BCP is current.

Compliance

- COMPANY Management is responsible for conducting periodic tests of the BCP to ensure the continued processing requirements of the Company are met.

9.7 Sample Business Continuity Plan Policy

See Table 9.10 for a sample business continuity plan policy.

9.8 Summary

Business continuity planning is the process of ensuring that your organization can continue doing business even when its normal facilities or place of business is unavailable. In earlier years, many companies undertook what they called "disaster recovery planning" — which was nothing more than making sure that their computer operations could be resumed as quickly as necessary when the data center was unavailable. When companies tested their "disaster recovery plans," some of them realized that being able to recover data center operations was all very well but pointless if the organization's offices and other places of business — where the functions provided by the data center were used — were also unavailable. Business continuity plans are notoriously difficult to sell to senior management, and that is a cause for frustration among information security professionals. Creating and testing a business continuity plan is a very significant commitment of resources and many executives take a wait-and-see approach to dealing with the risk of business interruption. An approach to convincing reluctant organization managers to undertake business continuity planning is to break the process into components and "sell" each component on its own values. This chapter examined the components of a business continuity plan.

Glossary

802.11 — Family of IEEE standards for wireless LANs first introduced in 1997. The first standard to be implemented, 802.11b, specifies from 1 to 11 Mbps in the unlicensed band using DSSS (direct sequence spread spectrum) technology. The Wireless Ethernet Compatibility Association (WECA) brands it as Wireless Fidelity (Wi-Fi).

802.1X — An IEEE standard for port-based layer two authentications in 802 standard networks. Wireless LANs often use 802.1X for authentication of a user before the user has the ability to access the network.

Abend — Acronym for abnormal end of a task. It generally means a software crash.

Acceptable use policy — A policy that a user must agree to follow to gain access to a network or to the Internet.

Access controls — The management of permission for logging on to a computer or network.

Access path — The logical route that an end user takes to access computerized information. Typically, it includes a route through the operating system, telecommunications software, selected application software, and the access control system.

Access rights — Also called permissions or privileges, these are the rights granted to users by the administrator or supervisor. These permissions can be read, write, execute, create, delete, etc.

Accountability — The ability to map a given activity or event back to the responsible party.

Administrative controls The actions/controls dealing with operational effectiveness, efficiency, and adherence to regulations and management policies.

Anonymous File Transfer Protocol (FTP) — A method for downloading public files using the File Transfer Protocol. Anonymous FTP is called anonymous because users do not provide credentials before accessing files from a particular server. In general, users enter the word "anonymous" when the host prompts for a username; anything can be entered for the password, such as the user's e-mail address or simply the word "guest." In many cases, an anonymous FTP site will not even prompt for a name and password.

Antivirus software — Applications that detect, prevent, and possibly remove all known viruses from files located in a microcomputer hard drive.

Application controls — The transaction and data relating to each computer-based application system. Therefore, they are specific to each such application, which may be manual or programmed, are to endure the completeness and accuracy of the records and the validity of the entries made therein resulting from both manual and programmed processing. Examples of application controls include data input validation, agreement of batch controls, and encryption of data transmitted.

Application layers — They refer to the transactions and data relating to each computer-based application system and are therefore specific to each such application controls, which may be manual or programmed processing. Examples include data validation controls.

ASP/MSP — A third-party provider that delivers and manages applications and computer services, including security services, to multiple users via the Internet or virtual private network (VPN).

Asymmetric key (public key) — A cipher technique whereby different cryptographic keys are used to encrypt and decrypt a message.

Asynchronous Transfer Mode (ATM) — A high-bandwidth, low-delay switching and multiplexing technology. It is a data-link layer protocol. This means that it is a protocol-independent transport mechanism. ATM allows very high-speed data transfer rates at up to 155 Mbps.

Audit trail — A visible trail of evidence enabling one to trace information contained in statements or reports back to the original input source.

Authentication — The act of verifying the identity of a system entity (user, system, network node) and the entity's eligibility to access computerized information. Designed to protect against fraudulent logon activity. Authentication also can refer to the verification of the correctness of a piece of data.

Availability — Relates to information being available when required by the business process now and in the future. It also concerns the safeguarding of necessary resources and associated capabilities.

Baseband — A form of modulation in which data signals are pulsed directly on the transmission medium without frequency division and usually utilize a transceiver. In baseband, the entire bandwidth of the transmission medium (cable) is utilized for a single channel.

Biometrics — A security technique that verifies an individual's identity by analyzing a unique physical attribute, such as a handprint.

Bit-stream image — Bit-stream backups (also referred to as mirror image backups) involve all areas of a computer hard disk drive or another type of storage media. Such backups exactly replicate all sectors on a given storage device. Thus, all files and ambient data storage areas are copied.

Brute force — The name given to a class of algorithms that repeatedly tries all possible combinations until a solution is found.

Business impact analysis (BIA) — An exercise that determines the impact of losing the support of any resource to an organization, establishes the escalation of that loss over time, identifies the minimum resources needed to recover, and prioritizes the recovery of processes and supporting systems.

Certificate authority (CA) — A trusted third party that serves authentication infrastructures or organizations and registers entities and issues them certificates.

Chain of custody — The control over evidence. Lack of control over evidence can lead to it being discredited completely. Chain of custody depends on being able to verify that evidence could not have been tampered with. This is accomplished by sealing off the evidence so that it cannot in any way be changed and by providing a documentary record of custody to prove that the evidence was at all times under strict control and not subject to tampering.

Cleartext — Data that is not encrypted; plaintext.

Cold site — An IS backup facility that has the necessary electrical and physical components of a computer facility, but does not have the computer equipment in place. The site is ready to receive the necessary replacement computer equipment in the event the users have to move from their main computing location to the alternative computer facility.

Confidentiality — Confidentiality concerns the protection of sensitive information from unauthorized disclosure.

Criticality analysis — An analysis or assessment of a business function or security vulnerability based on its criticality to the organization's business objectives. A variety of criticality may be used to illustrate the criticality.

Cyber-cop — A criminal investigator of online fraud or harassment.

Data classification — Data classification is assigning a level of sensitivity to data as they are being created, amended, enhanced, stored, or transmitted. The classification of the data should then determine the extent to which the data needs to be controlled or secured and is also indicative of its value in terms of its importance to the organization.

Data diddling — Changing data with malicious intent before or during input to the system.

Data Encryption Standard (DES) — A private key cryptosystem published by the National Institute of Standards and Technology (NIST). DES has been used commonly for data encryption in the forms of software and hardware implementation.

Data normalization — In data processing, a process applied to all data in a set that produces a specific statistical property. It is also the process of eliminating duplicate keys within a database. Useful because organizations use databases to evaluate various security data.

Data warehouse — A generic term for a system that stores, retrieves, and manages large amounts of data. Data warehouse software often includes sophisticated comparison and hashing techniques for fast searches as well as advanced filtering.

DDoS attacks — Distributed denial-of-service attacks. These are denial-of-service assaults from multiple sources.

Decryption key — A piece of information, in a digitized form, used to recover the plaintext from the corresponding ciphertext by decryption.

Defense-in-depth — The practice of layering defenses to provide added protection. Security is increased by raising the cost to mount the attack. This system places multiple barriers between an attacker and an organization's business-critical information resources. This strategy also provides natural areas for the implementation of intrusion-detection technologies.

Degauss — To have a device generate electric current (AC or DC) to produce magnetic fields for the purpose of reducing the magnetic flux density to zero. A more secure means of destroying data on magnetic media.

Digital certificates — A certificate identifying a public key to its subscriber, corresponding to a private key held by that subscriber. It is a unique code that typically is used to allow the authenticity and integrity of communications to be verified.

Digital code signing — The process of digitally signing computer code so that its integrity remains intact and it cannot be tampered with.

Digital signatures — A piece of information, a digitized form of signature, that provides sender authenticity, message integrity, and non-repudiation. A digital signature is generated using the sender's private key or applying a one-way hash function.

Disaster notification fees — The fee a recovery site vendor usually charges when the customer notifies the vendor that a disaster has occurred and the recovery site is required. The fee is implemented to discourage false disaster notifications.

Discretionary Access Control (DAC) — A means of restricting access to objects based on the identity of subjects and groups to which they belong. The controls are discretionary in the sense that a subject with certain access permission is capable of passing that permission on to another subject.

Disc mirroring — This is the practice of duplicating data in separate volumes on two hard disks to make storage more fault tolerant. Mirroring provides data protection in the case of disk failure, because data is constantly updated to both disks.

DMZ — Commonly, it is the network segment between the Internet and a private network. It allows access to services from the Internet and the internal private network, while denying access from the Internet directly to the private network.

DNS (Domain Name Service) — A hierarchical database that is distributed across the Internet and allows names to be resolved to IP addresses and vice versa to locate services such as Web and e-mail.

Dual control — A procedure that uses two or more entities (usually persons) operating in concert to protect a system's resources, such that no single entity acting alone can access that resource.

Dynamic Host Configuration Protocol (DHCP) — DHCP is an industry standard protocol used to dynamically assign IP addresses to network devices.

Electronic signature — Any technique designed to provide the electronic equivalent of a handwritten signature to demonstrate the origin and integrity of specific data. Digital signatures are an example of electronic signatures.

Enterprise root — A certificate authority (CA) that grants itself a certificate and creates a subordinate CAs. The root CA gives the subordinate CAs their certificates, but the subordinate CAs can grant certificates to users.

Exposure — The potential loss to an area due to the occurrence of an adverse event.

Extensible Markup Language (XML) — A Web-based application development technique that allows designers to create their own customized tags enabling the transmission, validation, and interpretation of data between application and organizations.

Fall-through logic — Predicting which way a program will branch when an option is presented. It is an optimized code based on a branch prediction.

Firewall — A device that forms a barrier between a secure and an open environment. Usually the open environment is considered hostile. The most notable open system is the Internet.

Forensic examination — After a security breach, the process of assessing, classifying, and collecting digital evidence to assist in prosecution. Standard crime-scene standards are used.

Guidelines — Documented suggestions for regular and consistent implementation of accepted practices. They usually have less enforcement powers.

Honeypots — A specifically configured server designed to attract intruders so their actions do not affect production systems; also known as a decoy server.

Hot site — A fully operational off-site data processing facility equipped with both hardware and system software to be used in the event of disaster.

HTTP — A communication protocol used to connect two servers on the World Wide Web. Its primary function is to establish a connection with a Web server and transmit HTML pages to the client browser.

IDS (intrusion detection system) — An IDS inspects network traffic to identify suspicious patterns that may indicate a network or system attack from someone attempting to break into or compromise a system.

Information security governance — The management structure, organization, responsibility, and reporting processes surrounding a successful information security program.

Information security program — The overall process of preserving confidentiality, integrity, and availability of information.

Integrity — The accuracy, completeness, and validity of information in accordance with business values and expectations.

Internet Engineering Task Force (IETF) — The Internet standards setting organization with affiliates internationally from network industry representatives. This includes all network industry developers and researchers concerned with evolution and planned growth on the Internet.

Intrusion detection — The process of monitoring the events occurring in a computer system or network, detecting signs of security problems.

IP Security Protocol (IPSec) — A protocol in development by the IETF to support secure data exchange. Once completed, IPSec is expected to be widely deployed to implement virtual private networks (VPNs). IPSec supports two encryption modes: Transport and Tunnel. Transport mode encrypts the data portion (payload) of each packet but leaves the header untouched. Tunnel mode is more secure because it encrypts both the header and the payload. On the receiving side, an IPSec-compliant device decrypts each packet.

ISO 17799 — An international standard that defines information confidentiality, integrity, and availability controls.

Internet service provider — A third party that provides organizations with a variety of Internet and Internet-related services.

Mail relay server — An e-mail server that relays messages where neither the sender nor the receiver is a local user. A risk exists that an unauthorized user could hijack these open relays and use them to spoof their own identity.

Mandatory access control (MAC) — MAC is a means of restricting access to data based on varying degrees of security requirements for information contained in the objects.

Masqueraders — Attackers that penetrate systems by using user identifiers and passwords taken legitimate users.

Message Authentication Code — Message Authentication Code refers to an ANSI standard for a checksum that is computed with keyed hash that is based on DES.

Mirrored site — An alternate site that contains the same information as the original. Mirrored sites are set up for backup and disaster recovery as well to balance the traffic load for numerous download requests. Such "download mirrors" are often placed in different locations throughout the Internet.

Mobile site — The use of a mobile/temporary facility to serve as a business resumption location. They usually can be delivered to any site and can house information technology and staff.

Monitoring policy — The rules outlining the way in which information is captured and interpreted.

Nonrepudiation — The assurance that a party cannot later deny originating data, that it is the provision of a proof of the integrity and origin of the data which can be verified by a third party. A digital signature can provide nonrepudiation.

Nonintrusive monitoring — The use of nonintrusive probes or traces to assemble information and track traffic and identity vulnerabilities.

OSI 7-layer model — The Open System Interconnection seven-layer model is an ISO standard for worldwide communications that defines a framework for implementing protocols in seven layers. Control is passed from one layer to the next, starting at the application layer in one station, and proceeding to the bottom layer, over the channel to the next station and back up the hierarchy.

Off-site storage — A storage facility located away from the building, housing the primary information processing facility (IPF), and used for storage of computer media such as offline backup data storage files.

Packet filtering — Controlling access to a network analyzing the attributes of the incoming and outgoing packets and either letting them pass or denying them based on a list of rules.

Passive response — A response option in intrusion detection in which the system simply reports and records the problem detected, relying on the user to take subsequent action.

Password cracker — Specialized securities checker that tests user's passwords, searching for passwords that are easy to guess by repeatedly trying words from specially crafted dictionaries. Failing that, many password crackers can brute force all possible combinations in a relatively short period of time with current desktop computer hardware.

Penetration testing — A live test of the effectiveness of security defenses through mimicking the actions if real-life attackers.

Port — An interface point between the CPU and a peripheral device.

Privacy — Freedom from unauthorized intrusion.

Procedures — The portion of a security policy that states the general process that will be performed to accomplish a security goal.

Proxy server — A server that acts on behalf of a user. Typical proxies accept a connection from a user, make a decision as to whether or not the client IP address is permitted to use the proxy, perhaps perform additional authentication, and complete a connection to a remote destination on behalf of the user.

Public key — In an asymmetric cryptography scheme, the key that may be widely published to enable the operation of the scheme.

RADIUS — Remote Authentication Dial-In User Service. A protocol used to authenticate remote users and wireless connections.

Reciprocal agreement — Emergency processing agreements between two or more organizations with similar equipment or applications. Typically, participants promise to provide processing time to each other when an emergency arises.

Recovery point objective (RPO) — A measurement of the point prior to an outage to which data is to be restored.

Recovery time objective (RTO) — The amount of time allowed for the recovery of a business function or resource after a disaster occurs.

Redundant site — A recovery strategy involving the duplication of key information technology components, including data, or other key business processes, whereby fast recovery can take place. The redundant site usually is located away from the original site.

Residual risks — The risk associated with an event when the control is in place to reduce the effect or likelihood of that event being taken into account.

Risk assessment — A process used to identify and evaluate risks and their potential effects.

Risk avoidance — The process for systematically avoiding risk. Security awareness can lead to a better educated staff, which can lead to certain risks being avoided.

Risk mitigation — While some risks cannot be avoided, they can be minimized or mitigated by putting controls into place to mitigate the risk once an incident occurs.

Risk transfer — The process of transferring risk. An example can include transferring the risk of a building fire to an insurance company.

RSA — A public key cryptosystem developed by Rivest, Shamir, and Adleman. RSA has two different keys: the public encryption key and the secret decryption key. The strength of RSA depends on the difficulty of the prime number factorization. For applications with high-level security, the number of the decryption key bits should be greater than 512 bits. RSA is used for both encryption and digital signatures.

Secure Socket Layer (SSL) — A protocol developed by Netscape for transmitting private documents via the Internet. SSL works by using a public key to encrypt data that is transferred over the SSL connection.

Security metrics — A standard of measurement used to measure and monitor information security-related information security activity.

Sniffing — An attack capturing sensitive pieces of information, such as a password, passing through the network.

Social engineer — A person who illegally enters computer systems by persuading an authorized person to reveal IDs, passwords, and other confidential information.

Split knowledge — A security technique in which two or more entities separately hold data items that individually convey no knowledge of the information that results from combining the items. A condition under which two or more entities separately have key components that individually convey no knowledge of the plaintext key that will be produced when the key components are combined in the crypto-graphic module.

Spoofing — Faking the sending address of a transmission to gain illegal entry into a secure system.

Stand-alone root — A certificate authority that signs its own certificates and does not rely on a directory service to authenticate users.

Standard — A set of rules or specifications that, when taken together, define a software or hardware device. A standard is also an acknowledged basis for comparing or measuring something. Standards are important because new technology will only take root once a group of specifications is agreed upon.

Steering committee — A management committee assembled to sponsor and manage various projects, such as an information security program.

Steganography — A technology used to embed information in audio and graphical material. The audio and graphical materials appear unaltered until a steganography tool is used to reveal the hidden message.

Symmetric key encryption — In symmetric key encryption, two trading partners share one or more secrets, and no one else can read their messages. A different key (or set of keys) is needed for each pair of trading partners. The same key is used for encryption and decryption.

TACACS+ — Terminal Access Controller Access Control System Plus is an authentication protocol, often used by remote-access servers or single (reduced) sign-on implementations. TACACS and TACACS+ are proprietary protocols from CISCO®.

TCP/IP — Transmission Control Protocol/Internet Protocol is a set of communications protocols that encompasses media access, packet transport, session communications, file transfer, electronic mail, terminal emulation, remote file access, and network management. TCP/IP provides the basis for the Internet.

Threat analysis — A project to identify the threats that exist over key information and information technology. The threat analysis usually also defines the level of the threat and likelihood of that threat to materialize.

Two-factor authentication — The use of two independent mechanisms for authentication; for example, requiring a smart card and a password.

Virus signature files — A file of virus patterns that are compared with existing files to determine if they are infected with a virus. The vendor of the antivirus software updates the signatures frequently and makes them available to customers via the Web.

Virtual private network (VPN) — A secure private network that uses the public telecommunications infrastructure to transmit data. In contrast to a much more expensive system of owned or leased lines that can only be used by one company, VPNs are used by enterprises for both extranets and wide area intranets. Using encryption and authentication, a VPN encrypts all data that passes between two Internet points, maintaining privacy and security.

Warm site — A warm site is similar to a hot site; however, it is not fully equipped with all the necessary hardware needed for recovery.

Web hosting — The business of providing the equipment and services required to host and maintain files for one or more Web sites and to provide fast Internet connections to those sites. Most hosting is "shared," which means that the Web sites of multiple companies are on the same server in order to share costs.

Web Server — Using the client/server model and the World Wide Web's HyperText Transfer Protocol (HTTP), Web Server is a software program that serves Web page files to users.

Worm — With respect to security, a special type of virus that does not attach itself to programs, but rather spreads via other methods such as e-mail.

Bibliography

1. International Standards Organization. Information Technology — Code of Practice for Information Security Management, ISO/IEC 17799:2000(E). Geneva, Switzerland: ISO, 2000.
2. Ford, Warwick and Michael S. Baum, *Secure Electronic Commerce*. Upper Saddle River, NJ: Prentice Hall, 1997.
3. King, Christopher M; Curtis E. Dalton; and T. Ertem Osmanoglu. *Security Architecture: Design, Deployment and Operations*. New York: Osborn/McGraw-Hill, 2001.
4. Summers, Rita C. *Secure Computing: Threats and Safeguards*. New York: McGraw-Hill, 1997.
5. Tudor, Jan Killmeyer, *Information Security Architecture*. New York: Auerbach Publications, 2001.
6. Hutt, Arthur E.; Seymour Bosworth; and Douglas B. Hoyt. *Computer Security Handbook, Third Edition*. New York: John Wiley & Sons, 1995.
7. National Institute of Standards and Technology. *An Introduction to Computer Security: The NIST Handbook, Special Publication 800-12*. Washington, D.C.: U.S. Government Printing Office,
8. Pfleeger, Charles P. *Security in Computing, Second Edition*. Upper Saddle River, New Jersey: Prentice Hall, 1996.
9. Summers, Rita C. *Secure Computing: Threats and Safeguards*. New York: McGraw-Hill, 1997.
10. Vallabhaneni, Rao S. *CISSP Examination Textbooks*. Schaumburg, IL: SRV Professional Publications, 2000.
11. Devlin, Ed and Cole Emerson. *Business Resumption Planning, 1999 Edition*. New York: Auerbach Publications, 1999.
12. Hare, Chris. CISSP Certified CBK Study Guide: Business Continuity Planning Domain. Posted at http://www.cccure.org, March 1999.
13. Hutt, Arthur E.; Seymour Bosworth; and Douglas B. Hoyt. *Computer Security Handbook, Third Edition*. New York: John Wiley & Sons, 1995.

14. Tipton, Harold F. and Micki Krause, Editors. Information Security Management Handbook, 1996–97 Yearbook Edition, New York: Auerbach Publications.

15. Atkinson, R. "Security Architecture for the Internet Protocol," *RFC 1825*, Naval Research Laboratory, August 1995.

16. Guttman, E.; L. Leong; and G. Malkin. "Users' Security Handbook," *RFC 2504*, Sun Microsystems, February 1999.

17. Housley, R.; W. Ford; W. Polk; and D. Solo. "Internet X.509 Public Key Infrastructure Certificate and CRL Profile," *RFC 2459*, SPYRUS, January 1999.

18. Krawczyk, H.; M. Bellare; and R. Canetti. "HMAC: Keyed-Hashing for Message Authentication," *RFC 2104*, IBM, February 1997.

19. Piper, D. "The Internet IP Security Domain of Interpretation for ISAKMP," *RFC 2407*, Network Alchemy, November 1998.

20. Postel, Jon, and Joyce Reynolds. "File Transfer Protocol," *RFC 959*, ISI, October 1985.

21. Schneier, Bruce. *Applied Cryptography*. New York: John Wiley & Sons, 1996.

22. Ermann, M. David; Mary B. Williams; and Michele S. Shauf. *Computers, Ethics and Society, Second Edition*. New York: Oxford University Press, 1997.

23. Imparl, Steven D., JD; *Internet Law — The Complete Guide*; Specialty Technical Publishers, 2000.

24. Stephenson, Peter. *Investigating Computer-Related Crime*. New York: CRC Press LLC, 2000.

25. Economic Espionage Act of 1996; U.S. Congressional Record of 1996; http://cybercrime.gov/EEAleghist.htm.

26. Depuis, Clement. *CISSP Study Booklet on Operations Security*. Posted at http://www.cccure.org. April 5, 1999.

27. Kabay, Michel E. *The NCSA Guide Enterprise Security,* McGraw-Hill Computer Communications Series, 1999.

28. National Institute of Standards and Technology. *An Introduction to Computer Security: The NIST Handbook, Special Publication 800-12.* Washington, D.C.: U.S. Government Printing Office, 1995.

29. National Institute of Standards and Technology. NIST Generally Accepted Principles and Practices for Securing Information Technology Systems, Special Publication 800-14. Washington, D.C.: U.S. Government Printing Office, September 1996.

30. National Institute of Standards and Technology. *Risk Management Guide for Information Technology Systems, Special Publication 800-30.* Washington, D.C.: U.S. Government Printing Office, January 2002.

31. National Institute of Standards and Technology. *Contingency Planning Guide for Securing Information Technology Systems, Special Publication 800-34.* Washington, D.C.: U.S. Government Printing Office, June 2002.

32. National Research Council. *Computers a Risk: Safe Computing in the Information Age.* Washington, D.C.: National Academy Press, 1991.

33. Summers, Rita C. *Secure Computing: Threats and Safeguards*. New York: McGraw-Hill, 1997.

34. Tipton, Harold F. and Micki Krause, Editors. *Information Security Management Handbook, 1996-97 Yearbook Edition*, Auerbach Publications.

35. U.S. Department of Defense. *Technical Rationale Behind CSC-STD-003-85*. Washington, D.C.: U.S. Government Printing Office, 1985.
36. U.S. Department of Defense. *Trusted Computer System Evaluation Criteria* Washington, D.C.: U.S. Government Printing Office, 1985.
37. U.S. Department of Defense. *Trusted Network Interpretation of the Trusted Computer System Evaluation Criteria*. Washington, D.C.: U.S. Government Printing Office, 1987.
38. Carroll, John M. *Computer Security, Third Edition*. Woburn, MA: Butterworth-Heinemann Publishers, Ltd., 1996.
39. International Standards Organization. Information Technology — Code of Practice for Information Security Management, ISO/IEC 17799:2000(E). Geneva, Switzerland: ISO, 2000.
40. _____. Common Criteria for information Technology Security Evaluation, Version 2.1. August 1999.
41. King, Christopher M; Curtis E. Dalton; and T. Ertem Osmanoglu. *Security Architecture: Design, Deployment and Operations*. California: Osborn/McGraw-Hill, 2001.
42. Pfleeger, Charles P. *Security in Computing, Second Edition*. Upper Saddle River, NJ: Prentice Hall, 1996.
43. Tudor, Jan Killmeyer, *Information Security Architecture*. New York: Auerbach Publications, 2001.
44. Vallabhaneni, Rao S. *CISSP Examination Textbooks, Volume 1*. Schaumburg, IL: SRV Professional Publications, 2000.
45. Bryson, Lisa C. "Protect Your Boss and Your Job: Due Care in Information Security," *Computer Security Alert, Number 146*. San Francisco, May 1995.
46. D'Agenais, Jean and John Carruthers, *Creating Effective Manuals*. Cincinnati, OH: South-Western Publishing Co., 1985.
47. Glass, Robert L. *Building Quality Software*, Englewood Cliffs, NJ: Prentice Hall, 1992.
48. Icove, David; Karl Seger; and William VonStorch. *Computer Crime: A Crimefighter's Handbook*. CA: O'Reilly & Associates, 1995.
49. International Information Security Foundation. *Generally Accepted Systems Security Principles (GASSP) Version 2.0*. Gaithersburg, MD, June 1999.
50. International Standards Organization. Information Technology — Code of Practice for Information Security Management, ISO/IEC 17799:2000(E). Geneva, Switzerland: ISO, 2000.
51. Jackson, K.M. and J. Hruska. *Computer Security Reference Book*: Boca Raton, FL: CRC Press, 1992.
52. National Institute of Standards and Technology. *An Introduction to Computer Security: The NIST Handbook, Special Publication 800-12*. Washington, D.C.: U.S. Government Printing Office.
53. National Security Agency. *Online Course: Overview and Risk Management Terminology*. Posted at www.ncisse.org/Courseware/NSAcourse/lesson1/lesson.PPT. 1997.
54. Parker, Donn. "Risk Reduction Out, Enablement and Due Care In," *Computer Security Institute Journal, Volume XVI, Number 4*, Winter 2000.

55. Peltier, Tom. "How to Build a Comprehensive Security Awareness Program." *Computer Security Institute Journal*, Volume XVI, Number 2, Spring 2000.
56. Peltier, Thomas R. Information Security Policies, Standards, Procedures and Guidelines. Boca Raton, FL: CRC Press, 2001.
57. Peltier, Thomas R. *Information Security Risk Analysis*. New York: Auerbach Publications, 2001.
58. Russell, Deborah and G.T. Gangemi Sr. *Computer Security Basics*. CA: O'Reilly & Associates, 1991.
59. Tipton, Harold F. and Micki Krause, Editors. *Information Security Management Handbook, 4th Edition*. New York: Auerbach Publications, 2000.
60. Anonymous. *Maximum Security: A Hacker's Guide to Protecting Your Internet Site and Network, Second Edition*. Indianapolis: Sams Publishing, 1998.
61. Scambray, Joel; Stuart McClure; and George Kurtz. *Hacking Exposed: Network Security Secrets & Solutions, Second Edition*. New York: Osborne/McGraw-Hill, 2001.

Index

A

Tier 3 policies, 97–99
timecard policy example, 100
topic-specific policies, 75, 83–97
utility company information protection
    policy example, 84–85
utility company information security
    policy example, 79
Information security professional, job
    description for, 5–9
Information security program, 240
    business unit responsibilities, 41–45
    developing, xv
    infrastructure, 48–54
    security awareness program, 45–47
    structure of, 39–41
Information Security Risk Analysis, 11
Information security software tools, 50–51
Information security triad, 22–23
Information System Security Information
    (ISSA), 106
Information Systems Audit and Control
    Association (ISACA), 106
Information Systems Security Officer
    (ISSO), 1
Information Technology department, 60–61
Information users, 117–118
    example policies, 124
Insider fraud/theft, 10
Insider security breaches, 21–22
Insulation breakdowns, 172
Insurance, as compensatory control, 220
Integrated approach, 2
Integrity, 156, 240
    as goal of information security, 22
Integrity technology, 27
Interleave parity, 24
Internal audit, 40, 48
Internal use information, 106
    example of, 110, 120, 122, 123, 125
    vs. public information, 106–107
International service provider, information
    classification categories for, 109
Internet Engineering Task Force (IETF), 240
Internet service providers, 241
Internet usage and responsibility statement,
    93
Internet usage policy example, 89–90
Interviews, in business impact analysis,
    216–217
Intrusion detection systems, 34, 69, 154,
    177–179, 240

Intrusion prevention systems, 154
IP Security Protocol (IPSec), 240
ISO 17799, 64, 240
    control list using, 198–201

J

Jargon Dictionary, 34
Job descriptions
    access permissions based on, 142–143
    incorporating information security into,
        57
    for information security professional,
        5–9
    role in personnel security, 18
    as Tier 3 policy, 98

K

Kassebaum-Kennedy Act, 68
Kerberos, 145
Kerckhoff. Auguste, 157
Key clustering, 157
Known plaintext attacks, 162

L

Labeling
    in access control, 141
    of electronically stored information, 131
    of printed documents, 130
Least privilege, 25, 142
Legal requirements, 65–68
    contractor agreements, 176
Line testing
    of business recovery plans, 229
    review table for, 230
Load balancing, 23, 24
Local area networks, 13
Log analysis, 153
Log-in scripts, 144
Logging procedures, 179
Logic bombs, 31–32
Losses, sources of, 9–10
Loyalty, duty of, 1–2